T0380664

INFERNO!

And the Miracles of the Colorado Marshall Fire

TOM GORMLEY

Order this book online at www.trafford.com
or email orders@trafford.com

Most Trafford titles are also available at major online book retailers.

www.trafford.com

North America & international
toll-free: 844 688 6899 (USA & Canada)
fax: 812 355 4082

Our mission is to efficiently provide the world's finest, most comprehensive book publishing service, enabling every author to experience success. To find out how to publish your book, your way, and have it available worldwide, visit us online at www.trafford.com

ISBN: 978-1-6987-1297-0 (sc)
ISBN: 978-1-6987-1314-4 (hc)
ISBN: 978-1-6987-1298-7 (e)

Library of Congress Control Number: 2022917760

Print information available on the last page.

Trafford rev. 12/28/2022

Firefighters' Prayer[1]

When I am called to duty,
God wherever flames may rage,
give me strength to save a life,
whatever be its age.

Help me to embrace a little child before it's too late,
or save an older person from the horror of that fate.

Enable me to be alert to hear the weakest shout,
and quickly and efficiently to put the fire out.
I want to fill my calling and to give the best in me,
to guard my neighbor and protect his property.

And if according to your will I have to lose my life,
bless with your protecting hand my loving family from strife.

[1] Adapted from "Firemen's Prayer" by A. W. "Smokey" Linn, circa 1850, and posted at Louisville Fire Department at https://www.louisvillefire.com/about/history/.

Overview Map of the Marshall Fire

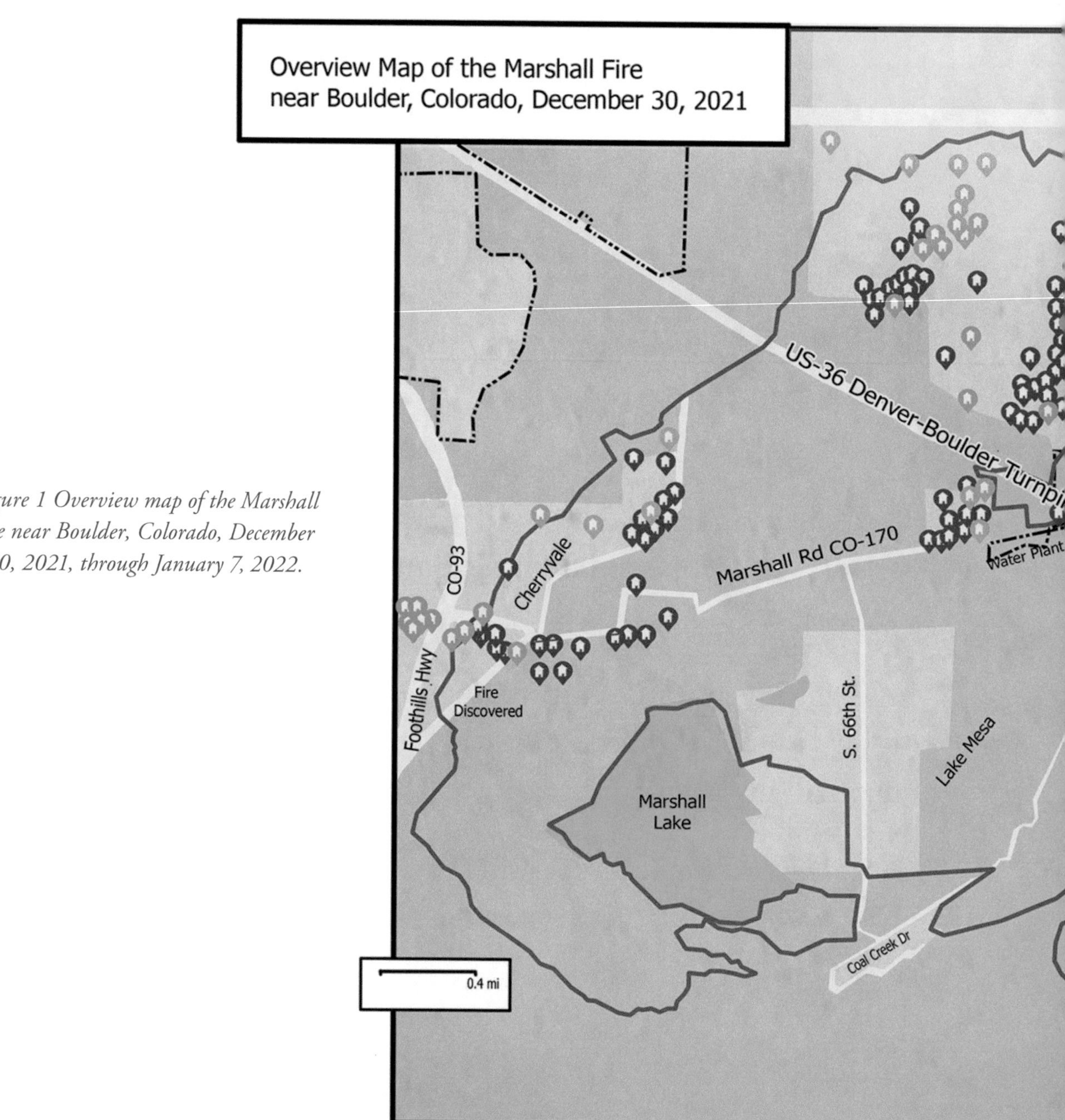

Figure 1 Overview map of the Marshall fire near Boulder, Colorado, December 30, 2021, through January 7, 2022.

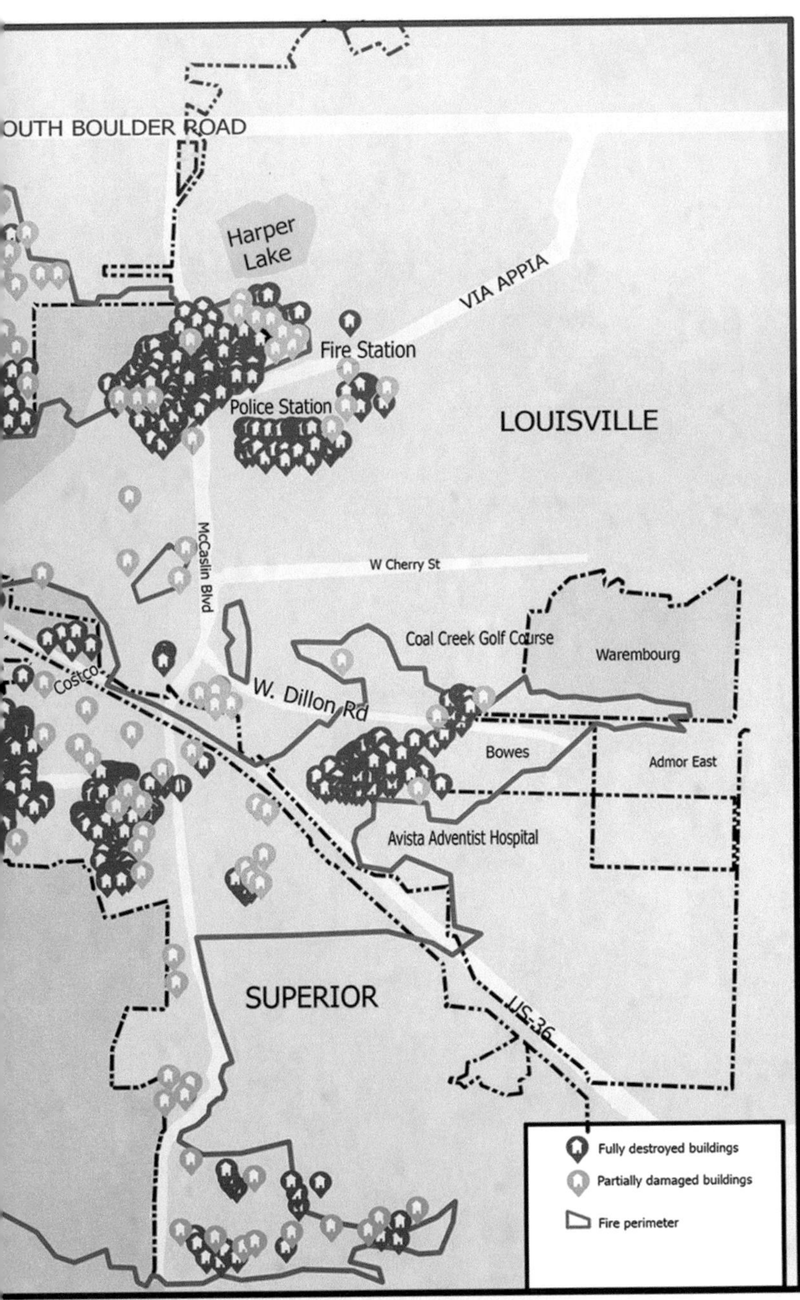
OUTH BOULDER ROAD
Harper Lake
VIA APPIA
Fire Station
Police Station
LOUISVILLE
McCaslin Blvd
W Cherry St
Coal Creek Golf Course
Warembourg
Costco
W. Dillon Rd
Bowes
Admor East
Avista Adventist Hospital
SUPERIOR
US-36
Fully destroyed buildings
Partially damaged buildings
Fire perimeter

Contents

Preface ix

Message from Chief John Willson, Louisville Fire Protection District xi

Message from Commander Randy Wilber, Boulder County Sheriff's Office xii

Introduction xv

Marshall, December 30, 2021, 8:00 a.m., Wind NW 4 mph, Gusting to 19 mph, 30°F 1

Louisville, December 30, 2021, 8:45 a.m., Wind E 10 mph, Gusting to 18 mph, 41°F 10

Superior, December 30, 2021, 10:00 a.m., Wind WSW 30 mph, Gusting to 65 mph, 41°F 18

Marshall, December 30, 2021, 11:00 a.m., Wind WSW 98 mph, Gusting to 98 mph 40°F 28

Superior, December 30, 2021, 11:46 a.m., Wind SSE 12 mph, Gusting to 39 mph 44°F 42

Louisville, December 30, 2021, 12:46 p.m., Wind SSE 25 mph, Gusting to 55 mph 44°F 57

Marshall, December 30, 2021, 1:56 p.m., Wind W 68 mph, Gusting to 84 mph 40°F 77

Louisville, December 30, 2021, 2:58 p.m., Wind W 32 mph, Gusting to 68 mph 48°F 89

Louisville, December 30, 2021, 3:46 p.m., Wind E 12 mph, Gusting to 17 mph 46°F 101

Louisville, December 30, 2021, 4:59 p.m., Wind NNE 9 mph, Gusting to 19 mph 43°F 114

Louisville Manorwood, December 30, 2021, 5:53 p.m., Wind NW 5 mph, Gusting 6 mph 43°F 121

NREL, December 30, 2021, 7:00 p.m., Wind WSW 35 mph, Gusting to 47 mph 41°F 132

Louisville Middle School, December 30, 2021, 8:08 p.m., Wind E 1 mph, Gusting to 12 mph 42°F 141

Louisville Manorwood Lane, December 31, 2021, 8:01 a.m., Wind Calm 29°F 149

Rocky Mountain Metro Airport, January 1, 2022, 8:45 a.m., Wind Calm 5°F.......154
Superior, January 2, 2022, 8:45 a.m., Wind Calm 5°F.......160
Louisville and Superior Cleanup, Early January.......167
Assistance and Aid.......179
Rebuilding and Rebirth.......189
Cause and Effects.......194
Conclusion and Final Thoughts.......200
About the Author.......203
Appendix A—Partial List of the Marshall Fire Miracles.......205
Appendix B—Statistics and Fire Responders.......208
Partial Bibliography.......211
Index.......217

Preface

The December 30, 2021, Marshall fire outside of Boulder will be remembered as the most destructive inferno in Colorado history and one of the top fifteen worst fires in the Western United States. In a little over four hours, the fire, fueled by high velocity Chinook winds, burned 6,026 acres, consumed 1,084 structures, and damaged many more. The fire caught everyone living nearby by surprise. No one thought a fire could cause so much destruction in so short a time. Few residents thought Superior and Louisville at risk to a wildfire. During a holiday shutdown, with many firefighters and police on vacation, when fires rarely occur, during the COVID-19 pandemic, and with many open employment positions, firefighters and law enforcement officers from around Colorado miraculously stopped a raging firestorm with the help of Mother Nature. Only two people were confirmed dead, and only eight were reported injured.

Some 37,500 residents, plus many more business customers and employees, evacuated from the spreading flames. Though everyone's story is unique, those affected by the fire share common experiences. They all fled with little warning from the encroaching flames. They all located temporary shelter. They all must decide whether to rebuild or start over someplace new. Many events occurred during and after the fire that can only be called miracles.

The book is based on the Boulder County fire and law enforcement dispatch tapes, interspersed with interviews and stories of participants, with history tales thrown in for context. Chapters are headed by the area's National Oceanic and Atmospheric Administration hourly weather reports as the winds played a powerful part. All events are factual and written without bias.

I wish to express my gratitude to those who helped me gather these stories and put them to paper. First off, to my wife, for allowing me to hole up in my office for six months pounding away on the computer. Then to those firefighters and law enforcement officers who provided firsthand accounts and insight into the logistics that went into battling such a large conflagration. And to Code 10 Photography for allowing me to use so many of their pictures. And of course, a big thanks to those who shared their individual stories.

Hopefully, *Inferno!* will provide all those reading it with a greater appreciation of the history of the area, the events that took place around the fire, and the bravery shown by those who helped fight it.

Message from Chief John Willson, Louisville Fire Protection District

Louisville, Colorado, has a rich firefighting history. From its first hose cart in 1887 pulled by ten strong men, Louisville Fire has protected the community and surrounding areas. Brave Louisville firefighters have always responded quickly and trained hard for calls without showing fear for themselves. Louisville's largest fire prior to Marshall occurred in November 1926 and almost destroyed wooden downtown. But with the help of neighboring firefighters, the fire was contained, and damage was limited to four buildings.

Our motto, Our Family Serving Your Family, captures our sprit of a motivated and dedicated crew providing help no matter what. Our career and volunteer firefighters are driven by passion, innovation, and serving the needs of all. We operate our three fire stations twenty-four hours a day, seven days a week, ready to respond to any need. We train continuously to be able to serve in any situation.

The December 2021 Marshall fire challenged our training to the utmost. Our crews valiantly stayed in service fighting the conflagration for almost twenty-four hours straight. But with perseverance and the help of neighboring firefighters, the most destructive fire in state history was over. Though many structures were damaged and destroyed in our city, we will rebuild better and stronger. I am honored to serve as their fire chief.

Message from Commander Randy Wilber, Boulder County Sheriff's Office

Wildland fires in Colorado are rare in December. But December 30, 2021, was not a typical December day. The Chinook winds were blowing, and the vegetation was tinder dry. The North Broadway fire in the 5000 block of Boulder started just before 10:00 a.m. Fire crews responded quickly and contained it within a few minutes to less than a couple of acres. Then dispatch called out a grass fire near Middle Fork Road at 10:27 a.m. Firefighters already deployed diverted to it within minutes, but the wind caused the fire to burn rapidly with flames reaching four-foot high. By 11:04 a.m., almost forty acres were involved. As structures were threatened, I arrived on-site to coordinate evacuations. The wind was horrendous. Over thirty-six fire trucks were deployed from seventeen different fire stations to fight the fire. During lulls in the extremely high winds, we saw a large plume of smoke to the south and heard chaotic and frantic radio calls. The Marshall fire had begun. We soon understood that we were dealing with the wrong fire.

During my twenty-four years of service with the Boulder County Sheriff's Department, I assisted with many wildfires—the 2003 Overland fire, 2009 Old Stage fire, 2010 Fourmile fire, 2016 Cold Springs fire, and 2020 Cal-Wood and Lefthand Canyon fires. In all of these, we collaborated with the firefighters, predicted how the fire would behave, and deployed our deputies accordingly, issuing pre-evacuation notices, knocking on doors, and closing the few mountain roads affected. We had time to coordinate our efforts. That was not the case with the Marshall fire.

The Marshall fire was the fastest, craziest fire ever. It was discovered as a grass fire about 11:20 a.m. and started burning homes within ten minutes as the high winds pushed it eastward. We could hear the frantic radio calls as the fire exploded. By noon, Costco and the Sagamore subdivision in Superior were under attack.

The fire spread over three miles in half an hour. I thought for sure we would lose many civilians, firefighters, and deputies.

But the quick-thinking actions of our deputies and firefighters spared many lives. Even though the smoke was intense, everyone in the Costco shopping center, Original Superior, and the Sagamore subdivision safely evacuated due to their actions. The hard work of the sergeants and deputies saved many lives. I joined Marshall Command at FlatIron Crossing Mall later that day and helped coordinate firefighting and evacuations. We received support from all over the state. But it is due to the heroic efforts of the sheriff sergeants and deputies who performed the early evacuations and traffic control during those first frantic minutes that saved lives. They deserve credit and our thanks.

Everyone involved in the Marshall fire said it was the fastest-moving and the most destructive fire they have ever experienced. Add in the complications of a fire going through the wildland-urban interface, thick smoke, extremely high winds, very limited visibility, and crossing from county jurisdiction into municipality jurisdiction, and then consider that the fire is part wildland and part structure fire, and you have the recipe for an "unprecedented" fire.

Introduction

The December 30, 2021, Marshall fire outside of Boulder will be remembered as the most destructive inferno in Colorado history and one of the top fifteen worst fires in the Western United States. In a little over four hours, the fire, fueled by high-velocity Chinook winds, burned 6,026 acres,[2] consumed 1,084 structures, and damaged an additional 149 more. Over 37,500 residents evacuated. Most fled without receiving any warning, leaving with little more than the shirts on their backs, escaping a fire burning minutes behind them. And yet miraculously, only two persons were confirmed killed and eight reported injured during the fire.

The Marshall fire began as a field fire discovered just after 11:10 a.m. near CO-93 S. Foothills Highway and CO-170 Marshall Road. Fanned by tremendous Chinook winds, it expanded to over two thousand acres and attacked the Sagamore subdivision in the town of Superior in under an hour, blossoming into an urban interface fire. It jumped the large US-36 Boulder-Denver Turnpike firebreak at least twice and first attacked western then southern Louisville, before devastating the Spanish Hills and Harper Lake areas. Grasslands to the south and west were devoured in its relentless march guided by the winds and bone-dry vegetation. Scenes during the fire were surreal with one house engulfed in flames while its neighbor sat quietly displaying Christmas lights. The fury of the wind decided what burned and what stood safe.

Records of windstorms fanning fires in the region go back as far as 1876, when the Boulder *Colorado Banner* in an April 6 article entitled "The Prairie Fire" discussed the winds and a winter wildfire east of Boulder burning a similar swath. Likewise, the Boulder *Daily Camera* reported damage and fires in Marshall and near present-day Superior on January 26, 1910. The nearby *Lyons Recorder*, February 10, 1917, stated that "the second fire in less than a week was raging up Noland Canon [*sic*] Saturday afternoon . . . The fires were started from sparks thrown from the freight engine, and the strong winds fanned the flames over the dry

[2] An additional 54 acres were consumed over the next few days for a total of 6,080 acres burned.

grass rapidly and swept over 60 acres of land in short order." High winds called Chinooks and grassland fires are not unusual in Boulder County; but one exploding so rapidly, occurring so late in the year, and causing so much damage, has never happened. This is the story of the fire, the area history, and the many miracles that transpired along the way.

Marshall, December 30, 2021, 8:00 a.m., Wind NW 4 mph, Gusting to 19 mph, 30°F

Native Americans, Spanish explorers, and fur trappers were the first humans to visit Colorado and see its spectacular mountains before the early 1800s. With the Louisiana Purchase in 1803, Colorado became a possession of the United States when President Andrew Jackson dealt with France's Napoleon Bonaparte to purchase the lands west of the Mississippi River. In 1806, Zebulon Pike led an expedition through the southern portion of the territory along the Arkansas River and partway into Colorado toward his namesake peak to explore this new acquisition. The western edge of the purchase was unknown as Spain claimed the lands east of the Pacific Ocean and France never set a western boundary.[3]

In 1820, Lt. Stephen Long of the US Topographical Corps explored the South Platte to present-day Denver. Failing to find a path through the mountains, he turned south and called the Colorado plains the "Great American Desert" and the entire region "almost wholly unfit for cultivation." The western half of Colorado joined the American territories in 1848 when the United States won the Spanish-American War, eliminating Spain's claim to the west. Originally part of the Kansas and Nebraska Territories, Colorado did not become its own territory until the Pikes Peak gold rush. During the 1840s, explorer John Fremont led five expeditions through the Colorado region looking for a possible transcontinental train route from St. Louis to the Pacific coast. John Gunnison followed him with the same objective in 1853. His party explored the Arkansas River into the San Luis Valley, then west to the Gunnison River. He left his name on a river and his scalp with the natives but never found a suitable train route. These explorers mapped the new Colorado region but didn't discover anything to entice settlers to stay. During the mid-1800s, most pioneers went around or passed through Colorado on their way to riches in California.

[3] Due to this discrepancy, the "kingdom" of Breckenridge celebrates Kingdom Days every year, commemorating it being left off US maps through the 1930s.

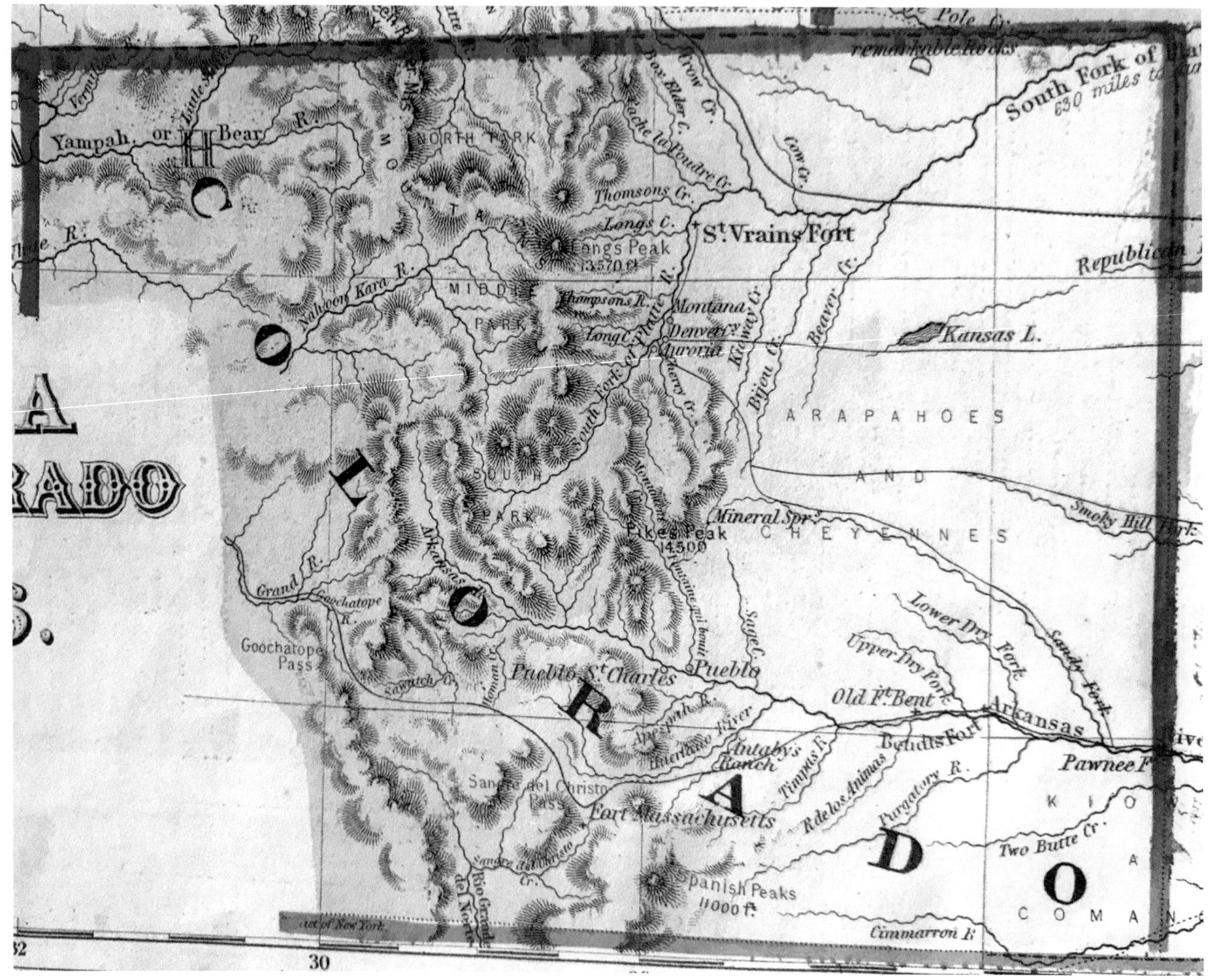

Figure 2 1863 Colorado Territory map from Johnson's New Illustrated Family Atlas.

Cherokee argonauts, traveling to the California gold fields, found gold along the Platte River before they crossed the mountains. In Sacramento, they told William Green Russell of their find, and he organized a small party to venture into Colorado in 1858. Just north of the confluence of Cherry Creek and the South Platte River near present-day Denver, Russell discovered placer gold. Additional gold discoveries soon followed up Boulder

Canyon near Gold Run (today's Gold Hill), Clear Creek Canyon near Idaho Springs, and in the "richest square mile on earth," near Black Hawk and Central City. The 1859 gold rush began, and over one hundred thousand prospectors rushed to the Colorado Territory planning to strike it rich. An 1863 map[4] of the Colorado Territory shows little details but a few towns, rivers, and mountains with the entire southwest corner of Colorado blank. Gold mining brought a great influx of settlers to the area, and these people needed to stay warm.

Coal was first discovered about five miles south of Boulder by William Kitchens in 1859 near today's Marshall. At that time, the area was a lush valley where the tall prairie grass grew belly-high to horses and game was plentiful. The coal formed in seams from one to twelve feet thick beneath the Laramie sandstone formation. Due to uplifts and faults created when the Rocky Mountains formed, the coal seams bent and twisted and stood exposed at the surface in this area. Kitchens named his coal find the Washington Lode. It was soon used as a wagon mine, where clients drove their teams to the area to scrape the coal from the exposed seam and took it home to fire their hearths and stoves. The Northern Coalfield, as it became known, stretched from Marshall, through Superior, Louisville, Erie, and Lafayette in Boulder County, to Serene, Frederick, and Firestone in Weld County.

Due to the faults and rock thrusts, iron ore (hematite) was also discovered in the area. Joseph Marshall collected the hematite; and his friend and partner, Augustine Langford, opened a foundry at Seventeenth and Larimer in Denver. Using the Washington Lode coal and nearby iron ore, they cast the first canon produced in the Colorado Territory in May 1861. It fired its first shot on July 4, 1861, and is now stored at the Denver History Museum. Expecting to capitalize on the coal and iron ore, Joseph Marshall and investors purchased the Washington Lode from William and Nancy Kitchens in 1866. He was granted a US land grant in 1868, signed by then president Andrew Johnson, which gave him legal rights to all the coal lands in the vicinity.

Marshall established a smelter south of Boulder fired by the nearby coal and using the local hematite. Famous travel writer Bayard Taylor of the *New York Tribune* wrote in 1866, "The furnace is not only substantially but handsomely built and has thus far done a thriving and successful business for its owner."[5] Marshall's smelter produced one ton of excellent gray pig iron for every 4,400 pounds of iron ore mixed with limestone and charcoal. But mining the iron ore was labor intensive, and Marshall soon discovered it was cheaper to

---

[4] Johnson & Ward, *Johnson's New Illustrated Family Atlas*, 113 Fulton St., New York, 1863, owned by author.

[5] Joanna Sampson, *Walking Through History on Marshall Mesa* (2008), 7.

buy worn-out farm equipment and recast it rather than mine iron ore. After processing about 500 tons of hematite, the smelter closed, and Marshall concentrated on mining coal.

Figure 3 The Virginia reel folk dance was performed in Langford (Marshall) on April 6, 1887. Courtesy of the Carnegie Library for Local History / Museum of Boulder Collection.

A thriving community developed around the coal mine. Miners from all over the world came; and miners' shacks, dugouts, company houses, and sturdy rock homes soon filled the valley. Boarding homes, blacksmiths, and numerous saloons, including a branch of the Zang Brewery Company, were soon built, joined by a meat market and a post office. The area never hosted a cemetery or a church, but there was always a school. The town was originally called Langford in honor of Augustine B. and Nathaniel P. Langford,[6] who were early investors. It was also called Gorham during the early 1900s. But finally, Marshall became its name.

Fifty-one coal mines operated in the vicinity of Marshall per official Colorado mining records. Soon railroads connected Marshall to Golden, Boulder, and Denver, transporting the coal during the cooler months for heating, power plants, railroads, and steam engines.

Figure 4 Coal mining in Marshall circa 1885. Note Flatiron Mountains and burning coalfields in the background. Courtesy of the Carnegie Library for Local History, Boulder.

[6] Nathaniel Langford became the governor of Montana and later the first superintendent of Yellowstone National Park after its founding in 1872.

Being a low-grade subbituminous coal, the mines only operated in the winter, and the miners scraped out a living elsewhere during the summer. The coal mined contains a significant moisture content, and when it dries, the coal falls apart or spontaneously combusts, and thus does not keep. Mining is a hard life and living in a company town means paying exorbitant prices in the company store. Miners purchased their own tools, carbide lights, and black powder for blasting the coal seams. They paid monthly fees to fund the company doctor and blacksmith. Usually, they received no more than fifty cents per ton of coal they mined. When payday came and the miner spent more than he earned at the company store, he received a "bobtail" check stating the amount he owed the company.

Mining was dangerous and many miners died working. Falling slabs of coal and rock killed the most, but many were taken by being crushed against a wall or run over by a loaded coal car. Miners died in explosions, by being buried alive in collapses, and some were electrocuted. Miners formed unions to increase wages and improve working conditions, but the companies retaliated harshly, evicting entire families without providing back pay.

At the beginning of the Long Strike in 1910, twenty-five miner families were evicted into the winter night in Marshall. Machine guns and searchlights swiveled on the mining tipples and water tanks to keep the strikers at bay. The governor sent in the state militia (now the National Guard), not to negotiate, but to protect the company property from the strikers. Untrained scabs were brought in to replace the miners, and accidental deaths skyrocketed. During the strike, Boulder County sheriff's department tried to remain impartial but was called to the mines and communities almost daily. The strike continued for four long years, and at the end, the miners gained little.

Coal mining stagnated until the need for coal boomed with the US entry into World War I. But the bottom fell out with the stock market crash of 1929 and the beginning of the Great Depression. The Gorham Mine that opened in 1898 closed in 1939. Coal lands sold for back taxes. Rail lines were pulled up for scrap metal. Except for a few small operations, mine property was abandoned, and the population of Marshall dwindled from a high over two thousand to just a handful.

Today, Marshall is a quiet and unassuming part of unincorporated Boulder County. Many of the coal mines have filled with water or collapsed. Only a few homes are occupied in this once-thriving town. Starting in 1971, the City of Boulder acquired land around the old mining community; and most of it is now Marshall Mesa, part of Boulder's Open Space and Mountain Parks land system. Though some of it is grazed by cattle, most of this land is left natural by the City of Boulder with tall prairie grasses predominant.

Marshall today is best known for the underground coal fires that still burn among the coal seams. Originating as early as 1869, these fires have sometimes raged and at others just smoldered, sending plumes of smoke up from the mesa. In 1883, Colorado coal mine inspector John McNeil wrote, "There are three collieries in this state in which spontaneous combustion is going on. The most fierce of these mine fires can be found in the Marshall coal field, Boulder. This fire in part originated fourteen years ago (1869) and now extends over many acres."[7]

Figure 5 Burning coal seams Langford (Marshall) circa 1890s. Courtesy of the Carnegie Library for Local History, Boulder.

[7] Joanna Sampson, *Walking Through History on Marshall Mesa* (2008), 18.

The US Geological Survey verified these problems again in 1986, and smoke can still be seen occasionally when walking the trails of the Open Space even today. The Colorado Division of Reclamation, Mining, and Safety confirmed in 2018 that the fires still burned at a "very low" level in the Marshall 1 and 2 mining areas. Located just across from the Twelve Tribes property, this coal seam fire was rated the nineteenth most active of thirty-eight known underground fires in the state. On December 20, 2005, a brush fire started from a "hot vent" near the smoldering coal seam adjacent to the open space trailhead. It was quickly extinguished, but a temperature reading at the vent afterward read 373°F. Over 275 tons of gravel were dumped into that seam in 2006 to lessen the danger. In 2016, additional excavating, compacting, and backfilling occurred in areas of concern. Other remediation work followed in both 2013 and 2018, including taking ground temperatures and mapping fissures, snowmelt, and surface features. Additional seam fire vents are in the vicinity, but their surface temperatures only measured 90°F. Nearby where Marshall Road meets Cherryvale Road were the Lewis 1 and 2 mine sites that were also on fire. This was confirmed in February 2018 from inconsistent surface snowmelt. Measurements of the vent above this fire barely registered above ambient air temperature but were hot enough to melt snow. Three coal seam fire locations are being investigated as the potential source of the Marshall fire.

A coal seam fire ignited a blaze in Glenwood Springs in 2002 that quickly spread and consumed 12,000 acres and 29 homes[8]. The South Canyon coal seam fires that started this blaze were south of Glenwood Springs on County Road 134 and had been burning since before 1900. They were considered "highly active," with new vents opening often and surface temperatures reaching 700°F. Even today, signs are posted along trails in the area telling tourists not to call 911 upon spying the smoke venting from these fires. Glenwood fire sends crews out each summer to clear the vegetation within one hundred feet of known fire vents. They don't need to remove vegetation from over each vent as the heat kills anything growing. After the Marshall fire, the state Division of Reclamation, Mining, and Safety may recommend increasing that one-hundred-foot clearing zone if it is shown that a coal seam fire initiated the Marshall fire.

Extinguishing an "eternal flame" coal fire is extremely difficult. One fire in Australia is dated over six thousand years old. Water can douse a surface fire, but if injected into a subsurface mine fire, it can cause a steam explosion. In Colorado, the only coal seam fire extinguished successfully transpired because the seam was close to the surface, and it was strip-mined to remove the burning coal.

---

[8] Mary Shinn, Evan Wyloge, and Stephanie Earls, "Dangerous Legacy: Tens of Thousands of Coloradans Live Near One of the State's Many Underground Coal-Mine Fires," *Denver Gazette*, February 20, 2022.

Another concern fighting coal seam fires is that many coal beds also emit methane gas. In 1976, the Eagle mine, outside of Erie, emitted seven thousand cubic feet of methane per day (twenty-eight cubic feet of gas per ton of coal). It closed in 1978 due to a fire. In 1983, Tremain and Toomey[9] drilled pilot holes near the Marshall 2 mine and took three samples for methane gas. No gas was found at the forty-foot depth. But one cubic foot of methane gas per cubic ton of coal was identified in the Gorham bed at both eighty-four-foot and ninety-one-foot depths. This is a low gas content as other drill test sites in the region measured gas from four to twenty-four cubic feet per ton of coal in the same Gorham seam. Later studies hypothesized that the gas at these relatively shallow depths dispersed into the numerous abandoned mining shafts in the area. These gases occasionally fed the burning seams and can result in fire plumes soaring high into the air as documented happening in 1986.

Currently, Colorado budgets $3 million a year to monitor coal mine issues. This is to increase to almost $10 million a year for the next fifteen years based on the 2021 Infrastructure Investment and Jobs Act, once the government decides how to distribute it. Currently, a survey of all known coal fires is conducted every five years, and each fire is ranked according to a risk assessment. The last survey was completed in 2018. During that survey, the three fires burning near Marshall rate as "low activity" fires but are in above-average "wildfire hazard potential" risk areas with more than six thousand inhabitants living within two miles. With the additional funding, extra surveys and new techniques can be applied to reduce the risk of wildfires caused by coal seam fires. Boulder County and the City of Boulder both received copies of the 2018 survey.

The National Weather Service issued a high wind warning for Boulder County at 7:00 a.m. on December 30, 2021. High winds coming off the mountains and foothills to the west are called Chinooks and are not unusual near Boulder. Since 1967, at least 15 windstorms have recorded velocities over 100 miles per hour and an additional 20 or so exhibit wind speeds in the 70 to 90 mph range. The highest recorded gust of 137 mph occurred during the great windstorm of January 16–17, 1982, which caused more than $17 million in damage and had 20 other gusts over 120 mph. With the wind building, Xcel Energy received the first notifications of electrical power outages around the county by 8:30 a.m. The first wisps of smoke were noticed by the residents of Marshall around 9:00 a.m.

[9] Stephen B. Roberts, "Coal in the Front Range Urban Corridor," US Geological Survey, 2007, 20.

Louisville, December 30, 2021, 8:45 a.m., Wind E 10 mph, Gusting to 18 mph, 41°F

The day before New Year's Eve in Louisville, Colorado, started out partly cloudy and cool at 30°F. School was closed for the holidays, and many parents took time off to spend with their children. With a population of 21,226, Louisville is a suburban residential community with most workers commuting to jobs nearby or working remotely from home. This year had been particularly dry, with no significant rain or snowfall occurring since September, or even earlier. The town was relatively affluent, and old homes were often scraped and replaced with new "McMansions."

But this wasn't always true. Most of the land that became Louisville was originally owned by farmers and speculators who believed that once the steam trains from the first transcontinental railroad up by Julesberg (now Julesburg) made it south to Golden Town (now Golden), the territorial capital,[10] coal will be needed to fire them. One of these speculators was William A. Davidson, who with investors from Iowa purchased upward of six thousand acres east of Boulder by 1870. By April 1873, grading for a railroad from Julesberg to Golden was complete, and Davidson incorporated his company on April 24, 1873, to "mine for coal and iron and other ores in the County of Boulder Colorado, to construct and maintain canals, ditches & flumes for mining, manufacturing and agricultural purposes, to buy, sell and lease coal, iron, agricultural and other lands in the county of Boulder."[11] An "adit" mine, where the shaft goes horizontally into the hillside instead of vertically down, was proposed near the current Louisville North water treatment plant north of today's S. Boulder Road. The Davidson irrigation ditch was built to provide the mine with water across what is now known as Davidson Mesa and through the current Spanish Hills housing development. Competitive investors filed a similar mining claim nearby called Excelsior Coal. Louis Nawatny was hired to manage it. Both mines only operated for a short time as the coal delivered was of subquality and crumbled to dust soon after being mined. However, Nawatny's mining and management expertise caught the eye of Charles Welch, a prominent Golden investor who was working with Union Pacific, and Nawatny was soon working for him.

[10] Golden Town (now Golden) was the Colorado territorial capital from 1862 to 1867.

[11] *Louisville Historian*, Issue #88, Fall 2010.

With Welch's financial backing, on July 25, 1877, Nawatny leased mineral rights from David Kerr of 240 acres northwest of the current intersection of Highway 42 and Ninety-sixth Street. On August 26, he entered a land contract to purchase 240 acres north of Kerr's property for the inflated price of $20 per acre. He then built a two-story home on government property just west of the railroad tracks at the southwest corner of today's Front and Pine Streets. Welch appointed Nawatny the first superintendent of the mine. Digging soon commenced in early 1878 north of today's Empire Road near the Louisville wastewater treatment plant to reach the rich coal seam 210 feet below. The mine was soon named the Welch mine.

On February 18, 1878, Nawatny purchased the forty-acre site on which his home was built for $2.50 per acre from the federal government. In a series of convoluted transactions, Welch and Nawatny traded properties that resulted in Nawatny maintaining the surface rights of what was to become Old Town Louisville plus $100 and Welch retaining the underground mineral rights. An application was filed for a post office on May 7, 1878, for Louisville stating that seventy-five residents lived in the area. Kate Nawatny, Louis's wife, became postmaster. The plat for the town of eighty-five lots on twenty acres was filed with Boulder County on October 24, 1878. When filed, Welch, his wife, or one of their relatives owned 22 percent of the new town. The borders of the original plat today are the railroad to the east, the alley west of Main, South Street to the north, and Elm Street on the south.

Figure 6 1919 Louisville with Acme Mine. Courtesy of the Louisville Historical Museum.

In speculation that the Welch mine and Louisville will succeed, Welch purchased forty acres to the west of town from Edward Autrey for $40 per acre on February 1, 1879. He filed a plat for twenty of those acres as the Jefferson Place expansion to Louisville on October 12, 1880. Meanwhile, the Wall Street baron Jay Gould, who owned controlling interests in the Union Pacific Railroad, acquired the Welch mine on February 20, 1879. By 1880, it was the largest producing mine in Colorado, employing 179 men and producing 600–700 tons of coal daily. Union Pacific sold the mine to the Marshall Consolidated Coal Mining Company in 1885.

Almost 500 residents called Louisville home, and another 130 lived in the surrounding farms in 1880. By 1882, there were four general merchandise stores, the miners' cooperative store, and eight saloons in town. A school opened in the Jefferson Place development in 1881. The married residents wanted to incorporate into a town, but many single miners did not. But on May 26, 1882, the town of Louisville was legally recognized, and John H. Simpson was elected the first mayor.

A second mine, the Acme Mine, opened in 1888, where Hutchinson and Roosevelt Streets now meet. This mine became the primary mine in Louisville due to its central location and long life. It produced 1,729,282 tons of coal[12] and employed hundreds of men over its forty years of operation. Digging on two levels, the shaft reached 186 feet, and two veins were worked directly under Louisville: the first at 90 feet and later at 185 feet. Based on its success, the Acme Place subdivision was platted in 1893, building Louisville farther to the south and west. Orrin Welch platted the Pleasant Hill addition to the west of Jefferson Place and north of Acme Place in 1894. Three other mines opened near Louisville by 1890—the Hecla, the Caledonia, and the Ajax. Louisville seemed destined to grow along with the need for energy and coal.

But then the bottom fell out. The town began to sink. In the late 1880s, land east of downtown first started to settle from the collapse of part of the old Welsh mine. The railbed was raised by bringing in rock to counter the sinking. Then in October 1893, additional mine timbers collapsed, and the ground sank two to three feet in downtown and disrupted the water supply. In 1895, shallow works in the Acme mine resulted in areas sinking three to four feet. Then in 1896, downtown businesses and residences, including the post office, dropped by as much as six feet.

> Alarmed at the Sinking of Lots and Property. The citizens of Louisville are becoming very anxious as to their future location and what shall become of their homes. For a year or two, the operators of the Acme coal mine have been working under the town of Louisville and lots and residences have been affected by this work as the mine is not a very deep one. During the last few months, the residence lots of quite a number of citizens have commenced to cave in, the bottoms of wells have dropped out and a farsicle [*sic*] return to the method of living of old time cave dwellers is threatened. Some property has already sunk down three or four feet and it would seem that the people would soon find themselves without homes and their property destroyed unless heroic action is taken.[13]

[12] Carolyn Conarroe, *Coal Mining in Colorado's Northern Field.*

[13] *Boulder Daily Camera*, July 22, 1895, in an article titled "Will Protect Their Homes."

Many thousands of wagonloads of dirt and rock were used to prop up the sinking buildings. Through 1923, numerous lawsuits were filed and out-of-court settlements made against the mines that caused the sinkage.

Thirty mines opened and operated around Louisville with twelve operating during the peak years of 1907 to 1909. Louisville's population grew to about seventeen hundred. With the City of Boulder voting to become dry in 1907, thirteen saloons operated in a four-block stretch on Front Street within walking distance of the train to Boulder. When national Prohibition passed in 1916, most of these saloons officially became pool halls or soda parlors, though the alcohol still readily flowed. Bosses with connections to the mob made sure that booze was available, and the miners supposedly tunneled from saloon to saloon so that when the law showed up at one, the party moved to another without being disrupted. Prohibition officially ended in 1933, but Boulder remained dry through 1967, supplying a steady stream of customers to Louisville who wanted a drink with their meal. Rumor has it that three retired mafia "dons" reigned in one local restaurant up through the early 1980s.

Figure 7 Hecla mine cottage and tower riddled with bullet holes. Courtesy of the Carnegie Library for Local History / Museum of Boulder Collection.

Louisville miners also participated in the 1910–1914 Long Strike.[14] The Hecla mine, located near where King Soopers now stands on S. Boulder Road, built twenty-six cottages, a boardinghouse, and a casino to entice scabs to mine and break the strike. A security force patrolled the high fence enclosing the compound with searchlights and machine guns. The strikers could only picket outside under the taunts of the guards. The scabs could only leave the compound when accompanied by armed guards.

Though bad in Louisville, the conditions were worse in the southern coal mines. Violent clashes were bitter and claimed many casualties. This culminated in the Ludlow Massacre on April 20, 1914, when the state militia fired on the strikers, killing at least five miners and thirteen women and children in Ludlow, Colorado. Hearing of the carnage, the strikers in Louisville fired shots at the Hecla mine on April 26, 1914. The guards returned fire with machine guns. The shooting continued for eighteen hours, with bullets whizzing downtown

[14] Base in part from *Louisville Historian*, Fall, 2014, in an article titled "Fear Rules Cities and Fight is On at Louisville Mines."

and into the compound. No townsfolk or strikers were injured, but one death and two injuries occurred inside the Hecla compound.

The governor sent the state militia to Louisville to protect the mines and restore order, but the townsfolk met them with gunfire due to their actions at Ludlow. Federal troops were then called in from Fort Robinson, Nebraska. When their train arrived, the city greeted them with a marching band and a parade and thumbed their noses at the departing militia. The strike ended in December 1914, and the troops moved out. A small wage increase was granted, but mining conditions worsened.

Figure 8 Federal troops camping in Louisville 1914. Courtesy of the Louisville Historical Museum.

One more major strike occurred in the fall of 1927 that affected the northern coal mines.[15] Due to the poor economic conditions, the mines all closed, except the Columbine mine in Serene (located just east of Lafayette off today's SR-7, where the only remains of the two-thousand-plus-person town are a small monument and a bench on the south side of the road). The International Workers of the World (IWW) or "Wobblies" marched daily from Louisville and the surrounding mines to demand that the Columbine close. On November 8, almost two hundred autos

Figure 9 Columbine mine in Serene with train. Courtesy of the Carnegie Library for Local History / Museum of Boulder Collection.

[15] Based in part from *The 1927 Columbine Mine Massacre: Trouble in Serene* by P. Eberhart

blocked the roads to Serene; and on Saturday, November 19, an estimated one thousand two hundred strikers, including women, marched outside the fortress that was Serene. On the following Monday, an estimated six hundred strikers marched on Serene by six thirty in the morning. Supposedly rocks were thrown and warning shots fired. The miners claimed that the guards opened up with machine guns. In what is to become known as death alley, twenty-three strikers were seriously wounded (including two women), and five eventually died. The state militia was again called out, and they camped in Serene and later Louisville and Frederick. Then the strike just petered out . . .

The decline of the coal mines accelerated when the first natural gas pipelines came to Colorado from Texas in 1928. Natural gas was cleaner, cheaper, and easier to use than shoveling coal to heat homes and cook food. Louisville turned to restaurants and taverns for revenue. Under the watchful eye of wise guys, local restaurants served alcohol and hosted backroom gambling. This did not sit well with the county government. In 1951, the Boulder County district attorney filed suit to close the Bugdust Pool Hall, a notorious rigged gambling place on Main Street.

In 1952, natural gas finally reached Louisville, and the residents readily installed it even though coal founded the town. The Boulder Turnpike (now US-36) was completed in 1952, providing four-lane traffic between Boulder and Denver for a quarter. In 1953, a bond was passed to install a sewer system. The original sewer pipes installed were made from rolled tar paper and lasted for more than seventy years. The last coal mine in Louisville, the Crown Mine, closed in 1955; but only twenty miners lost their jobs. The rest commuted to mines in Lafayette or Erie or worked for the secretive Rocky Flats nuclear plant south of town. In February 1958, over four thousand people visited Louisville each Sunday. Its three main restaurants, the Blue Parrot, Colacci's, and the Hacienda, served over two thousand three hundred meals, mostly homemade spaghetti, served with a glass of wine or liquor. Street paving replaced the practice of oiling gravel when a bond passed in 1959. Louisville finally became a city.

Jesse Aweida, Juan Rodriguez, Tom Kavanagh, and Zoltan Herger formed Storage Technology Corporation as a spin-off from the IBM plant located north of Boulder in 1970. They purchased forty acres of land south of Louisville along US-36 for its headquarters and manufacturing site. The company planned to invest $1M to develop computer tape drives and hire one hundred local employees. So started Louisville's transition into a high-tech haven. In response to Boulder's land grab for open space to surround it, Louisville annexed several parcels of land, including what became Via Appia, McCaslin Boulevard, and the 715 acres destined as the Colorado Technology Center. Following Boulder's lead, Louisville designated the land around Harper Lake as the Leon A. Wurl Wildlife Sanctuary and set aside land for the North Open Space in 1979.

The population in Louisville in 1980 was 5,593 and grew to 12,361 by 1990. Fueled mostly by the high home prices in growth-limited Boulder, young families flocked to Louisville to enjoy its mounting infrastructure and historic downtown. Why buy a small, cramped town house in Boulder when a new home twice the size with land was available in Louisville for the same price? Louisville put in a golf course and a recreation center and started plans for building Centennial Valley along McCaslin Boulevard in 1993. Growth continued to 18,937 by 2000, and Louisville became a home rule charter in 2001. The first downtown street fair occurred in 2004, and by 2005, *Money Magazine* started listing Louisville as one of the five best places to live in the United States. By 2010, the population was 18,376, and the art district began the first Friday art walk.

The one-thousand-year flood of 2013 took out the Coal Creek Golf Course and sections of County Road and Dillon Road and damaged homes throughout the city when eighteen inches of rain fell over seventy-two hours. Fifth graders from Fireside Elementary on a field trip in the mountains were airlifted by helicopter back home from Jamestown when the flood cut them off. But Louisville built back quickly. By 2020, Louisville topped 20,154 in population and the COVID-19 pandemic hit. The city blocked off part of Main Street to allow restaurants to serve outside, and life continued.

By December 30, 2021, Boulder County still had COVID restrictions in place, with masks required for all public indoor activities. SARS-CoV-2, the virus that causes COVID-19, was first recorded in Boulder County in March 2020 and after almost two years showed little signs of stopping. The Delta variant peaked in February 2021, and the Omicron variant was the dominant strain in the community on December 30, 2021. With milder but more virulent symptoms, Omicron cases in the county expanded rapidly. As of January 20, 2022, Boulder County counted 53,052 total confirmed COVID cases and reported 339 deaths caused by or related to COVID-19.

Figure 10 The Boven residence in Louisville prior to the fire.

Retired volunteer fireman Larry Boven[16] lived with his wife, Mary, in the Centennial Heights West subdivision on Hillside Lane in Louisville in a home that they built for $179,000 in 1993. The two-story, two-car-garage home boasted five bedrooms and three-and-a-quarter baths tucked away in its 1883 square feet. Its walkout finished basement looked out to the south. In their almost thirty years living there, they accumulated many knickknacks and heirlooms. Every Christmas they hosted a heritage Swedish smorgasbord party for their friends and neighbors, highlighting Mary's collection of forty Simpich Character Dolls that she collected every year in Old Colorado City with their daughter, Anna. Larry was an avid runner, participating in many marathons even though he was pushing seventy years young. Mary was more reserved, suffering from a version of Multiple Sclerosis that often left her mentally challenged. Zillow's "zestimate" value for their home was $1.1M, with its back deck overlooking the Centennial Valley of Louisville and spectacular view of the mountains.

Mary enjoyed structure and routine and went to the Louisville Recreation and Senior Center most weekday mornings. When it was nice, she walked the five blocks down the hill and across McCaslin then along Via Appia. But this late December morning was a bit nippy with a brisk breeze, so Larry drove her. He thought about running but decided that it would not be pleasant in the wind. He thought he might be able to run later.

[16] Interview with Larry Boven at LaMar's Donuts, Louisville, May 11, 2022.

Superior, December 30, 2021, 10:00 a.m., Wind WSW 30 mph, Gusting to 65 mph, 41°F

Figure 11 Williamson dream home in Superior.

R. Paul Williamson,[17] 74, spent many years in the US Navy and teaching as a professor at the University of Montana but finally retired to build his dream home in Original Superior. An inventor and author, he purchased two third-of-an-acre lots on W. Maple Street, south of Whole Foods and west of McCaslin in 2010. He designed the house himself and ensured that it was energy efficient and fully sustainable with solar panels and a wind turbine. To be safe in Colorado's stormy environment, he used prebuilt insulated sections covered with Hardie Backer Cement Board siding and a steel roof to construct his dream home. He started building in 2014. Spending ten hours a day of his own labor and with the help of a general contractor, he completed the building within a year and a half. The only exposed wood on the entire house was the particle board eaves under the roof and a small stoop. Everything else was nonflammable cement board and metal roofing. He added solar panels and raised garden beds and a gazebo in the back. The house was a showcase of sustainability, and Paul often referenced it in his advocacy promoting mass transportation for the northern Front Range. He called it the Sustainable Smart Home Living Learning Center and often opened it up for tours. On this fateful Thursday morning, Paul was driving back to Superior from a visit to Denver.

[17] Interview with R. Paul Williamson at Cristos Coffee, Erie, February 4, 2022.

Undoubtedly, prehistoric natives were the first settlers to live along Coal Creek and the Superior area. The Folsom and the Clovis people as far as 7000 BC visited the area and left many of their distinctive spear points. An archaeological dig at the Goodhue Farm, where Rock Creek flows under US-287 south of Lafayette, dated dwellings to six thousand two hundred years ago. Countless stone rings outlining teepees and fire pits exist along the length of Coal Creek. The Ute traditionally roamed all of Colorado starting in the 1650s when they acquired horses from the Spaniards. Later natives who inhabited east of the Rockies include the Southern Arapaho, Southern Cheyenne, Kiowa, and Comanche. The Arapaho and Cheyenne came to the area late, in the early 1800s, when they fled the white immigration into Minnesota. They joined forces to combat the Ute to control the great hunting grounds along the Front Range.

The Southern Arapaho settled in the Boulder Valley for the good hunting and therapeutic Eldorado Springs. Being nomadic, they ranged from Boulder Canyon out to present-day Brush, including the confluence of Cherry Creek and the South Platte (present-day Denver). Not just hunters and warriors, the Arapaho were also adept traders. Because of this, they were known as diplomats and language artists.

Figure 12 Reputed picture of Chief Niwot of the Arapaho. Courtesy of AboutBoulder.com.

One of the best of these who became chief was a boy who favored his left hand and was called Niwot[18] (which means left hand in his native language). Through trade, Niwot became proficient in many native languages and even learned English from his sister's husband, a fur trapper named John Poisal. Born in the early 1820s, he was a handsome man, broad in shoulder, at least six feet in height. Per the Treaty of Fort Laramie in 1851, the Arapaho were promised the lands between the Platte and Arkansas Rivers. In the fall of 1858, the Arapaho discovered gold seekers at the mouth of Boulder Creek. Captain Thomas Aikens and gold seekers from Fort St.

[18] Based on https://aboutboulder.com/blog/chief-niwot-and-the-curse-of-boulder-valley/ and other sources. Note no picture is proven to be Chief Niwot, and this picture may be of another chief with the same name from Oklahoma in the 1890s.

Vrain thirty miles east came to winter at the mouth of the creek while searching for gold. Chief Niwot issued his legendary curse of the Boulder Valley to Captain Aikens, "People seeing the beauty of this valley will want to stay, and their staying will be the undoing of the beauty." Though tensions were high that fall, no fighting ensued, and to keep the peace, Chief Niwot moved his people east.

A treaty in 1861 guaranteed the Arapaho and Cheyenne hunting grounds in eastern Colorado. But raids against white settlers were blamed on these natives, and Territorial Governor John Evans called out the Colorado Volunteer Cavalry led by Col. John Chivington. They mercilessly attacked an encampment of Arapaho and Cheyenne in November 1864 at Sand Creek, killing 150, mostly women, children, and old men. Most of these troops came from the Boulder area and trained at Fort Chambers, located near Valmont, a small town east of Boulder north of sacred Valmont Butte.[19] Chiefs Black Kettle, White Antelope. and Niwot all died. In a sad and tragic twist, the survivors moved to a reservation in Oklahoma only to be attacked again by troops led by Lt. Col. George Custer along the banks of the Washita River in 1868.

The first English settlers to the Coal Creek Valley were William C. Hake and his wife, Emmaline.[20] They came to the Colorado Territory in 1860 from Superior, Wisconsin, planning to provide agricultural supplies to the gold mining towns in the mountains west of Boulder. Hake planted crops and apple trees and raised livestock along the creek. In the spring of 1864, the creek flooded, and a vein of coal appeared. He continued farming for another thirty years before hiring Jim Hood to sink a 265-foot shaft to tap the coal seam in 1892. The mine was named the Industrial, and from then on, Hood was the engineer and manager and Hake its owner. Over four million tons of coal were extracted from the Industrial until it finally closed in 1945. The remains of the shaft can be found west of today's McCaslin Boulevard south on the hillside above the irrigation ditch along the Mayhoffer Singletree Trailhead. A second Superior coal mine, the Enterprise, is located east of McCaslin closer to US-36.

---

[19] The Arapaho and Chief Niwot were camped at Valmont Butte when Capt. Thomas Aikens came to Boulder Creek. It is still sacred to the Arapaho today.

[20] Based on https://downtownsuperior.com/a-superior-transformation/

Figure 13 1889 picture of William Hake farm. Courtesy of the Carnegie Library for Local History / Museum of Boulder Collection.

Hake advertised in regional publications urging miners to move to Superior to find "lovely, cheap homes," the best coal in the state, and an "elegant climate and water pure." He predicted the town will boast a population of 600 within two years (by 1898). He missed his forecast as only 135 lived in Superior in 1900. The town incorporated in 1904 and soon boasted a general store, several saloons, the Miner's Trading Company, a candy and fruit shop, a boardinghouse for single miners, and a house on the way to Marshall for "working girls."

No one is certain why Hake named the town Superior. The obvious reason is because he came from Superior, Wisconsin. Others say he chose Superior because he advertised the coal from the Industrial as "having no superior in the State." A third version says he and his wife broke down in Superior, Nebraska. Being overwhelmed by the residents' generosity and helpfulness, he vowed to name any town he founded for them.

Superior coal miners also participated in the 1910–1914 Long Strike. The Industrial Mine by then was owned by the Rocky Mountain Fuel Company. They hired scabs to work the mine during the strike and the Baldwin-Felts detectives for protection. The Searcy family from Tennessee was hired as scabs to mine during the strike due to their ruthless reputation. Brothers Jim and John "Dude" Searcy worked the mine and were suspect in the dynamiting of a striking miner's cabin. During the strike, the brothers met about thirty picketers and Marshal Angelo D'Andrea at the Superior train depot on the evening of November 28, 1911. After exchanging words, a fifteen-minute gunfight ensued, and Dude Searcy was mortally wounded by Marshal D'Andrea. Boulder County sheriff M. P. Capp arrived the next morning and took D'Andrea to jail, where he was indicted for "killing with felonious intent."[21] The striking miners banded together and raised $10,000 bail. He was acquitted of murder in November 1912 during a jury trial because of his impeccable reputation and the statement of Canon City prison inmate William Adams, who testified that Searcy was brought to Colorado to break the strike and previously killed two men in West Virginia. Adams said Searcy went to town that evening to avenge words said about his mother by the strikers and drew his gun and fired at D'Andrea first. The jury found D'Andrea not guilty.

---

[21] "Shootout at the Superior Depot," *Superior Historian*, October 2004.

Figure 14 Evidence Photo from the D'Andrea trial of the Superior train depot. Courtesy of the Carnegie Library for Local History / Museum of Boulder Collection.

Coal mining in the Boulder-Weld coalfield occurred from 1859 through 1979.[22] The coalfield stretched in a +/-15-mile-wide belt running from Marshall northeast over 50 miles to just southeast of Greeley. More than 160 mines operated in the region and extracted over 170 million tons of coal. The coal throughout the region had seven major beds, each ranging from 1 to 14 feet thick. All the coal was a subbituminous grade, having heat-of-combustion values from 8,200 to +9,000 BTUs per pound. The lowest seam, no. 1, sat atop Fox Hills Sandstone and marked the base of the Laramie Formation. It was only 1 to 3 feet thick and usually not mined. Seam no. 2, also called the Sump seam, was located 11 to 65 feet above and was 1 to 8 feet thick. Seam no. 3, the Gorham seam, was the most mined in the region because of its lateral continuity and thickness ranging from 2 to 14 feet. In places it merged with seam no. 4, but elsewhere it was separated by as much as 30 to

[22] Stephen B. Roberts, "Coal in the Front Range Urban Corridor . . .," US Geological Survey, 2007.

35 feet of rock. Seam no. 4 typically ranged from 1 to 11 feet in thickness. The Middle seam, seam no. 5, ranged from 1 to 10 feet in thickness and was located 10 to 50 feet above no. 4 and 20 to 70 feet below no. 6. The Upper seam, seam no. 6, ranged from 1 to 8 feet thick and was typically 30 to 100 feet below the top no. 7 coal bed, which was 2 to 5 feet thick. All these coal beds were located at varying distances underground depending upon the local topography. Seam no. 7 breached the surface in certain areas near Marshall, Coal Creek in Superior and in Erie, and was as much as 700 feet below ground level elsewhere.

Coal mining brought settlers to this region, but water defined it. Colorado is considered semiarid and only averages 17 inches of precipitation a year statewide. By the end of 2021, Boulder County was in an extreme drought condition. When the snows finally came early in 2022, it quickly returned to average rainfall. Varying changes in rainfall in the region are normal, and Coal Creek flooded periodically. In 1935, Coal Creek flooded during spring runoff after a particularly heavy rainfall that included a large amount of hail. A more devastating flood hit in 1938, taking out both the Second Avenue and Third Avenue bridges in Superior and cutting off the town from Boulder and Louisville to the north until the water subsided and the creek could be forded. The thousand-year flood of 2013 also caused widespread damage throughout Superior and the Front Range.

The grasslands to the west of Superior and Louisville are part of Boulder-owned Open Space, partly put in place to protect one of the few remaining tallgrass prairies left in Colorado. On Davidson Mesa, fauna includes big bluestem grass, side oats grama, and blue grama.[23] Closer to Superior and Marshall, these are joined by switchgrass and Indian grass, which are all distant cousins of aspen. These grasses look bluish in the spring and early summer but appear reddish in September and become dried and brown by December. In wetter areas, prairie cordgrass grows, and in drier areas, little bluestem is common. Due to underlying rock and clay, the water table is quite high. In 2021, rains occurred in the spring through June when these grasses grow the best. Then the summer dried out with little moisture falling. This is almost perfect growing conditions for these grasses, accessing the water from below. The record-setting snowpack during the previous winter followed by a wet spring resulted in a 70 percent increase in grasses growing in the meadows near Marshall Lake. After a great growing season, drought followed, and these grasses were tinder-dry by December.

Frederick Clements in the early 1900s considered the grasslands to be "disclimax," requiring disruptive forces to maintain equilibrium. According to Owensby (1972), tallgrass prairies are "fire derived and fire maintained" with most fires occurring from fall to midspring when "vegetation is dormant, humidities are

[23] Grassland discussion from *The Boulder Tallgrass Prairies*, William L. Baker and Susan M. Galatowitsch, August 15, 1985.

low, soil surfaces are dry, and wind velocities are above average." Fires in early winter reduce warm-season perennial grasses while fires in early spring favor them. In contrast, fires in late spring favor bluestem grasses. Due to city and county controls, these grasslands had not been burned for at least the past thirty years.

A human-caused grass fire, the Oak fire, torched 152 acres near S. Kipling Parkway and C-470 two days prior to the Marshall fire in neighboring Jefferson County on December 27, 2021. The fire started around 2:15 p.m. near a popular hiking trail and quickly spread north and east. Pre-evacuation notices were posted for Ken Caryl Valley and the Westerly Apartment complex, but they were never evacuated. With the winds light, this fire was 70 percent contained by firefighters and a single-engine air tanker from Fort Collins within four hours. Though a suspect was identified, no arrests were made.

Similarly, the NCAR fire started on Saturday, March 26, 2022, near a trailhead south of the National Center for Atmospheric Research (NCAR) facilities in south Boulder, only a few miles from where the Marshall fire initiated. Over 8,000 homes were evacuated. Though the fire spread rapidly and put up a lot of smoke, no buildings were consumed, and no one was hurt. The fire was fully contained by March 31 at 190 acres burned. Fire officials stated the fire was human caused but no suspects have been identified.

During the 1920s, other fires that burned near Superior, Louisville, and Boulder included large wooden crosses. Founded in 1921 by Dr. John Galen Locke, the Kolorado Ku Klux Klan[24] dominated Colorado state politics, controlling the governor, secretary of state, US Senate, Denver mayor, and other offices in the 1922 election. Though race issues controlled the Klan in other states, here in Colorado the Klan intimidated Jews and Catholic immigrants, especially Italians, instead. In 1922, over 250 "Kleagles" or pledges were inducted into the organization near Lee Hill Road in north Boulder with burning crosses and a cult initiation service. Old-timers in Superior remember talking about cross burnings above the Industrial Mine. Crosses burned in Louisville and on the lawns of Catholics in Boulder. But the Klan was short-lived in Colorado. When it was discovered that Grand Dragon Locke used the organization's finances for his own benefit, membership in the Klan collapsed. Internal corruptions and dissension destroyed the Klan from within by 1925, though cross burnings did occur on Flagstaff Mountain as late as 1939 and during the civil rights movement of the 1960s. Although the Klan was a dark stain on Colorado history, it was short lived and did not result in any known deaths.

[24] Based in part from https://www.superiorcolorado.gov/home/showpublisheddocument/10569/636476249141770000

Figure 15 Industrial Mine Camp in Superior. Courtesy of the Louisville Historical Society.

After the Industrial Mine closed in 1945, Superior became a sleepy burg of about 250 until Richmond Homes petitioned the town to annex the Rock Creek Ranch subdivision in the late 1980s. By a town vote of 100 in favor and 20 opposed, the annexation was approved. A zoning application was submitted to the town in January 1987. In exchange for approving the zoning, Superior residents received an improved and consistent water supply and Original Town was paved.

During the coal mining era from 1890 through 1955, Superior boasted its own post office. Since then, Louisville has provided it with postal service, which is why Superior and Louisville share the same zip code, 80027. Since the 1950's, police protection has been provided by the Boulder County Sherriff. Louisville and Superior also share library facilities. Mountain View Fire and Rescue supply fire protection through its station 5, located on Indiana Street south of Coalton Road and Rock Creek. Superior, known as the "Gateway to Boulder Valley", is a statutory town and not a city, and covers four square miles. With the Rock Creek development, it boasts 594 acres of parks and open space and 27 miles of trails, many of which interconnect with the Boulder trail system through the extensive surrounding grasslands. By 2021, over 2,800 homes had been built in Superior, and the population in 2020 was 13,094.

Boulder County 911 County Dispatch received two calls for grass fires by 10:30 a.m. on December 30, 2021. Both calls referenced downed power lines and blown transformers. One was in the 5000 block of North Broadway, and it was 100 percent contained within an acre in fifteen minutes. The other burned at North Foothills Highway and Middle Fork Road. Boulder County Sheriff radio technician and photographer Chris Rodgers[25] first headed toward North Broadway fire hoping to take pictures but quickly diverted to Middle

[25] Chris Rodgers also operates Code 10 Photography. Based on an interview with author on May 5, 2022.

Fork Road. Sheriff Commander Randy Wilber drove directly to the Middle Fork Road fire. This one was stubborn, and US-36 north of Boulder was soon closed. Many fire units responded to help fight the Middle Fork fire. With the winds increasing, Boulder County opened its Office of Emergency Management as the Middle Fork fire threatened to become dangerous. The Marshall fire had not yet started to burn . . .

Marshall, December 30, 2021, 11:00 a.m., Wind WSW 98 mph, Gusting to 98 mph 40°F

New residents to the area, Bill and Karen Lerch,[26] moved to Frederick in the summer of 2021 to be closer to relatives. On December 30, they planned to meet Karen's brother for lunch at Woody's Pizza in Golden. They drove from Frederick through Erie and Louisville, taking South Boulder Road to Cherryvale, then turned south and joined up with CO-170 Marshall Road just before 11:00 a.m. Driving westbound on CO-170, they were stopped by Boulder Open Space ranger Kelly McBride near Marshall. She told them that there were downed power lines across the road ahead and asked them to divert. They detoured onto Old Marshall Road north and joined up with CO-93 Foothills Highway southbound a mile or so out of their way. Once on CO-93, they soon passed their first tipped-over semitruck. "Scary . . . the wind was so strong that it shook the car," stated Karen of their drive. A few miles south, CO-93 was closed due to high winds, and they were directed onto CO-128 and wound their way on the back roads to get to Golden. They missed the Marshall fire's beginnings by just minutes but made it to Golden in time for pizza.

Electricity came to Colorado earlier than most states. Walter Cheesman founded the Colorado Electric Company on February 21, 1881. The company purchased two thirty-five-horsepower, direct-current Brush-Swan dynamos. Soon, an arc light was mounted at the top of Denver's Union Depot tower, and large customers like the Daniels and Fisher Department Store had lights permanently installed. Others ordered lights for special occasions. The electric company furnished temporary wiring, batteries, and bulbs and placed them in gas chandeliers for an evening and then retrieved the next day. The February 24, 1882, *Boulder News and Courier* advertised Euler's, a local merchandiser, "That pure electric oil has arrived, the finest oil ever brought to this market, at Euler's where it can be seen burning nightly" referring to batteries and light bulbs that can be purchased or rented for special occasions. Other electric companies soon followed suit, resulting in ruinous competition. Through many mergers and acquisitions, the Denver Consolidated Electric Company emerged in 1889.

[26] Based on an interview with author on January 19, 2022.

In December 1892, the Mehollin Electric and Extraction Company filed for incorporation to extract metal ores by the electric process and furnish electric light to Boulder and its citizens.

Figure 16 Inside Wanaka Lake Power Plant 1914. Courtesy of the Carnegie Library for Local History / Museum of Boulder Collection.

Though funded with $100,000 common stock, the company folded in February 1893. But Mehollin went on to found the Western Electric Transit and Power Company in October 1895. This company intended to "construct electrical plants, railway lines and carry on the general business of an electric transit company."[27] Though again not successful, power plants went up in Louisville and Lafayette, built by the Consumers' Electric Company by 1898. These plants provided power to the mines, streetlights, and limited lighting for homes and businesses until they were acquired by the Northern Colorado Power Company in 1906.

The Consumers' Electric Company thought big. In a grandiose design, this company built a Westinghouse 10,000-horsepower alternating current plant, expandable to 35,000 horsepower, on Waneka Lake in Lafayette. With its own coal mine on-site and the water provided from the lake, the steam turbine plant soon produced 6,000 kilowatts of power. It was used to drive the Interurban passenger trolley service connecting Boulder to Denver. Soon over 167 miles of transmission lines were strung, supplying power to Lafayette, Louisville, Longmont, Loveland, Fort Collins, Boulder, and most of Northern Colorado and southern Wyoming, including many coal mines and sugar beet factories. It also drove the remote pumps needed to lift water to far-reaching irrigation ditches. This was one of the first successful generation and power distribution systems in the entire country. In 1914, it changed its name to Western Light and Power. It was acquired by Public Service Company in 1923. After the Valmont electric generation station in Boulder came online in 1924, the Lafayette plant was put on standby to fill peak periods of demand. It was last fired up in 1948 and was torn down in the early 1950s.

[27] Jefferson County Clerk and Recorder incorporation papers.

Through acquisitions and profitable management, Public Service Company soon controlled over 80 percent of Colorado's energy needs for both natural gas and electricity. It operated successfully through 1995 when it merged with Amarillo, Texas-based Southwestern Public Service Company. Together, they formed New Century Energies. That only lasted for five years when Northern States Power of Minneapolis gobbled up New Century in 2000 and formed Xcel Energy. Today, Xcel Energy is a large multistate utility electric-and-gas holding company with a diverse electric-generating profile and operations in many different markets. The company functions in Minnesota, Colorado, Michigan, New Mexico, North Dakota, South Dakota, Texas, and Wisconsin. It has five natural gas-powered generating plants in Colorado, plus numerous solar and wind generating sites.

Xcel filings show that in 2020, its power and transmission lines sparked 647 wildfires in Colorado high-risk areas, but none were among Colorado's most significant wildfires. In regulatory filings, Xcel reported that it spent $13,500,000 to track and mitigate fire risks in Boulder County alone in 2020. This included infrared screening of power lines, visual inspections, and wind analysis to determine vulnerabilities. Xcel also replaced vulnerable overhead lines and cleared away dangerous vegetation near poles and lines.

Marshall receives its electricity through aboveground wires hung on telephone poles. Power lines in the newer sections of Louisville and Superior are buried but still on power poles in the older sections. Many pictures exist of Christmas lights shining brightly on homes in Superior as the Marshall fire raged one or two houses beyond.

Xcel and its contractors also provide natural gas services throughout Colorado. Colorado has eleven out of the top one hundred of the country's largest verified natural gas reserves. Numerous natural gas wells exist in nearby Weld County. Xcel also contracts with two cities, Englewood and Littleton, to collect methane gas from each city's wastewater treatment plants to add to Xcel's natural gas supply.

Whether from a wellhead or collected methane, natural gas flows through ever-enlarging "gathering" pipelines. Like a tree, natural gas collection starts at the wellhead "twigs" and consolidates into larger "branches" the closer it approaches the central collection point "trunk." Compressors help push the increasing gathered gas through the lines. Impurities like water, carbon dioxide, sulfur, and inert gases are removed along the way to the collection point.

At the central collection point, the gas moves into the transmission system, composed of about 272,000 miles of pipeline throughout the United States. The transmission system moves liquefied natural gas to the local distribution companies throughout the country. Pressures in the transmission lines varied from 200 to 1,500 pounds per square inch, and gas can move through the system at speeds approaching 30 miles per hour. When the gas reaches a local distribution company, it passes through a gate station that reduces the pressure below 200 pounds, adds the distinctive sour egg scent, and measures the gas acquired by the local company for billing.

Figure 17 Natural gas arrived in Boulder on September 28, 1929, at Public Service Regulator Station at Twenty-eighth Street and Pennsylvania Avenue. Courtesy of the Carnegie Library for Local History / Museum of Boulder Collection.

From the gate station, the gas moves into local distribution mains ranging from 2 inches to 24 inches in diameter. Generally, the closer natural gas is to a customer, the smaller the pipe and the lower the pressure. Xcel continuously monitors flow rates and pressures to keep it within limits for each customer. Distribution mains are interconnected in multiple grid patterns. Strategically located shutoff valves help minimize service disruptions during service outages and emergencies. Natural gas runs from the main to the customer through a service line. Xcel is responsible for maintaining the service line from the main to the customer's gas meter, and the customer is responsible from the gas meter throughout the premises. Typically, the gas meter further reduces the gas pressure to below one-fourth pound per square inch. This ensures that the gas at the burner ignites in its familiar clean blue flame.

Boulder County Fire dispatch radio broadcasted a call to investigate smoke near the South Foothills (CO-93) and Marshall Road (CO-170) RTD Park-n-Ride at 11:09 a.m.[28]. Mountain View Fire and Rescue Engine 2209 and Brush 2232 were tasked to investigate, though only Engine 2209 initially responded.

At that same time, Boulder Dispatch coordinated another wildfire that had already spread to 30–40 acres—the Middle Fork fire burned where North Foothills and Middle Fork Road met north of Boulder near Left Hand Creek. With the wind forecast to increase, this fire could be explosive, and the Boulder All-Hazard Incident Management Team was already on-site, along with Sheriff Commander Randy Wilber, badge 514. Commander Wilber[28] had fifteen deputies evacuating houses and coordinating traffic along the path the Middle Fork fire was expected to follow. Most of the City of Boulder's firefighting equipment was already on site or enroute to help. The wind was atrocious, and a large sheet of loose corrugated metal almost took Commander Wilber's head off, missing him by just inches.

To keep communications clear, the Middle Fork firefighters used a separate tactical radio channel onsite so that the main dispatch radio channel remained open. Dispatch continued to send resources as needed to Middle Fork per Firefighting Plan 1. To send units, unique two-toned pitches were first broadcast over the radio. Each two-tone pitch was associated with a particular unit to help it readily identify an important tasking call following the tones. Dispatch information was simultaneously sent via an application to unit devices and, in most cases, personal cell phones. The 911 call about smoke near the South Foothills and Marshall Road intersection fell under the jurisdiction of Mountain View Fire Rescue and their Engine 2209 was the first to respond.

[28] Based on an interview at the Boulder County Sheriff's office June 2, 2022, with author.

Figure 18 Firefighters battled the Middle Fork fire before the Marshall fire began. Photo: Code 10 Photography.

Mountain View Fire Rescue (MVFR) is a full-service fire department that covers approximately 220 square miles in Boulder and Weld Counties, including the towns of Erie, Mead, Dacono, Niwot, Eldorado Springs, Flagstaff Mountain, and Superior. It has 10 firehouses, and its almost 200 employees proudly protect nearly 100,000 residents. Besides firefighting, the department provides emergency medical, ambulance services, wildland firefighting, rescue workers, training programs, smoke alarms, car seat checks, and COVID-19 KN95 masks and virus test kits. It acquired the Rocky Mountain Fire District in 2021.

The Rocky Mountain Fire District (RMFD) began January 1, 2007, by combining the Cherryvale Fire Protection District, the Eldorado Springs-Marshall Fire Protection District, and the former Rocky Flats Fire Department. An interagency agreement with the Lafayette Fire Department allowed sharing of personnel, medical calls, and fire equipment. Boulder County Dispatch coordinated 911 calls for RMFD. The department operated six stations: Boulder, Cherryvale, Superior, Flagstaff, Rock Creek, and Eldorado Springs. These all transferred to MVFR with the merger in 2021.

Started at its inception, RMFD published its Community Wildfire Protection Plan[29] to meet the Healthy Forest Restoration Act (HFRA) requirements to study wildfire protection needs in its community of service in 2010. The report covered the complete fire district, including Eldorado Springs, Marshall, Superior, and Rock Creek. These areas all rated "moderate risk" for a wildland-urban interface fire by the study. The study included specific recommendations to help minimize these risks, including at least a three-hundred-foot clear zone before developments, ensuring greenbelts are irrigated, and periodic prescribed burns of tall grasslands. It also recommended the development of a large animal evacuation plan for Marshall. RMFD merged with Mountain View Fire Department to defray costs. Even after being acquired by MVFR, the report remained unchanged and was not updated to reflect the large population growth that occurred in both Superior and Louisville.

Boulder County issued its own Community Wildfire Protection Plan[30] also in 2010. It stated that wildfires can occur any time of year, and they are a risk to residents of the plains as well as the mountain forests. The study quoted Boulder sheriff Joe Pelle as saying, "I don't live well anymore with wind. I can tell you we talk a lot about fire, but wind is my enemy." The report noted that fires tend to return to the same wildlands periodically and firefighters cannot protect every structure. It also agreed with the RMFD report that Superior/Rock Creek, Marshall, and Eldorado Springs all had a "moderate risk" rating for wildfires. The "Conditional Burn Probability" map on page 69, the "Wildfire Hazard" map on page 73, and the forecast "Areas of Concern 2011" map on page 74 all showed the grasslands west of Louisville and Superior as having the *highest probability of fire* of *any* region in the county when the report was written in 2010. Louisville Open Space issued its own wildfire hazard assessment in 2012 that agreed with the other two reports.

The combined firefighters of Rocky Mountain and Mountain View often practiced wildfire fighting by setting controlled burns on open space, farms, and along ditches. They proposed to both Boulder County

[29] Report issued by Rocky Mountain Fire in 2010 before merger with Mountain View Fire Rescue.

[30] See https://assets.bouldercounty.org/wp-content/uploads/2017/02/community-widfire-protection-plan-book-low-resolution.pdf.

and the City of Boulder that the Marshall Open Space areas be burned several times in recent years, but these government units either turned them down or ignored them.[31] During one conversation with Sheriff Pelle, he replied that his hands were tied as it was the responsibility of the county commissioners to approve and pay for a prescribed burn. Now the fire department "practiced" on a wildfire burn for real.

At 11:12 a.m., MVFR Engine 2209 arrived near Marshall and found a utility line partially down on Marshall Road about ten feet off the ground and assumed that it was an electrical power cable. At that time, winds in the area were a constant 95 miles per hour with higher gusts. Unit 2209 was a new, standard fire engine with 7,000 miles on the odometer, based out of station 9 in Eldorado Springs, less than a mile-and-a-half away. They saw no smoke. Boulder Open Space Ranger Kelly McBride, unit 5077, was nearby when they arrived. The wind was so powerful that when 2209 Commander Lt-1 opened his door to greet Ranger McBride, the door ripped from his grasp and bent so badly that it no longer closed. Fighting the wind, they blocked Marshall Road (CO-170) at Foothills (CO-93) and requested Xcel Energy and law enforcement to respond. About then, Bill and Karen Lerch drove by and were directed onto Old Marshall Road. Another call to respond to a blown over truck on CO-93 about a mile away was broadcast at 11:17 a.m.

While setting up the roadblock, Lt-1 noticed what appeared to be smoke and moved Engine 2209 south on a small dirt road between the homes nearby. At 11:21 a.m., they reported a small grass fire south of Marshall Road and deployed to fight it. The Marshall fire had been discovered. Knowing that the fire would burn rapidly, they requested that they be called South Foothills Command. The wind promptly ripped a firefighter's helmet off, never to be seen again. The fire spread quickly and soon was burning mulch in a garden.

Brush Truck 2232 arrived, and the wind also bent its passenger door and took its firefighters' helmets when they deployed. The crews shot water under 250 pounds of pressure at the spreading flames with no noticeable effect. The wind just blew the water away. Embers from the now inferno piled up against fences, homes and the tires of parked cars, and these soon caught fire. At 11:23 a.m., Engine 2209 called in that the wildland fire was now racing toward the east from CO-93, driven by the high winds. He reported that homes were in its path and requested additional fire units be dispatched. Sheds caught fire and soon were cartwheeling away, spreading flames and destruction as they fell apart. The first house started to burn, looking like the inside of a turbine engine. The fire hoses caught flying embers and started springing leaks.

[31] Telephone interview with a former Mountain View firefighter March 27, 2022.

Initial Fire Reports CO-93 and CO-170 Near Marshall

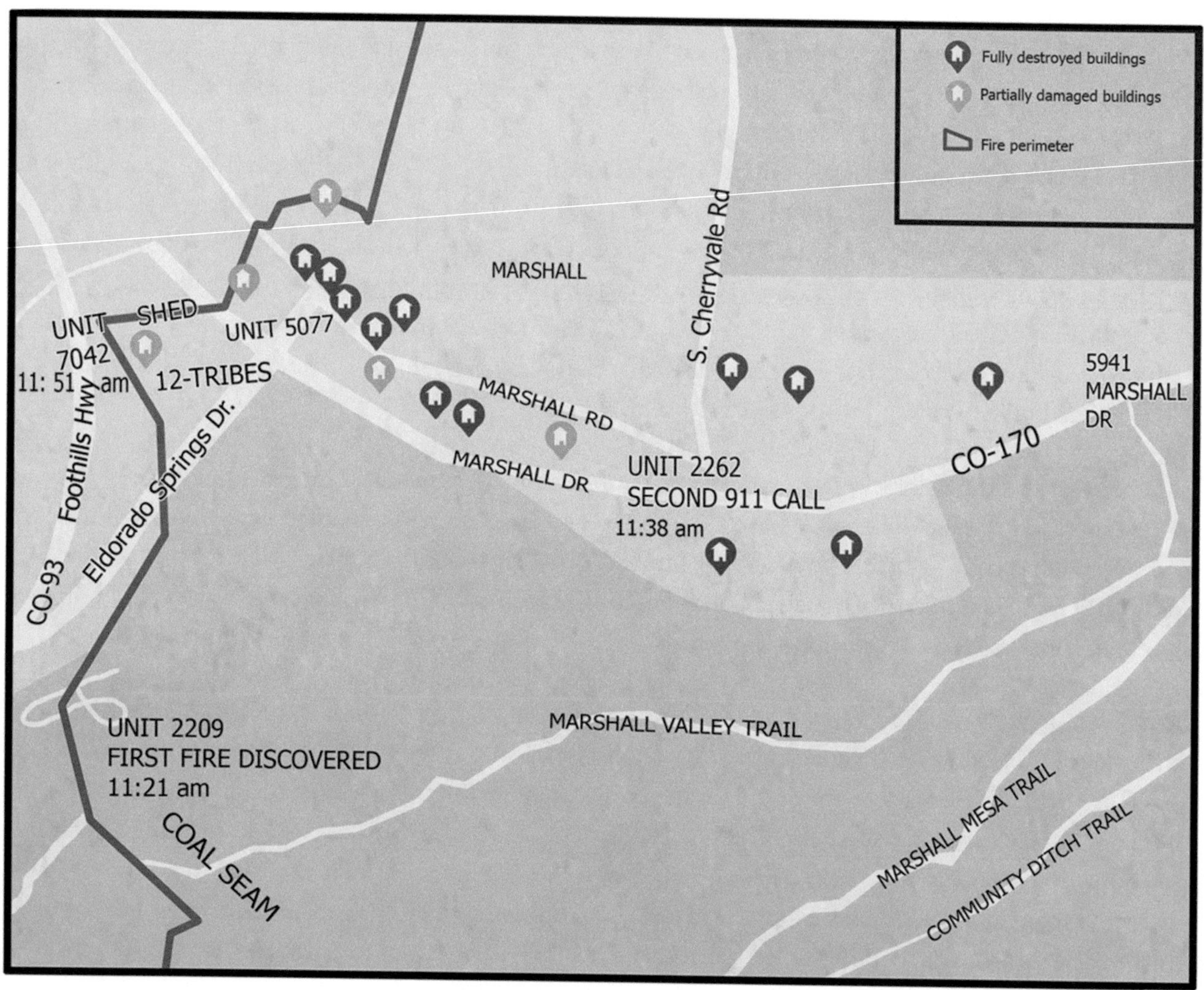

Figure 19 Initial fire reports CO-93 and CO-170 near Marshall

County Dispatch stated no additional sheriff resources were available for traffic control on Marshall Road at that time. Ranger 5077 radioed she would assume traffic control for the utility line and directed traffic westbound onto Old Marshall Road. While there, she filmed smoke rising from behind the Twelve Tribes property at 11:19 a.m.[32] Neighbor Anne Michaels filmed the fire south of the Twelve Tribes property at 11:25 a.m. Former state representative Jack Pommer also videoed the smoke and Ranger McBride's pickup in the intersection near that time. The Marshall fire began its devastating burn toward the east.

Ranger 5077 responded that she was evacuating the homes in the direct path of the fire. Dispatch played tones to send Lafayette Brush 2631 and Louisville Battalion 2760 to the fire at 11:24 a.m. Tactical channel 14 was assigned for ease of communications. To lessen confusion with the Middle Fork fire, the fire was relabeled from South Foothills Command to Marshall Command at 11:30 a.m. MVFR Engine 2209 assumed local tactical control. With the broken door, Engine 2209 soon had hot embers within, burning a notebook, a stuffed toy, a hat and melting the driver's seat. All the horizontal surfaces of the truck were covered with hot coals and the truck later would need extensive repairs. The fire raced to the east, sending up great plumes of smoke. Deputy 797 stated on the dispatch channel that she could already see the smoke from the Marshall fire from Airport Road near the county jail seven miles north at 11:30 a.m. At 11:31 a.m., it reached its first buildings.

At 11:30 a.m., County Dispatch received a second call for a fire at Marshall Road and Cherryvale about a half mile to the northeast of the original fire, possibly caused by a downed wire. Just then, wind gusts were clocked at over 105 miles per hour, and the fire exploded. Engine 2209 reported structures were now involved and requested additional fire units. County Dispatch toned Allenspark Engine 5202 and MVFR Command 2262 to assist at 11:34 a.m. Law Dispatch also sent four sheriff units to CO-93 and CO-170 to help and instructed them to use the Law 3 tactical channel. Three additional trucks, MVFR Tower 2215, Truck 2216, and Brush 2234, were dispatched at 11:37 a.m. for a total of seven trucks responding within fifteen minutes. At 11:38 a.m., MVFR Command 2262 reached the second wildfire at Cherryvale and Marshall and immediately requested additional units. MVFR Units Tower 2215, Brush 2238, and Lafayette Battalion 2660 were dispatched within a minute. Louisville Battalion 2760 assumed command of the Marshall fire at 11:42 a.m. from Engine 2209. County Dispatch directed Lafayette Battalion 2660 to assume command of the Cherryvale fire at 11:45 a.m. Later Boulder OEM maps of the Marshall fire showed two initial incident locations, one south of CO-170 along CO-93 on the east side and the other at CO-170 and Cherryvale. Satellite and overhead images of the fire burn area reviewed later showed three locations might be possible ignition sites.

[32] Denver 9News has compiled a version of the events at https://www.youtube.com/watch?v=khLjeE pqoy.

Figure 20 Marshall fire as seen from South Boulder early afternoon December 30, 2021. Photo: Steve Brown, NOAA NWS-Boulder.

Lafayette Battalion 2660 requested County Dispatch issue an evacuation notice for east of the Cherryvale fire for two or three miles along CO-170 at 11:44 a.m. The Boulder County Office of Emergency Management (OEM) issued the first evacuation order three minutes later at 11:47 a.m. for CO-93 east past Cherryvale Road to CO-170. It reached 215 contacts and recommended to evacuate to the Sacred Heart of Mary Church on S. Boulder Road. Marshall Command requested additional fire units from Boulder, but none were available as all were committed to the Middle Fork fire or working downed power lines at that time. MVFR Medic 2225 and Louisville Engine 2703 were toned to evacuate a hospice patient at 1613 Marshall Road with an ambulance as the fire raged nearby. AMR-2 responded that they would help with this evacuation. Additional tenders and brush trucks were requested from Coal Creek Regional Fire at 11:47 a.m., and Tender 7042 and Brush 7031 quickly responded. With the high winds, the fire jumped to both sides of Marshall Road in multiple locations and expanded rapidly by 11:50 a.m.

According to the National Oceanic and Atmospheric Administration (NOAA), the strongest winds occurred around noon. A peak gust of 115 mph was recorded at the base of the foothills just west of the fire's origin. The 12:00 p.m. surface plot (Figure 21) showed an 85 mph gust in south Boulder and 100 mph gust south along CO-93 at Rocky Flats. Winds in Louisville and Superior at that time were in the mid-40 mph range but swirling with the topography uplift. Humidity was low, around 20 percent, helping the fire to spread rapidly.

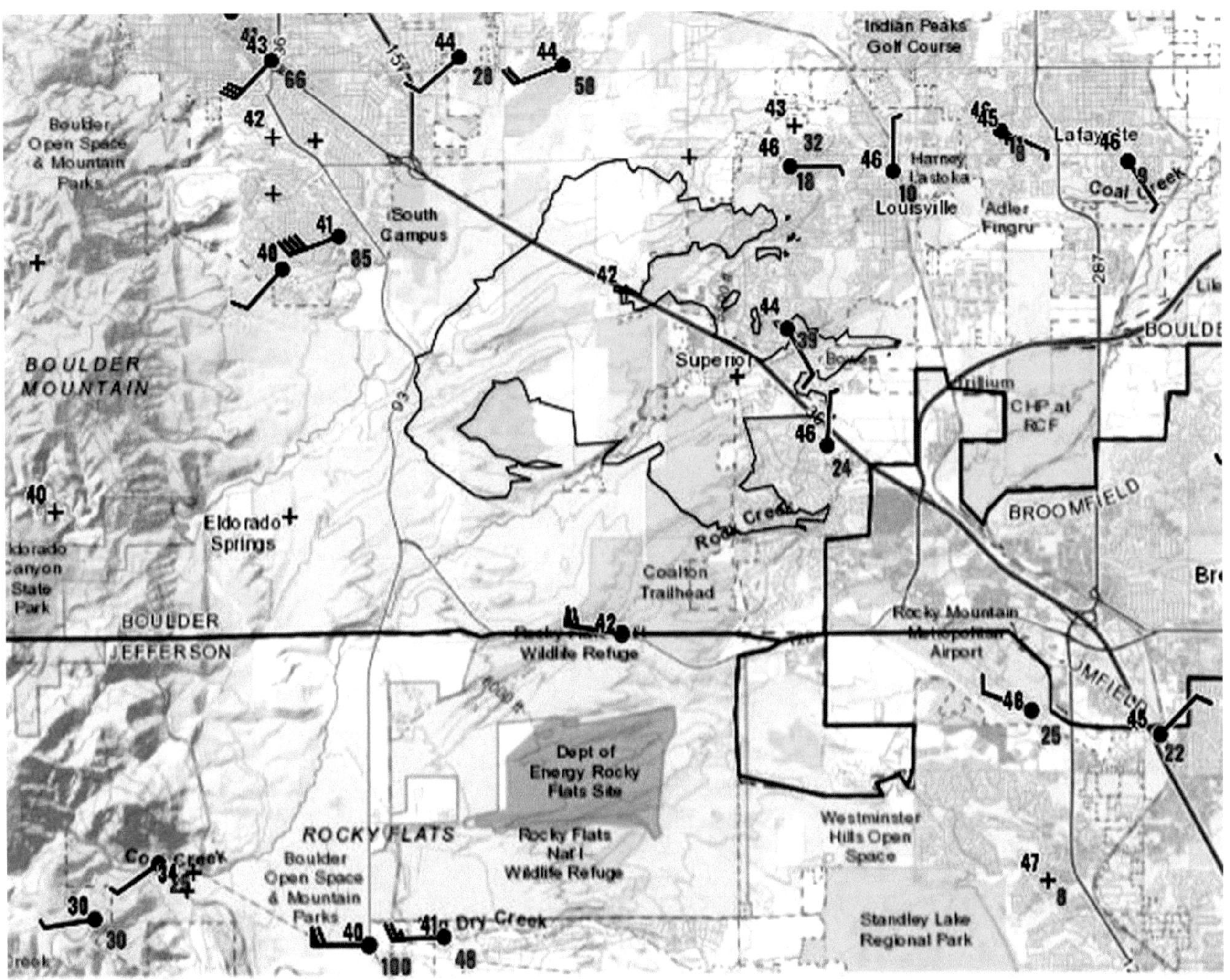

Figure 21 NOAA noon surface winds for Marshall fire. Courtesy of NOAA NWS-Boulder.

Boulder Utility 2552 stated they were headed to Cherryvale. The fire was burning uncontrolled in many locations. Marshall Command broadcast the first reference to a shed fire at 11:51 a.m. and asked the first arriving unit to attend to it. Coal Creek Canyon Tender 7042 arrived quickly at the shed fire, with Brush 7031 soon following. Videos showed the shed reduced to smoldering ashes within thirty minutes. Unit 1800 announced they must detour to make it to CO-170 and CO-93 due to CO-170 being impassable from smoke and fire at 11:52 a.m. At 11:54 a.m., an officer reported that he closed Cherryvale at Sixty-sixth, but the open flame had already raced past. County Dispatch broadcasted they had Cherryvale Command fighting the fire with six resources and asked if they needed more at 11:56 a.m. Lafayette Battalion (Cherryvale Command) replied that they were just trying to "wrap their head around it" and they could use three more units as the fire raged uncontrolled.

Along with Sheriff Deputy Sergeant 526, Louisville Battalion 2760 drove back east on CO-170 to Seventy-sixth Street west of the Costco gas station to strategically view the fire. There they were joined by MVFR Command 2262. From their vantage point, it was obvious that the fire was expanding out of control, and many more firefighting resources will be needed. In fact, they expected their position to be soon overwhelmed, so they moved east and north across US-36 to the KeyBank parking lot in Louisville about 12:15 p.m. They only stayed there a few minutes as it became clear that traffic and smoke will make this location untenable for anything other than as an observation post. Through discussions with the OEM, they decided firefighting resources will gather at Macy's parking lot at FlatIron Crossing Mall. The mall offered open parking areas and easy access to US-36 to allow firefighting resources to quickly deploy where needed. They traveled there by 12:30 p.m. and established the Incident Command Post for the fire. The mall allowed them use of the vacant Nordstrom's store as a command and communications center. These three units stuck together and operated as Marshall Command until the Boulder Type 3 incident management team assumed command after completion of their deployment at the Middle Fork fire at 3:40 p.m. Meanwhile, the fire raced uncontrolled through the open space grasslands toward Superior and Costco.

About noon, Sheriff Commander Randy Wilber realized the Middle Fork fire was coming under control but heard that the Marshall fire was exploding. He had already dispatched Sergeants 525 and 517 and additional deputies there to help with evacuations and traffic control. During a major fire, the Sheriff Department helps firefighters with three main tasks—traffic control, door-to-door evacuation notices, and emergency evacuations for persons who are unable to leave without assistance or when the fire is already nearby. Since the 2020 Cal-Wood fire, Boulder County Sheriff has used SWAT teams to help with these tasks as they already operate together, have the necessary equipment prepositioned, and can be deployed quickly. He put SWAT on alert. Major wildfires in Boulder County typically occur in the remote mountain forests, and these duties are usually limited to the few roads and inhabitants impacted. There has always been time to evaluate the expected fire spread and deploy deputies judiciously. This will not be the case today.

He decided to leave the Middle Fork fire and headed toward Louisville on US-36 through Boulder, planning to meet Marshall Command at the KeyBank. It was a typical traffic day in Boulder complicated by the occasional power outage. He finally made it through town and stayed on US-36, the Denver-Boulder Turnpike, heading up the hill toward McCaslin. The smoke was thick, and suddenly he can see sparks and flames shooting across the six-lane highway. He performed a U-turn across the median and exited back on S. Boulder Road to head east. His travels provided him with an unobstructed view southeastward of the tremendous smoke and flames. He made it to Louisville and started heading south through town. By this time, Marshall Command had moved to FlatIron Crossing Mall, so he drove through Louisville against the evacuating traffic and across the US-36 bridge. Driving was slow through the intense smoke and traffic. It took him almost an hour to navigate the eighteen miles from the Middle Fork fire to FlatIron Crossing Mall.

Built in 1990, Avista Adventist Hospital has 114 beds and 9 surgical suites. Known for its award-winning New Life Center and the area's largest neonatal intensive care nursery, Louisville's community hospital is also widely recognized for first-rate emergency services, world-class joint and spine program, comprehensive cardiac care, general surgery with the latest physician-driven robot technology, and its Primary Stroke Center. The hospital is part of the Seventh-Day Adventist hospital group that in fiscal 2021 provided $2.3M of uncompensated faith-based charity care at Avista. Employing 99 staff members, the hospital is located on a hill off Eighty-eighth Street near US-36 and the Monarch school complex in southeast Louisville. On this fateful Thursday, 51 inpatients were under care by the employees. Avista initiated its emergency center by noon and made the decision to start evacuations at 1:04 p.m.

Superior, December 30, 2021, 11:46 a.m., Wind SSE 12 mph, Gusting to 39 mph 44°F

Coming back from Denver, Paul Williamson stopped at Freddy's Frozen Custard and Steakburgers on Coalton Road near FlatIron Crossing Mall for a hamburger. He saw the smoke, and someone mentioned to him that a grass fire was burning south of 120th. After eating, he left there in his electric truck and drove the three miles toward his home. He only made it to the Phillips 66 gas station at McCaslin and Marshall Road due to the smoke and traffic. He parked his truck and decided to hike the three blocks west to his home, but the wind was so atrocious and the smoke, ash, and dust so bad that he couldn't see to walk. So, he closed his eyes and walked a few feet, opened his eyes to see where he was, and did that again and again. It seemed to take forever. He finally covered his left eye with his stocking cap and protected his right eye with his hand as he fought the intense wind and smoke walking the few hundred feet home. He could see and hear the crackling of the massive flames to the west only a couple of blocks away.

He finally arrived home and knew that he will have to evacuate. Being very well organized, he had gamed evacuating previously, but now his mind went blank. He can't recall what he planned to take in the rush and adrenaline of the moment. He grabbed his computer, his flash drives, his financials, and a windup portable radio. His passport, Social Security card, and other important documents were all protected in a firesafe rated to 2700°F, so he left them behind. Even if the fire reached his home, they should survive. Then he recalled his granddaughter's school project where she asked him if he could only take one item in an emergency, what would it be, and he remembered his journals and grabbed them. Just then, a sheriff deputy pounded urgently on the front door and screamed, "Get out now! The fire is coming!" Putting his few possessions in a bag, he headed out the door into the maelstrom not knowing if his home will survive.

Luckily, the wind was now to his back, and he could almost see. To save time, he decided to cut across Asti Park to get to his truck. As he walked through the blinding wind and smoke, he stumbled over the Christmas light wiring on the property line fence and fell, hurting his knee. He lay there for a moment and saw the flames devouring the homes to the west. Even this far away, he could feel the heat radiating from the inferno. He got up and limped his way to his truck and joined the traffic jam crawling south on McCaslin. The wind, smoke, and ash were so bad, he could barely see the road and the cars all around him. His truck crawled the few blocks to the roundabout at McCaslin and Main, and like a miracle, the smoke cleared, and the sky turned blue. He drove to Applebee's and spent the day there, wondering if his home would survive. While there, two strangers offered him a place for the night, but he responded that he planned to stay at his daughter's up in Loveland. He figured he will come back tomorrow to see how well cement board and steel roofing construction stood up to wildfire.

The Twelve Tribes, also known as the Commonwealth of Israel, owns several properties south of the City of Boulder at CO-93 and CO-170 along Eldorado Springs Drive. Google Maps showed a pin at that location titled *Community in Boulder* with a link to the website https://twelvetribes.org. One of the few groups surviving from the Jesus movement of the 1960s and 1970s, the Twelve Tribes live together in communities as described in the New Testament book of Acts. Per their literature, they share all resources and live in "simple devotion to the life, death and resurrection of the man Yahshua the Messiah."[33]

Approximately thirty members live on the main property, with many working at the Yellow Deli café on Pearl Street in Boulder. They believe that they are gathering the twelve biblical tribes per the book of Revelations in preparation for Christ's return. Members take Hebrew names and receive no pay because they work as volunteers and live communally. Because of their common treasury, they are classified by the IRS similar to monasteries. Worldwide, there may be two thousand to three thousand members of the Twelve Tribes, and there are more than twenty-four communities scattered around the United States. A second community in Colorado is based in Manitou Springs. Members dress like Amish or Mennonites, with males sporting simple beards and bound hair while women wear modest, homespun clothing. Each group is independent and typically led by one or more male "shepherds." They gather mornings and evenings for worship and welcome guests to their Friday evening services. They follow strict moral codes and practice corporal punishment on disobedient children (some locations have been accused of child abuse and labor violations as a result).

They teach that communal living is essential for salvation. They quote 1 John 5:19 when asked why other Christians don't live communally and say that the world outside their commune is controlled by the evil one.

[33] Derived from information at https://twelvetribes.org and other sources.

Members are free to come and go and may own cell phones to communicate with loved ones outside of the community. But with money controlled collectively, few resources exist for a member to step out on their own.

Neighbor Mike Zoltowski took three video clips and posted them to YouTube[34] January 2 that showed the high winds and a shed burning on the Twelve Tribes property on Eldorado Springs Drive. Another person posted a video taken from a car on CO-93 showing the same shed blazing from a different angle. News and social media immediately accused the group of accidentally causing the fire. Firefighters visited the Twelve Tribes property a week prior on December 24 because of a neighbor's complaint about burning trash in an open pit, but the fire truck stayed for less than a half an hour. The Twelve Tribes often burned their trash and covered the remains with dirt using a tractor. After the Marshall fire, the Boulder County Sheriff executed a search warrant of the property, erected large fences around parts of it, and took possession of certain items as possible evidence. No arrest warrants were executed based on that search. The fences were removed, and all property was returned to the owners a week later.

On December 30, Boulder County announced at 12:14 p.m. that the Boulder Emergency Operations Center (EOC) had been activated to respond to multiple wildland fires. The center opened earlier, but the announcement went out after noon when the center was fully manned. The first fire was the Middle Fork fire burning north of Boulder near the intersection of North Foothills Highway and Middle Fork Road. The second fire was south of Boulder[35] near the intersection of South Cherryvale Road and Marshall Drive and was called the Marshall fire.[36] Unlike most states, in Colorado, county sheriffs have statutory responsibility to coordinate wildland fire response within their county for any fire that crosses fire department jurisdiction lines.

Managed by the Boulder Office of Emergency Management (OEM), the EOC is where designated management personnel assemble during emergencies and disasters. The OEM operates the EOC to coordinate communications, provide resource mobilization and support, manage information, develop situational awareness to maintain a common operating picture, assist policy group members, support event management planning, provide operational support and coordination, and assist with continuity of government activities.

[34] Zoltowski's videos may be viewed at https://www.youtube.com/watch?v=8C-RTRlgqzc .

[35] The OEM announcement incorrectly reported the Cherryvale fire as the Marshall fire in their announcement of the opening of the EOC. The Cherryvale and Marshall fires are later merged into the Marshall fire.

[36] The following is adapted from the OEM functional descriptions at https://www.boulderoem.com.

In addition to large-scale emergencies and disasters, the EOC can also be activated to provide support for planned events and at the discretion of the Boulder OEM board of directors.

The EOC is a support and coordination center that primarily addresses consequence management issues and unmet needs. Operations and tactical planning are traditionally conducted at an Incident Command Post (ICP) or Department Operations Center (DOC) whereas the EOC supports these entities' activities. In the case of the Marshall fire, the ICP was located at the old Nordstrom's in FlatIron Crossing Mall. There the ICP made all tactical decisions to fight the fire while the OEM supplied them with the resources needed to make it happen.

The EOC is uniquely staffed by a group of subject matter experts known collectively as the Multi-Agency Coordination (MAC) group. The MAC group is made up of representatives from numerous City of Boulder and Boulder County departments, nonprofit organizations active in disaster, and the private sector. These dedicated professionals provide the foundation of the EOC.

The MAC group is organized into Emergency Support Functions (ESFs) that are divided into four main sections: Operations, Community Services, Situational Awareness, and Resource Mobilization.

One of the major operations groups is the Boulder All-Hazard Incident Management Team (IMT). The Boulder IMT is a Type 3 IMT, a partnership of professionals, trained and qualified in incident management. The team provides an organizational structure and competent management staff to support large-scale emergency responses in the City of Boulder and Boulder County. Founded in 2010, the team has responded to the Fourmile and Dome fires in 2010, the September 2013 floods, the Cold Springs fire in 2016, the Sunshine fire in 2017, and several smaller incidents through the years. With each activation, the team refines its processes, builds relationships with its stakeholders, and continues to increase capacity. At the time the EOC opening was announced, the Boulder IMT was deployed working the Middle Fork fire. It assumed command responsibility of the Marshall fire later that afternoon.

The Boulder Office of Emergency Management (OEM) coordinates with many first responder agencies based on the situational need for command, function, jurisdictional authority, and mutual-aid agreements. These partners include the following:

Law Enforcement Agencies: Boulder County Sheriff's Office (including Superior, Ward, and Marshall), Boulder Police Department, Erie Police Department, Lafayette Police Department, Louisville Police Department, and Nederland Police Department

Fire/EMS/Search and Rescue Agencies: Allenspark Fire, American Medical Response (AMR), Big Elk, Meadows Fire, Boulder County Sheriff's Office Fire Management, Boulder Emergency Squad, Boulder Fire Department, Boulder Mountain Fire, Boulder Rural Fire, Coal Creek Fire, Fourmile Fire, Front Range Rescue Dogs, Gold Hill Fire, Hygiene Fire, Indian Peaks Fire, Jamestown Fire, Lafayette Fire, Lefthand Fire, Longmont Emergency Unit, Louisville Fire, Lyons Fire, Mountain View Fire, Nederland Fire, Pinewood Springs Fire, Rocky Mountain Fire, Rocky Mountain Rescue Group, Sugarloaf Fire, Sunshine Fire, and Timberline Fire

Emergency Management is the function that plans, coordinates, and supports a wide range of activities that help communities to reduce vulnerability to hazards and prepare for and cope with disasters. This work is generally thought of in four phases: preparedness, response, mitigation, and recovery. Preparedness is focused on the development of plans and capabilities for effective disaster response. Response is the immediate reaction to a disaster. Mitigation consists of those activities designed to prevent or reduce losses from disaster. Recovery includes activities that help to restore critical community functions and manage reconstruction.

The Boulder OEM has emergency management responsibilities for both the City of Boulder and all of Boulder County. In addition, the Boulder OEM coordinates with state and federal partners, many city and county departments, public safety agencies, municipalities, nongovernmental organizations, and private businesses throughout Boulder County to facilitate coordinated planning and response to emergency situations. During the Marshall fire, Mike Chard was the Boulder County director of emergency services. Curtis Johnson was the manager in charge of County Dispatch.

Boulder County Communications includes police and fire dispatch and is staffed by the following:

- 24 full-time dispatchers
- 3–4 hourly dispatchers
- 6 supervisors
- Communications director
- Support services division chief

- 2 administrative personnel
- CAD system administrator
- 1 dedicated employee for Emergency Medical Dispatch (EMD) quality assurance
- 2 radio technicians
- Technical radio system supervisor
- Additional support as needed provided by the Sheriff Computer Support group

The Boulder County Communication Center is one of four Public Safety Answering Points (PSAPs) in Boulder County. The other three are the Boulder Police and Fire Communications Center, the Longmont Emergency Communication Center, and the CUPD's Communication Center on the University of Colorado campus in Boulder. After spending many years in a joint facility with City of Boulder Police and Fire Communications, Boulder County moved into a new facility in August 2008 on Airport Road near the county jail. All four dispatch centers manage incident responses using hosted Tri-Tech computer-aided dispatch (CAD) systems. A hosted Viper phone network for receiving and making phone emergency and nonemergency calls is shared between the four facilities. When a 911 call is received that necessitates an emergency medical response, dispatchers use ProQA software to provide emergency medical dispatch instructions. This program allows IAEMD-certified dispatchers to see pertinent questions to ask the caller that assist the patient and enhance information for emergency responders.

All radio communications are handled through a combination of a local VHF infrastructure and a 700/800 MHz digitally trunked system. This hybrid approach allows for a wide range of coverage within mountains and flatland areas. It also provides interoperability between neighboring agencies that may respond from other parts of the state for large incidents. Boulder County Law dispatch broadcasts on 155.145 MHz to cover sheriffs and all other county law officials, except for Boulder, Longmont, and Colorado State Patrol. Boulder County Fire dispatch broadcasts on 154.325 MHz to cover all county volunteer fire departments, EMS, and rescue, except for Boulder and Longmont. All these resources were challenged to the utmost during the Marshall fire.

Figure 23 Flames northeast of Cherryvale at 12:40 p.m. Photo: Code 10 Photography.

The flames burst across Cherryvale by 11:54 a.m. With five units already committed, Lafayette Brigade acting as Cherryvale Command requested an additional three firefighting units. The fire took advantage of the dry growth along the Goodhue and Davidson ditches and spread rapidly with the high winds toward the northeast. By 11:55 a.m., the fire had spread past 1271 S. Cherryvale. By 12:03 p.m., units responding reported that the fire had already expanded to Sixty-sixth and Marshall Road by following Cowdrey Draw. By 12:10 p.m., the fire was nearing the small power plant at 6937 Marshall and the next-door Louisville South Howard Berry water treatment plant, just a stone's throw away from US-36. The smoke plume by this time was visible for miles around, and 911 was inundated with calls about fire and smoke.

Behind the racing fire line, the flames intensified. Around noon, County Dispatch requested Marshall Command to send a unit to 5337 Marshall as the residence was about to be engulfed. At noon, Sheriff Sergeant 571 reported that residents at 5675 Marshall were refusing to evacuate. Their neighbor at 5941 Marshall also decided to stay. Unluckily, the Davidson Ditch ran behind both properties, and all the homes near it were doomed.

Robert Sharpe, 69, was a longtime resident of Boulder, a naturalist who was concerned with children's rights, and worked in the construction industry for years. Family members think he stayed at his home during the fire to protect his collection of family memories. According to his family's written obituary, "He had a life-time ambition to gather as much Sharpe memorabilia as he could find and over the years had amassed thousands of pages of documents that he kept in safes, file cabinets, and boxes." His remains were found in the 5900 block of Marshall Road on January 5, and he was positively identified using DNA technology. He was the first confirmed victim of the Marshall fire.

Figure 22 Family photograph of Robert Sharpe.

West Superior, Sagamore Subdivision and Costco.
The fire jumps US-36 and attacks Louisville

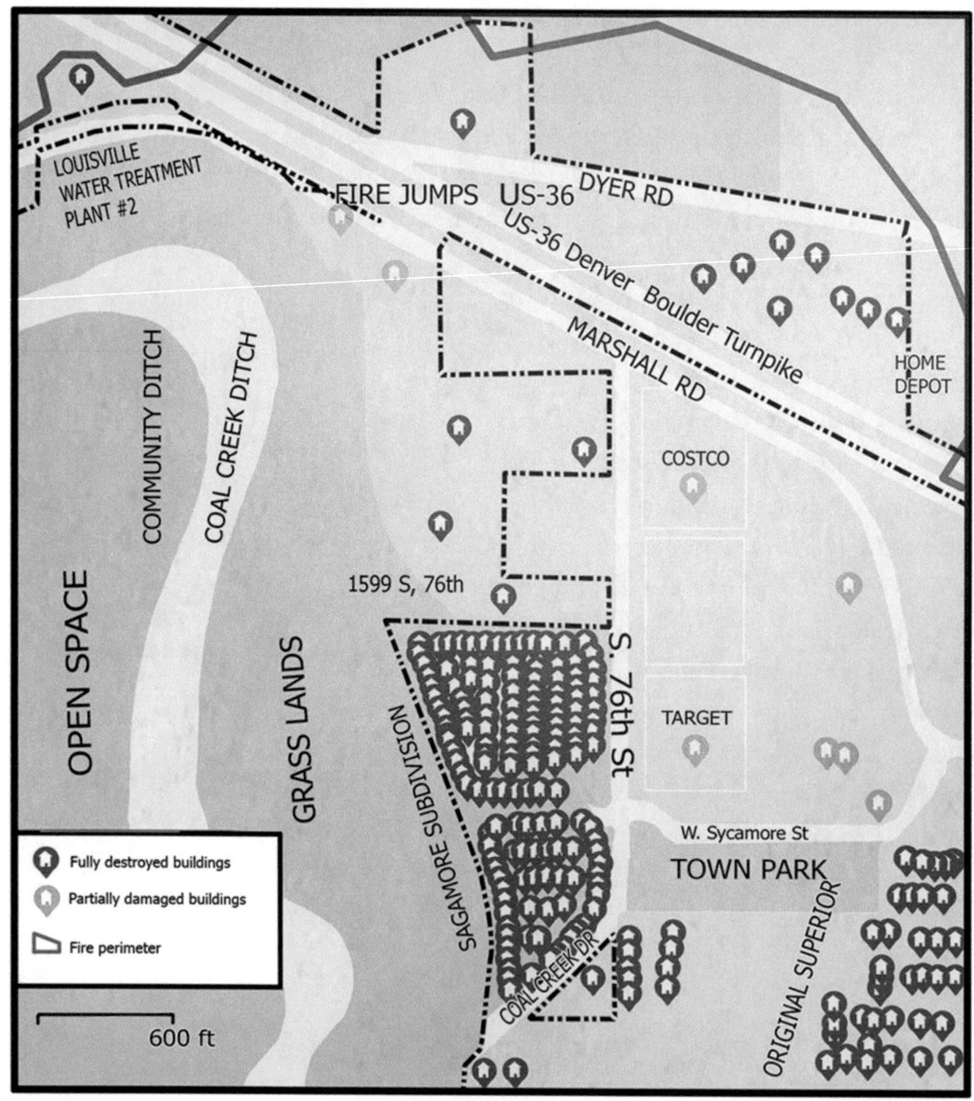

Figure 24 West Superior, Sagamore Subdivision, and Costco. The fire jumped US-36 and attacked Louisville.

Just after noon, a 911-fire call for Jasper Road diverted three units north to check it out. They found nothing and thought the callers saw the smoke from the exploding Marshall fire five miles away. By 12:15 p.m., the second evacuation notice went out for western Superior, including the Sagamore subdivision and the Costco shopping center. This evacuation notice reached 2,588 contacts and requested evacuees go north and east from the area. A minute later, the OEM ordered the shutdown of US-36 from east of Broomfield to Boulder. The OEM also asked for additional firefighting resources from nearby Broomfield County and small northern Hygiene. Marshall Road CO-170 became impassable by 12:15 p.m. due to smoke and fire. More firefighting aid was requested from Jefferson County, Arvada, and North Metro. Units from Jeffco and Arvada were first directed to come north on McCaslin and stage at the parking lot of the KeyBank in Louisville. As the fire exploded, Command quickly redirected these incoming units to stage at Macy's parking lot at FlatIron Crossing Mall. With the wind so intense, the fire quickly surpassed available firefighting capabilities.

By 12:20 p.m., the flames had reached the yard of 1599 S. Seventy-sixth Street, southwest of Costco, and County Dispatch broadcast a request for a disabled evacuation. The property was owned by ninety-one-year-old Edna Nadine Turnbull, who lived with her adult granddaughter, Layla Cornell, two dogs, two goats, and two horses. She came to Superior with her husband in 1965. Neighbor Scotty Roberts evacuated his nearby home with his wife but wondered whether Turnbull had made it out. Roberts spied Sheriff Sergeant 571 in a pickup nearby and convinced him to accompany him to the front door of Turnbull's old farmhouse, which faced west. When she opened the door, Roberts reported that the whole front of the house exploded in flames, forcing Sheriff Sergeant 571 to retreat. He grabbed Nadine and threw stuff out of the way to make it through the home to the north door. Granddaughter Layla Cornell left safely, but Nadine had the two dogs on leashes, and they got entangled around a table. Roberts sobbed, "She was tethered to the dogs that were wrapped around the table, and I couldn't pull all of them and the table with me at the same time." The two fell as he tried to pull her out. "And when I came back up like this, I fell off the step and hit the truck, and there was just

Figure 25 Family photograph of Edna Nadine Turnbull with granddaughter Layla Cornell. Courtesy of Amy Smith.

fire everywhere, and I just couldn't breathe no more, and I just looked, and I said, 'I'm sorry,' and I ran, and I couldn't go back into the fire."[37]

Cornell lamented later that she lost everything—her grandmother, her dogs, her horses, her clothing . . . She still had hope that the goats may have survived in early January, but they were never located. Bone fragments found in the ashes on January 19 were later identified as coming from Turnbull. Turnbull was the second confirmed victim of the Marshall fire.

James Montoya,[38] who worked in the tire center, was one of the first Costco employees to notice that the smoke and fire were coming closer and determined that Costco might have to evacuate. He notified Costco management around 11:40 a.m. of the threat and shut down operations in the auto shop. Meanwhile, Bob Guerreri was helping to unload a nine-thousand-gallon gasoline delivery truck at the Costco gas station on the north side near CO-170 when he saw that the fire growing dangerously close. He quickly instructed the driver to shut down the gas offload and evacuate. He then calmly closed the gas station and directed customers to evacuate back to the east. Miraculously, his quick thinking and sound judgment saved the building as well as the lives of numerous employees and members.

Associate Joe Cramer[39] received James Montoya's warning about the fire and walked back to the gas station and saw the intense smoke and fire. He quickly returned inside the store and helped coordinate Costco's evacuation. Hearing the announcement to evacuate, Associate George Emerson started directing members to leave their baskets and evacuate immediately. Checkout conveyors were stopped mid–checkout, and carts were left standing where they were as the shoppers fled. Associate Misty Vigil helped others to evacuate and then headed to her car. She commented, "It happened so quickly. But then we were stuck in the parking lot for twenty minutes." She also commented that she saw two or three Colorado Parks and Wildlife vehicles headed west on Marshall Road into the fire to evacuate large animals, and she couldn't believe their bravery. George Emerson said, "It was terrifying. The noise was ferocious. It sounded like the wind was tearing up the roof."

[37] Partially derived from the interview reported by Alan Gionet, January 5, 2022, 7:00 a.m. on CBS4 and other sources.

[38] James Montoya and Bob Guerreri stories based on Costco January 2022 employee newsletter.

[39] From author interview with Joe Cramer, George Emerson, and Misty Vigil at Costco on February 8, 2022.

At 12:10 p.m., Sheriff Sergeant 571[40] entered the store and yelled for everyone to evacuate. He walked past George Emerson (in a mask with beard sticking out below) and then Joe Cramer (in red vest) as he continued to urge employees and customers to leave immediately. Both Emerson and Cramer verified that the store was empty before they too exited with the belief it may be the last time that they would ever set foot in the store. As he was leaving, Cramer took one last picture of the empty aisles, the smoke accumulating in the rafters, and the checkout conveyors stacked with customers' gathered unpurchased merchandise.

[40] Body camera video of the evacuation from Sheriff Sergeant #571 is at https://www.youtube.com/watch?v=lyfPiBqq3Uk.

Figure 26 Smoke filling Costco rafters after evacuation. Note full checkout conveyors and carts. Courtesy of Joe Cramer.

Once outside, the associates found the parking lot a mess. Emerson helped an older sample sharer get to her car and then called other employees to make sure that they were OK. He knew of one employee who walked to work, and he telephoned her to make sure that she had a ride. Cramer also helped lost customers find their autos amid the smoke and confusion. The smell was horrible, the wind howled, and the fire was already raging in the gap with Target[41], just a few stores away. The parking lot was congested, and cars were barely moving east on Marshall Road as the traffic lights on McCaslin had traffic backed up. One video shot through a windshield leaving the parking lot showed hot embers bouncing off the windshield and smoke so thick the car just feet in front was obscured beyond the brake lights at 12:08 p.m. Later satellite imagery shows the fire burning fiercely on three sides of Costco by 12:19 p.m. and consuming the Sagamore subdivision to the southwest. It is a miracle that all the customers and associates made it out unscathed.

Bob Guerreri from the Costco gas station was also a volunteer fireman. He joined with the crew defending the shopping center and spent the night there putting out flames. A day later, as a fireman, he returned to the store and provided management with updates on the minor damage. Miraculously, the store reopened eight days after the fire following a special cleaning, removal of spoiled goods, and installation of temporary filter fans to cleanse the smoke smell.

[41] The nearby Target store was closed from fire and water damage until reopening on August 30, 2022.

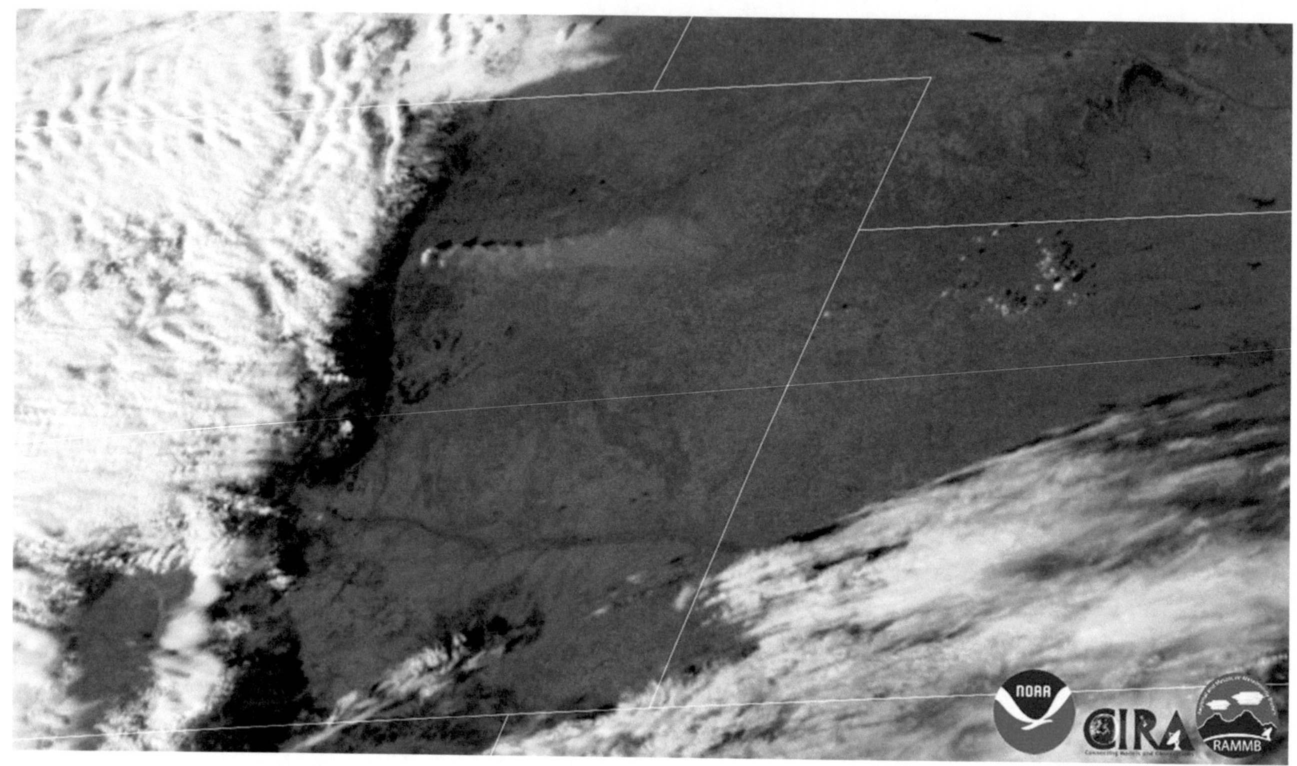

Figure 27 GOES East satellite image of the Marshall fire around 12:30 p.m. Note oscillations in smoke plume. Courtesy of NOAA.

Louisville, December 30, 2021, 12:46 p.m., Wind SSE 25 mph, Gusting to 55 mph 44°F

Jase and Jean H.[42] moved into a rental property in the Coal Creek Ranch subdivision of Louisville on Muirfield Circle six months earlier in June 2021. The rental was a beauty, a two-story built in 1990 valued at $890,000 and almost 2,600 square feet in size, with four bedrooms and three and a half baths—plenty of room for their two young sons ages two and three. They had collected many things during their marriage, and it took two large trucks to move all their stuff in, including Jase's large $5,000–$7,000 book collection. The finished basement included an office where Jase worked writing and an additional storage area that the kids used for play. The vaulted front living room led to a formal dining area. A glass door with a doggy hatch beside it led out onto the oversized deck in the immaculately landscaped enclosed backyard. Their twelve-pound black-and-white Chihuahua–Boston terrier mix Violet went in and out the doggy door and was safe in the backyard from coyotes. The neighborhood had almost 140 homes, and all were well-maintained. Coal Creek and the golf course were just to the west and north, and Avista Hospital can be seen through the trees up above on the hill to the east. St. Andrews Lane wound through this idyllic neighborhood and connected it to Dillon Road to the north and S. Eighty-eighth Street to the southeast. Jase thought

Figure 28 Jase and Jean's home in Coal Creek Ranch subdivision.

[42] Based on various personal interviews, included February 2, 2022, 6:00 p.m. The names have been altered at their request.

the home would be a great place to raise the boys and was close to Jase's elder son, 12, who lived with Jase's ex-wife and her family in nearby Lafayette.

Wednesday afternoon, Jase worked out as normal at the gym. While there, he invited a friend over Thursday evening to share a beer. This was to be the first time that he invited someone he met locally to visit socially. But when he got home Wednesday, he felt ill and went to bed about 3:00 p.m. He slept until 8:00 a.m. on December 30, got up, ate, and went back to bed still feeling off. He snoozed until 11:30 a.m. Jase was never ill and hoped it was only a twenty-four-hour bug. When he woke up, the house was shaking from the wind, and there was a light smell of smoke. His elder son spent most of Christmas week with them but was scheduled to be picked up by noon. Jase got up and looked outside. It was trash day, and the wind had blown trash cans and garbage everywhere. He also noticed that two neighbors' fences were down, and one fence section was down in his backyard. He thought he would have to call the rental company later to get it fixed. He looked on the internet to see where the smoke was coming from but didn't find anything about a fire near Louisville.[43] He hugged his elder son as his ex-wife picked him up. He had a premonition that the fire could be bad even though there was nothing on the internet, so he told Jean to pack overnight bags just in case. He called his friend from the gym and told him not to come tonight as he was feeling ill.

Jase and Jean had a virtual conference scheduled at 2:00 p.m. Jean packed a few personal and hygiene items into cloth grocery bags but then got distracted by the boys. They were fussy with the wind, and she put them down for a nap around 1:00 p.m. The dog also didn't like the wind and had disappeared, hiding someplace in the house she thought was safe. Jase looked for more information about a fire and found a small posting about a grass fire near Superior. Unbeknownst to Jase and Jean, by 1:38 p.m., the fire was already attacking neighboring homes in their Rock Creek Ranch subdivision.

With the smoke getting worse, Jase told Jean to cancel their 2:00 p.m. teleconference based on him feeling ill. She went onto the talk option on her computer and promptly got put on hold. At 1:52 p.m., Jase's eldest son texted Jase saying that Superior was being evacuated and asked what they planned to do. Jase looked out the window and saw police cars across Dillon Road with sirens and lights blazing, and the smoke looked ominous. He yelled at Jean that they were going to evacuate and to pack whatever she can and get the kids up and going. Jase headed to the basement and grabbed a few things, including his computer. Jean got her computer and backup drive and then headed upstairs to get the boys up. The youngest was easy to wake up

[43] News of the Marshall fire was not picked up by social media and local networks until midafternoon.

from a nap, but the eldest wanted to sleep once he was down. As Jase was gathering things up, he heard a pounding at the front door. A police officer screamed, "Evacuate now! Do not hesitate! Just go NOW!" Jase grabbed the cloth grocery bag full of personal items and the one next to it (full of cloth grocery bags) and his computer and put them into the back of their SUV in the garage. He then went to help Jean get the kids up and took the youngest and buckled him into the car. Jean, meanwhile, tried to convince the eldest to get up so that he can see the firetrucks. He loved firetrucks and even dressed as a fireman last Halloween. When he got up, Jase grabbed him and buckled him into the car while Jean looked for their dog, Violet. The police wailed again to evacuate now, but Jean couldn't find Violet. Jase lay on the horn in the garage to speed Jean up. Crying, she climbed into the car without Violet. As they pulled out onto Muirfield, they can see the houses at the other end of their street already burning . . .

Fighting the wind and the traffic, they crawled out of Louisville and called Jase's folks in Texas. They asked his parents to find them an Airbnb nearby to spend the night. Jean cried about leaving the dog. She was Jean's before they met, then Jase took care of the dog for six months before they got married. She was a real rascal and a mutt, but everyone loved her. Jase's folks called later with the address for the Airbnb. They also asked if they had checked their online security cameras. The security cameras and internet went blank twenty minutes after they evacuated. What an ominous sign.

They made it to the Airbnb and took stock of what they grabbed from the house. They had a few personal things, a change of clothes, and some hygiene items, but nothing for the kids. Jase took off to the local big box based on Jean's list of necessities and came back with those, plus enough food to make dinner. They settled in for one of the worst nights of Jase's life. They booked another Airbnb close by for New Year's Eve, but friends confirmed their worst fears that their house and all their possessions were gone. So they canceled the Airbnb and decided to drive to Jase's folks in Texas. Jase commented, "Really hard to process that it really happened. But we are all safe, and it is just stuff." As they were driving south and feeling relieved to be safe, he told Jean, "Hey, babe, at least we don't have to take the Christmas decorations down."

Figure 29 Sheriff deputies blocked traffic at Sycamore Street and S. Seventy-sixth Street east of the Sagamore subdivision in Superior about 1:00 pm. Photo: Code 10 Photography.

Water is king in Colorado. The early settlers recognized this and began building ditches to transport water from the rivers to the fields where it is needed for crop irrigation. The first recorded irrigation ditch in Colorado is the People's Ditch in the San Luis Valley at eight thousand feet in elevation and built in 1852. It diverts water from the Culebra Creek. In Colorado, the older the water rights, the more access to water. As such, the People's Ditch is the highest priority ditch and thus receives the most water from Culebra Creek. Other irrigation ditches on the same creek will be shut off as summer water supplies dwindle, but the People's Ditch will continue to receive water.

> Ditches were dug with teams of oxen or horses pulling plows or ditchers (V-shaped chisels that cut deep trenches in the soil). Many of the earliest ditches, such as the Holland Ditch near Altona, were dug with a team and walking plow. They were carefully designed to allow the water to flow gently across the entire field. Levels were attached to the plow, allowing a farmer to judge the proper angle so that the water did not flow too rapidly. A drop of one

> inch per twenty feet was common and that distance was often measured by tying a rag on the wagon wheel spoke. A predetermined number of revolutions of the wheel indicated the distance traveled.[44]

In the late 1860s, Abner Goodhue diverted the first water from South Boulder Creek. He neglected to register it properly, and the later Davidson and South Boulder Canon ditches now have more senior rights. Ditches in the Marshall fire zone include the Coal Creek Ditch, the Davidson Ditch, the Marshallville Ditch, the William C. Hake Ditch, and the Community Ditch. Shareholders in a ditch receive water based on the ditch's seniority and then on their seniority with the ditch company. In the spring when water is plentiful, all the gates along the ditch may open, and farmland saturates. As the water supply dries up, younger water rights are shut off and gates close. In Colorado, water and mineral rights can be sold independent of land ownership. Even though a ditch may cross someone's land, that does not mean the landowner has access to the water. Ditch companies are responsible for the maintenance of each ditch. Some are more careful than others, clearing vegetation and ensuring leaks are promptly sealed. Others are not so careful.

[44] Derived from https://bcn.boulder.co.us/basin/history/irrigation.html, Dyni, 2005.

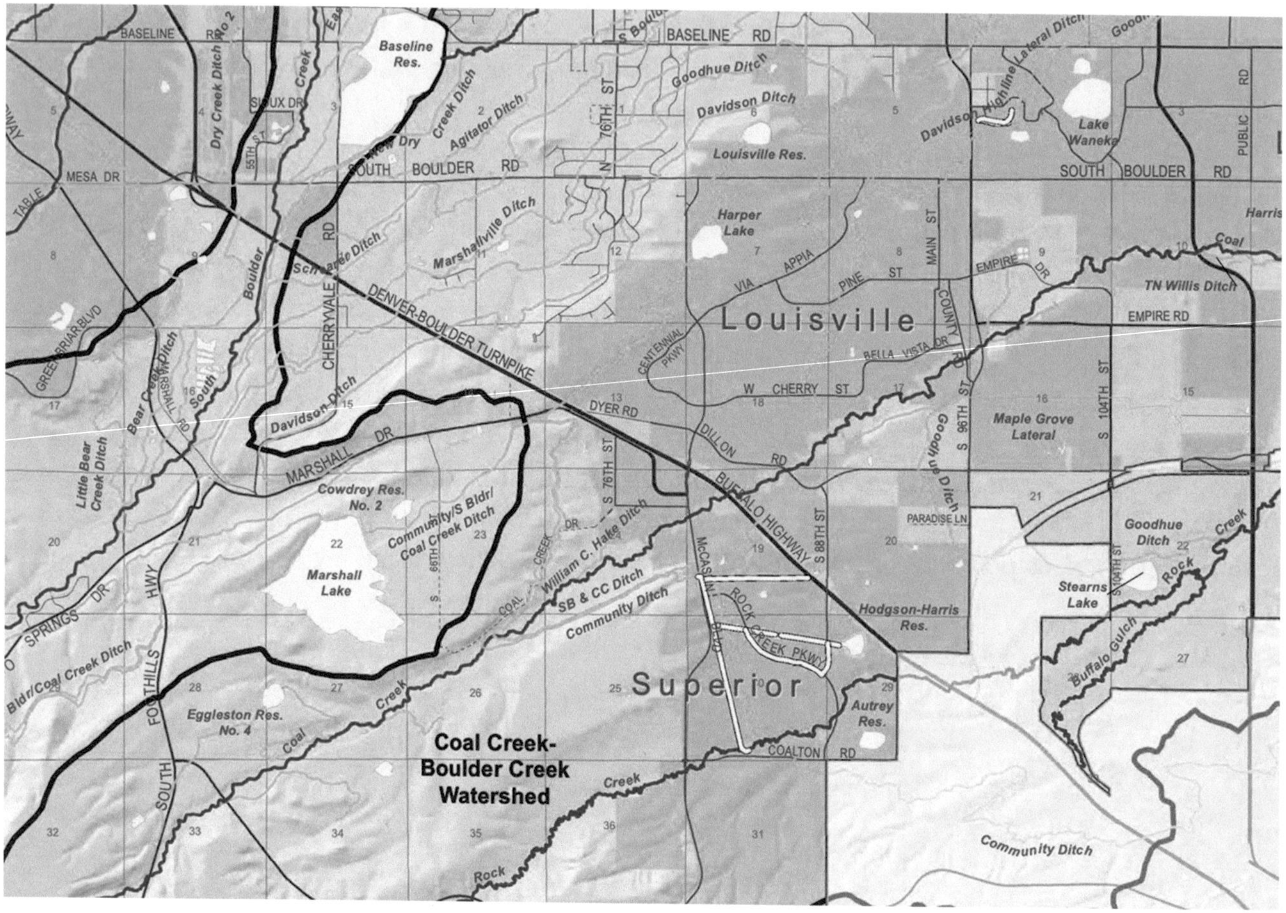

Figure 30 Active ditches in Marshall fire area 2020. Courtesy of Boulder County.

Water stealing and diversion has a rich and colorful history in Colorado. One famous old saying goes, "You can fool around with my wife, but not my water rights." Early water commissioners wore badges and carried guns to enforce gate closures and diversions. Along the nearby Dry Creek–Little Davidson Ditch, battles over water involved pitchforks, hatchets, weeds, and even bees, as one farmer placed a beehive on his headgate to discourage the water commissioners from turning it off. By December 2021, with no rain since summer, all the ditches in Boulder County were parched, and many had an overgrowth of tall dry plants and grasses along the sides.

By 12:30 p.m., County Dispatch sent additional units to 320 Cherokee Avenue in the Sagamore development of Superior just west of Target as the home was fully engulfed in flames. Five homes nearby burst into flames within a minute. Responding units reported that it sounded like a war zone with the blare of propane tanks venting then exploding in the extreme heat. County Dispatch requested units to rescue a trapped person in a burning house at 181 Mohawk Circle southwest of Target in Superior. Most of the 370 homes on the west side of Superior were now surrounded by flames and will be destroyed by the fire. With the winds at gale force, Lafayette Truck 2619 frantically radioed that they must back out of the Sagamore neighborhood as the fire encircles them. They cut their hoses tapped to the fire hydrants with axes and backed out of the neighborhood. Near that same time, OEM requested additional firefighting resources from Arvada. A reverse 911 was initiated for the Panorama Parks area in Original Superior. Traffic leaving the Costco shopping area came to a standstill due to the volume, traffic lights, and heavy smoke. With the strong winds, the fire started burning between TJ Maxx and Target at 12:36 p.m. while people were still in the parking lots and others still in the stores.

Figure 31 Superior Sagamore subdivision, November 10, 2021, before fire (Target store upper left). Courtesy of the Maxar Open Data Program.

Figure 32 Superior Sagamore subdivision during fire (Target store upper left). Courtesy of the Maxar Open Data Program.

A minute later, Marshall Command ordered all the fire trucks to withdraw from the Sagamore neighborhood due to the fierce blaze caused by the 100 mph winds. By this time, most of the homes at the south end and west side of the development were fully engulfed. The flames and heat were too intense to fight with the few hoses and trucks available. They decide to let the fire burn through the subdivision and fight it from the backside. Firefighters also pulled back from the Costco gas station due to the risk of it exploding. Traffic finally started moving again out of the Costco parking lot when sheriff's deputies opened both lanes on Marshall Road eastbound and stopped traffic on McCaslin coming southbound across the bridge from Louisville.

Sheriff deputies also directed traffic, ensuring that the traffic lights there were ignored. At 12:46 p.m., the third evacuation notice was pronounced for original and eastern Superior. This notification only reached 254 contacts and directed them to evacuate east on US-36 or southbound on McCaslin. Three minutes later, the OEM issued the fourth notice announcing pre-evacuation for the rest of Superior south to CO-120. It reached 4,173 contacts. CR-170 Marshall Road and CO-93 S. Foothills Highway both closed due to the winds and fire.

At 12:45 p.m., a fire broke out behind the Home Depot in Louisville, and resources responded to check it out. The powerful winds caused the fire to jump the natural firebreak of the wide, six-lane highway US-36 just northwest of Costco where the road was below grade. Homes and vegetation along Dyer Road started to burn on the north side. The city of Louisville was now threatened. Fire command requested evacuations for the southern half of Louisville, but these were not issued by OEM for another twenty minutes. Additional fire units started to arrive from Longmont and north. The Quality Inn in Louisville east of the Home Depot reported fire at 12:50 p.m., and La Quinta further east across McCaslin also reported flames a minute later.

In Louisville, initial responding fire crews described the scene as chaotic. The fire moved so fast, and the smoke was so thick that it was difficult to determine where to fight it. Crossing over US-36 on McCaslin heading north, visibility was next to zero, and the road and units ahead were totally obscured. They instead deployed west of the Louisville Recreation Center and attacked a grass fire south of the skate park. For a short time, traffic was stalled on Via Appia in front of Fire Station 2, and the fire jumped Via Appia and approached the fire station. Crews successfully put it out, and the traffic was able to move on.

Due to the traffic streaming out of Superior, arriving fire trucks coming from the southeast could not make it into town. Command ordered them to stage at FlatIron Crossing Mall to the east and had them deploy using now-closed US-36. A pre-evacuation notice was announced for all of Louisville. At 12:55 p.m., County Dispatch tasked Boulder Rural Brush 2236 to attempt rescuing the disabled party at 1599 S. Seventy-sixth (Turnbull residence). County Dispatch noted special equipment may be needed as the property was engulfed.[45] Units from the north Middle Fork fire broke off as it became under control and routed south to aid with the Marshall fire. By 1:00 p.m., west Superior was burning, and Louisville was vulnerable.

From the first call at 11:09 a.m., the fire consumed over two thousand acres in two hours. Businesses were threatened, and homes were now burning. But catastrophe was averted as the major Costco shopping center,

[45] This is thirty-five minutes after the initial call for help, and it is unclear if this is prior or after neighbor Scottie Robert's rescue attempt.

with Target, TJ Maxx, Petco, and other merchants, was safely evacuated. The wind-driven flames did not overrun the jammed traffic on Marshall Road and McCaslin Boulevard in Superior and did not result in a large loss of life. Another miracle!

Evacuations started in western and southern Louisville and all Superior. It was obvious that the number of evacuees could not be handled by the Sacred Heart of Mary Church on S. Boulder Road, so the OEM started contacting other larger locations. Finally, new evacuation centers opened at 12:43 p.m. at the South Boulder Recreation Center and Longmont Senior Center. Due to the high winds knocking down power lines, all of south Boulder promptly lost electricity, which remained out for many hours. The OEM continued to contact additional locations as the Longmont Senior Center was quite a distance away, and the South Boulder Recreation Center may have to close with no lights.

In most cases, evacuees received no warning or evacuation notice. Residents saw smoke and flames or received texts or shouts from neighbors, and they quickly hightailed it out. In many areas, law enforcement was unavailable to direct traffic, but the evacuation progressed slowly but smoothly in both cities.

Boulder County has more than thirty outdoor warning sirens for "flood, tornado, or other disaster" according to the Office of Emergency Management (OEM) website.[46] These sirens are to wail for a short period and then "broadcast a voice message immediately following the siren signal" to indicate why the warning and what action to take. The actual tones used and the length of the tones vary depending upon the emergency. For whatever reason, these sirens in Louisville and Superior were never employed during the fire.

Boulder County also utilizes a service by Everbridge of Burlington, Massachusetts, to provide emergency alerts. Hardwired phones from CenturyLink and VoIP phones from Xfinity/Comcast are automatically enrolled based on the registered household address. At the time of the Marshall fire, cell phones and all others had to be manually added by the household to be notified at https://member.everbridge.net/453003085612231/login. Messages from the system are of two types—prepare to act or immediate action is required. These can be further expanded to Advisory (an emergency may impact a registered address), Warning (prepare to act), and Order (act now). The most common actions broadcast are "climb to higher ground" (during a flood), "evacuation" (for wildfire, law enforcement, or HAZMAT reasons), "shelter in place" (law enforcement or health), "missing/endangered person" (public safety), and "all clear." Tornado and flash flood warnings issued

[46] Per https://www.boulderoem.com/preparedness/informed/sirens/.

by the National Weather Service are also automatically broadcast through the same system. The Boulder OEM used this system for pre-evacuation and evacuation notices for Louisville and Superior nine times during the fire, and they reached 40,657 contacts.

Nurse Galina Gilbert house-sat and watched a small dog and a cat for a friend in central Louisville while not working over the holidays. As she was out walking the dog late that fateful Thursday morning, she witnessed a friend on a bicycle get blown over by the horrific winds. She smelled smoke but didn't think much about it. Just then, she received a text. The homeowners, who were vacationing in St. Martin in the Caribbean, received the pre-evacuation notice on their registered cell phone and asked if Galina knew what was happening. They texted back and forth, but then texts became blocked due to network congestion. Finally, the owners called and told Galina to evacuate. Galina returned to the house; packed up her belongings, the dog, and the cat; and headed to a friend's place in Lafayette.[47] The emergency phone notification system did work, but in a roundabout way in Gilbert's case.

Another emergency notification system is called Wireless Emergency Alerts, or WEAs. This system broadcasts an emergency message to all cell phones attached to the cell phone towers in the region of interest. All the major cell phone companies participate in this arrangement with the federal government. The state of Colorado uses it for Amber Alerts for missing minors. The Federal Emergency Management Agency (FEMA) also uses it in their Integrated Public Alert & Warning System (IPAWS). But most Colorado counties and cities do not participate due to the cost and logistics involved. Though the state offered the Boulder OEM the ability to use a WEA broadcast during the Marshall fire, the offer did not come until after the first seven evacuation alerts had already been sent. The Boulder OEM decided that using WEA that late may confuse residents by providing possibly conflicting information. In a later update,[48] Boulder County explained the limitations of WEA:

> In a wildfire scenario, a WEA is likely to warn residents over a larger geographic area than intended, causing traffic congestion and egress issues for those closest to the danger attempting to evacuate. WEA notifications, if unclear to residents, will increase calls into the 911 center, resulting in additional call volume at the communication centers likely taxing 911 resources. When evacuating areas during a wildfire, it must be stressed that individuals near the evacuation zones need to evacuate immediately and emergency responders have to consider the transportation routes needed for areas evacuating immediately due to the encroaching fire.

---

[47] Interview with Galina Gilbert, January 13, 2021. The home she was house-sitting survived with little damage.

[48] https://assets.bouldercounty.org/wp-content/uploads/2022/01/marshall-fire-emergency-notification-system.pdf updated after Marshall fire.

In the event of an evacuation with only five minutes' notice, experts recommend that evacuees grab the six *P*s—people and pets, plastic, paper, prescriptions, pictures, and personal computer. People and pets are self-explanatory. Plastic implies money and credit cards. Paper means to grab important and hard-to-replace financial, medical, and personal information, including driver's license, health insurance information, and legal documents. Personal prescriptions include medications, eyeglasses, and important vitamins. Pictures means personal mementos that cannot be replaced. And today, important electronics and memory devices should be added to the list of items to grab in an emergency, including a personal computer. Unluckily, most evacuees aren't prepared and don't think in advance about what to do in an emergency. They are unprepared when the emergency occurs and lose too much time trying to determine what to take and often forget important items that are then lost. Like Paul Williamson, the adrenaline of the moment overshadows the planning from before. Post the six *P*s prominently in a location you will remember so that when disaster strikes, you have a handy reference available of what to grab.

The federal government maintains an information website (ready.gov[49]) and a FEMA phone application that covers most anticipated situations that require evacuating. Emergency and disaster situations from avalanche to bioterrorism to wildfires to floods and hurricanes are covered. Basic information about each situation and how to react and what to expect are listed. Another section covers how to "make a plan" that includes information on how to be prepared. The website also has sections on getting involved, business readiness, how to prepare children, and a section on additional resources and links. The website is well organized and informative. It should be visited before a disaster occurs and not during the disaster.

Balfour Senior Living hosts six communities in Louisville, making it the most comprehensive continuum for senior care in Colorado. The Lodges and the Residences offer independent living in apartments and cottage homes. The Villa and Lavender Farms provide assisted living. The Club provides skilled nursing. These communities are located on the east side of Louisville at the original site of the Hecla Mine casino. The sixth site, Cherrywood Village, offers memory care and is located off McCaslin Boulevard just north of W. Cherry Street. When Balfour received the first evacuation notice for west Louisville, it began the tedious task of individually preparing to move the fifty-four mentally challenged seniors from their Cherrywood Village home. Luckily, the second floor of the Club (Wellshire) in east Louisville was vacant. Around 1:00

[49] See https://www.ready.gov.

p.m., Balfour sent its eight buses and vans from the east side of Louisville to Cherrywood to start packing the patients and moving them to safety at the Club.

Figure 33 The Villa at Balfour assisted living facility in eastern Louisville.

Becki Siemers is the executive director of Balfour's Villa and Club facilities and has been in skilled nursing her entire career starting when she was licensed in 1996.[50] Previously, she directed a facility in Grand Junction, Colorado. She knows that Balfour's buildings are designed to withstand major emergencies, including wildfires. But she also knows that a site in New Orleans that did not evacuate during Hurricane Katrina

[50] Becki Siemers's interview, February 1, 2022, at the Villa at Balfour, Louisville, Colorado.

in 2005, lost residents when the levees broke and their first floor flooded. Though Balfour's buildings may survive the wildfire, other support functions may be lost during the emergency, and staying in place may not be the best solution. FEMA rolled out new regulations for all regulated assisted and nursing facilities in 2008, requiring updated disaster recovery plans, including how to perform evacuations. Balfour's disaster recovery plans were up to date, and the staff ran through them periodically. While the buses were at Cherrywood, Siemers dusted off the evacuation plans for skilled nursing and assisted living just in case. Balfour was not required to assist evacuating residents in independent living.

Siemers told a humorous story about the first disaster plans she developed while in Grand Junction. FEMA, in its wisdom, sent notification that her facility there required a disaster recovery plan for avalanches, since they were in mountainous Colorado. But Grand Junction is in the high desert, miles from the nearest mountains, and only receives an average of sixteen inches of snow a year. Surely FEMA was wrong. Becky and staff reviewed the request and decided that it was possible that an avalanche could sever I-70 and important supplies might not be available to the facility for quite some time. So they developed a detailed plan of how the facility could survive with the roads blocked and no direct contact to the east. They submitted their plan to FEMA. Many weeks later, they received notice from FEMA that they were not in compliance and will be heavily fined if an avalanche disaster recovery plan was not submitted promptly.

As the second floor of the Club had been vacant, none of the rooms were prepared to receive the Cherrywood patients. The Balfour staff began the task of moving beds and mattresses to the empty rooms and cleaning and making beds to prepare for their arrival, expecting that they will be needed immediately.

By 1:00 p.m., the fire was moving quickly in western Louisville. County Dispatch issued a request to rescue trapped personnel at the KinderCare facility on McCaslin, south of the Boven home. Louisville Brush 2718 arrived within two minutes and began hosing down a grass fire. As it was the holiday season, no children were on-site. They cleared KinderCare and were available for their next tasking within three minutes. Additional evacuation notices were broadcast, and Centennial Peaks and Avista Adventist Hospitals started emergency evacuation procedures on the southeast side of Louisville. The Costco evacuation finished by 1:08 p.m. As employees and customers left, the visibility in the parking lot was almost zero due to the smoke and wind.

The OEM issued the fifth evacuation notice at 1:08 p.m. for Louisville McCaslin Boulevard east to S. 104th Street between Cherry Street / Belle Vista / Empire Road to the north and US-36 / Disc Drive / Northwest Parkway to the south. This notice reached 7,251 contacts and instructed evacuees to go north or east from Louisville. Satellite imagery at that time showed the fire burning fiercely west of the Home Depot in Louisville, around Costco in Original Superior and near the Element Hotel. Hygiene firefighting resources began arriving at 1:10 p.m. from the north and deployed along McCaslin in Louisville. Erie and Dacono units arrived a few minutes later. A new law enforcement command net was established for Louisville as McCaslin Command and operated out of the Louisville Police Station. This command was dedicated to helping law enforcement coordinate evacuations and direct traffic. The first structure fire on Hillside Lane at the base of Davidson Mesa across from McCaslin and Via Appia was reported at 1:12 p.m., and Louisville Truck 2702 responded. A unit called in that "the whole west side of Louisville is completely smoked out and we cannot see anything." Evacuation order 6 was issued for Louisville north of US-36 to S. Boulder Road from Cherryvale Road east to McCaslin at 1:15 p.m. It reached 2,509 contacts and did not include where or how to evacuate in the announcement, even though County Dispatch recommended that the evacuees head either north or east. Unluckily, it didn't reach the Bovens or their neighbors.

On the western side of Louisville, Larry Boven drove the few blocks to pick up his wife, Mary, at the Louisville Rec Center about 12:30 p.m. As a previous firefighter, he noticed the thick cloud of swirling smoke to the west and knew that his friends with the Louisville Fire Department will be busy. He's not too concerned as the smoke appeared to be south of the natural firebreak of US-36, and besides, Louisville had those loud sirens that would be blaring if it was a real emergency. They drove back home, and he saw that the wind had knocked over several trash cans and Christmas wrapping paper was blowing all over the neighborhood. He pulled in the driveway, and Mary went in while he wandered down the street gathering up trash. Neighbors were out doing the same thing, and one suddenly screamed out pointing to the west. He looked up and saw a huge wall of flame bearing down on the Global Healthcare Exchange complex nearby. As a former firefighter, he knew the grass was tinder-dry and ready to explode. He dialed 911 to report what he saw, but the line was busy. He raced back home, jumped into the car, and frantically drove across McCaslin along Via Appia to the Louisville Fire Station 2 four blocks away to report the fire. They let him into the station, and the receptionist responded that all of Louisville's equipment was already committed and asked if he received the reverse 911 call to evacuate. His face drained of color as he raced back home, passing a tree burning at the end of Hillside Lane, not three houses away. He feared the worst for his home of almost thirty years.

He knew that it would take time and effort to convince Mary to get into the car to leave. He ran in the house and told her, "We must leave right now!" He gathered up the dogs and put them into the car. Mary said she had to go to the bathroom. Larry said, "We will stop along the way! Just get in the car!" He was more concerned about her than any physical possessions and left behind everything—his computer, important documents and memories, and even a change of clothes. All stayed in the house. They got in the car and headed down Hillside Lane past the first house to the west, which was now on fire. They turned up McCaslin to the north, and Mary said she really had to go, so Larry took her to Enclave Park to use the facilities. While she was inside, he saw houses burning to the southwest and the fire closing in on his house.

He really thought that the fire department will get ahead of the flames and save his home, so they left the park and headed north a couple of blocks and watched the fire with many others at the Leon A. Wurl Wildlife Sanctuary parking lot south of Harper Lake. A Longmont fire engine barricaded McCaslin to the north to keep traffic from heading to the south. He called a neighbor, and they assured him that they had evacuated safely. Before leaving, the neighbor used a hose on the spreading fire with no effect and then left. The Bovens stayed at Harper Lake for quite some time and saw the flames jump McCaslin and start burning the many homes in the Hillside neighborhood. After that, Larry decided it was time to go.

Unbeknownst to them, their daughter Anna drove to their house while they were at Harper Lake to make sure that they had evacuated safely. Risking the flames and burning homes nearby, she frantically searched the house, saw that it was empty, and grabbed a few sentimental pictures off the wall before fleeing. With the fire intense outside, she miraculously made it safely back to Longmont. She didn't tell Larry and Mary about her visit until that evening when they were all gathered safely in her home. Later, Larry called Louisville Fire chief Willson. He confirmed Larry's worst fears with these simple words: "It's gone, Larry. It's all gone."

A call went out at 1:17 p.m. requesting five units go to a structure fire at 7520 Coal Creek Drive Superior, south of the Sagamore subdivision, where three men were missing. The fire was bearing down on that area of Superior. Marshall Command added the call to the board and continued evacuations and firefighting. The fire in Superior, meanwhile, started leaping east across McCaslin Boulevard; and civilians were trapped in Original Superior at Main Street and Rock Creek.

At 1:20 p.m., MVFR Brush 2236 was redeployed to 400 block of W. Sycamore Court in Louisville to evacuate a fourteen-year-old female home alone. MVFR Medic 2225 stated they would cover the Sycamore evacuation, and County Dispatch routed Brush 2236 to 459 S. McCaslin in Louisville. This was in a small strip mall with eateries like Qdoba, Marco's Pizza, and Organic Sandwich Company. Luckily, only a few bushes and shrub were burning from flying embers, and the facility was not damaged.

Additional units arrived from the south metro area and staged at FlatIron Crossing Mall in front of Macy's, which became the incident command center for the fire. The Harper Lake area of Louisville was ordered evacuated at 1:25 p.m. when evacuation order 7 was issued. This order reached 276 contacts and directed them to head east or north from the area. County Dispatch also broadcasted a request for a chief level fire official to come to the dispatch center to help handle the volume of incoming 911 calls at 1:25 p.m. Boulder Rural Chief 2360 responded he would come to the dispatch center to help.

About that time, Marshall Command requested that Xcel cut electrical power from Foothills Highway east to Louisville and in all Original Superior. Power in Original Superior was still provided to homes using overhead power lines and poles. With the wind and the fire, too many loose hot wires were falling and causing additional problems. Unluckily, cutting electricity included turning off power to Superior's water plant, meaning hydrant pressure would then be based on the remaining pretreated water still in the water tanks. By 1:35 p.m., the fire attacked the Element Hotel in Superior, and Deputy 564 stayed at the roundabout at McCaslin and Main to pick up a woman who was fleeing the hotel on foot with fire in hot pursuit. The Tesla dealership nearby caught on fire. It was full of cars for sale as well as those in for repairs. The wall of fire was consuming western and Original Superior and following Coal Creek and other plant growth to spread further east. Radar beams reflected from the fire's smoke cloud indicated a "hydraulic jump" formed, where whirling turbulence from the +60-mile-per-hour winds and flames and created a "rotor" of multidirectional gusts. This spread the heat and embers in all directions from the burning buildings and caused more destruction.

Figure 34 The Element Hotel in Superior burned. © Trevor Hughes—USA TODAY NETWORK.

Though no incoming 911 calls were announced by County Dispatch, large heavy smoke was first noted in Spanish Hills at 1:30 p.m. Sheriff Deputy 558 was sent into the area for reconnaissance. Longmont Command 2167 requested a reverse 911 to evacuate all of Louisville south of South Boulder Road at 1:35 p.m. By 1:38 p.m., the fire started to cross Dillon Road at the golf course while Dillon Road was still heavy with evacuation traffic. Following the undergrowth and trees between US-36 and Dillon Road, the fire started to burn in the Coal Creek Ranch subdivision by St. Andrews Lane. An unoccupied car caught fire on McCaslin, blocking southbound traffic. By 1:40 p.m., the fire was entrenched in the field west across from McCaslin and Via Appia. The Louisville Police Department building was directly in its path with Fire Station 2 and the Louisville Recreation Center not far behind. Marshall Command announced personnel evacuation and traffic flow were now the highest priority and firefighting secondary. At 1:43 p.m., the Louisville Police Department abandoned its headquarters building on Via Appia and set up a temporary command post in the King Soopers parking lot at Ninety-fifth and S. Boulder Road east of town at the old Hecla Mine site. Boulder Sheriff SWAT was in transit and decided to stage at Centaurus High School on S. Boulder Road in Lafayette just east of there.

Sometime around 1:40 p.m., Balfour received a reverse 911 call telling them that eastern Louisville had been placed on pre-evacuation status. Balfour decided to send the Cherrywood patients to their new facility in Longmont, and Becki Siemers quietly started staff looking for other locations for the skilled nursing and assisted living residents in case they had to evacuate.

The fire spread to 115 Cherrywood Lane in Louisville south of the police station at 1:45 p.m., and County Dispatch sent Louisville Unit 2732 to fight it. Unluckily, Unit 2732 was a brush truck, and it was redirected to Marshall Command, and other units were sent into the Cherrywood subdivision by McCaslin Command. Sheriff Deputy 558 reported buildings engulfed at Spring Drive and Empire Drive in Spanish Hills at the same time. The fire jumped US-36 again someplace west of the scenic Davidson Mesa overlook and raced through the grasslands to the southwest of Spanish Hills. Fire Dispatch sent MVFR Engine 2203 and Big Elk Meadows Brush 4934 to check on the Element Hotel in Superior to ensure it had been evacuated if they could reach it. The Element Hotel was the only hotel accommodations in Superior, having recently opened in July 2019. The units reported the hotel was totally engulfed in flames at 1:55 p.m. Units from the south metro area started pouring into Macy's parking lot for assignment. Fire trucks picked up evacuees as they went through Superior's streets, but no place had been established to drop them off. Many were let out at Community Park on the east side of town. Southbound traffic was stopped on Ninety-fifth Street at Baseline north of Louisville at 2:00 p.m. From 2:00 p.m. onward, only outbound traffic was allowed from the two towns of Louisville and Superior.

At 1:52 p.m., the fire spread to the brush west of Avista Adventist Hospital.

Marshall, December 30, 2021, 1:56 p.m., Wind W 68 mph, Gusting to 84 mph 40°F

After a delightful lunch with Karen's brother and sister, Bill and Karen Lerch started the drive back from Golden after 1:30 p.m. Karen planned to stop at the Superior Costco to pick up a few items they needed. Knowing that CO-93 was windswept and might be closed, they headed east on CO-58 and started north on Indiana Street. They saw the large dark smoke cloud in the sky but thought nothing of it. Diverted twice due to construction, they continued to W. 120th Avenue, turned left, then turned right onto McCaslin heading into Superior. They made it to Coalton Road before they were diverted eastbound with all the evacuation traffic leaving Superior. There they realized that the fire was bad. Their trip to Costco was forgotten, and they headed for home. It took them an extra hour fighting the traffic winding through Broomfield and then onto Washington Street northbound. They saw no flames, just smoke and masses of humanity, and again miraculously missed the fire by mere minutes.

With its emergency center opened, Avista Adventist Hospital began executing plans to evacuate its fifty-one patients, including ones on COVID ventilators and preemies in the neonatal intensive care. Avista would be the first hospital to evacuate in 36-years. They first reviewed cases to see who could be released, and twenty-one patients were deemed well enough to send home. Their standard evacuation plan called to transfer the remaining thirty patients to the closest facility, Good Samaritan Exempla SCL Health, six miles away along US-287 near the Northwest Parkway in Lafayette.

Good Samaritan is a larger hospital facility with 183 inpatient beds and 664 employees. But Good Sam is also surrounded by grasslands and was in the direct path of the fire if the winds continued unabated. They declined to take any patients from Avista and instead also initiated their emergency plans to start evacuation procedures. They first shut down visitation and closed the emergency room (ER). All noncritical operations were immediate canceled. They started reviewing cases and, like Avista, released all the patients that they could. They called for ambulances to transport the most critical patients, and soon almost fifty responded and lined up in their parking lot. Using these ambulances, Good Sam identified fifty-five critical patients and evacuated them to other SCL facilities nearby. They then decided to wait before taking additional actions to see what the wind and fire chose to do.

With Good Sam not accepting patients, Avista decided to send its remaining thirty patients to other Centura hospitals—twenty-five to Saint Anthony North and five to Longmont United. The evacuations began with NICU, ICU, and ED patients, then progressed to medical-surgical patients and finally staff. All the patients were first moved from their rooms to the now-closed ER area where ambulances arrived to transport them. Nurses and aides accompanied each patient and carefully embraced the critical infants. The five NICU babies were taken to St. Anthony North where software was overridden to take care of them in the two available NICU beds. No Critical Care Transport ambulances were available during the evacuation, but miraculously, there were just enough ambulances with transport ventilators to handle the patients needing intubation. Only one ICU patient traveled without a critical drip medication that could not be administered by the ambulance and made it in time before his blood pressure dropped. The smoke was horrendous as the fire was close, but all staff and patients moved steadily without panic. Within two hours, all patients were successfully evacuated. As the final patients left, islands in the parking lot were burning and the fire was on three sides of the hospital.

Meanwhile, hospital workers fought the onrushing flames with garden hoses and buckets of water. With the fire fully engaged in the nearby Coal Creek Ranch subdivision,[51] the staff prayed that it didn't reach the large oxygen tank outside. The fire burned within four feet of the oxygen supply, which could have leveled the hospital had it exploded. Weather Service maps showed that the wind near Avista came from the south-southeast during that critical time while the wind blew from the west and southwest in the rest of Louisville. The flames burned three sides around the hospital. With the divine help of the wind, the dedicated employees of Avista evacuated the hospital within three hours and kept it safe, all during a pandemic over a holiday weekend where severe weather was expected the next day, another miracle.

Though the hospital was not hurt by fire, it did receive significant smoke damage. And the electricity and gas were cut off due to the fire. Emergency diesel generators were employed to maintain heat until the utilities returned. Avista called in Servpro,[52] who deployed over one hundred specialists working twenty-four hours a day to clean up and sterilize the smoke-ravaged hospital. Twelve Avista employees lost their homes to the fire, and many others had damage. Miraculously, Avista reopened nineteen days after the fire on January 18 with a prayer and blessing ceremony.

[51] See https://vimeo.com/661507003?embedded=true&source=vimeo_logo&owner=105818696 for a view of the fire in the Coal Creek Ranch subdivision from the hospital roof.

[52] For information on Servpro, see https://www.servpro.com.

Coal Creek Ranch Subdivision and Avista Hospital

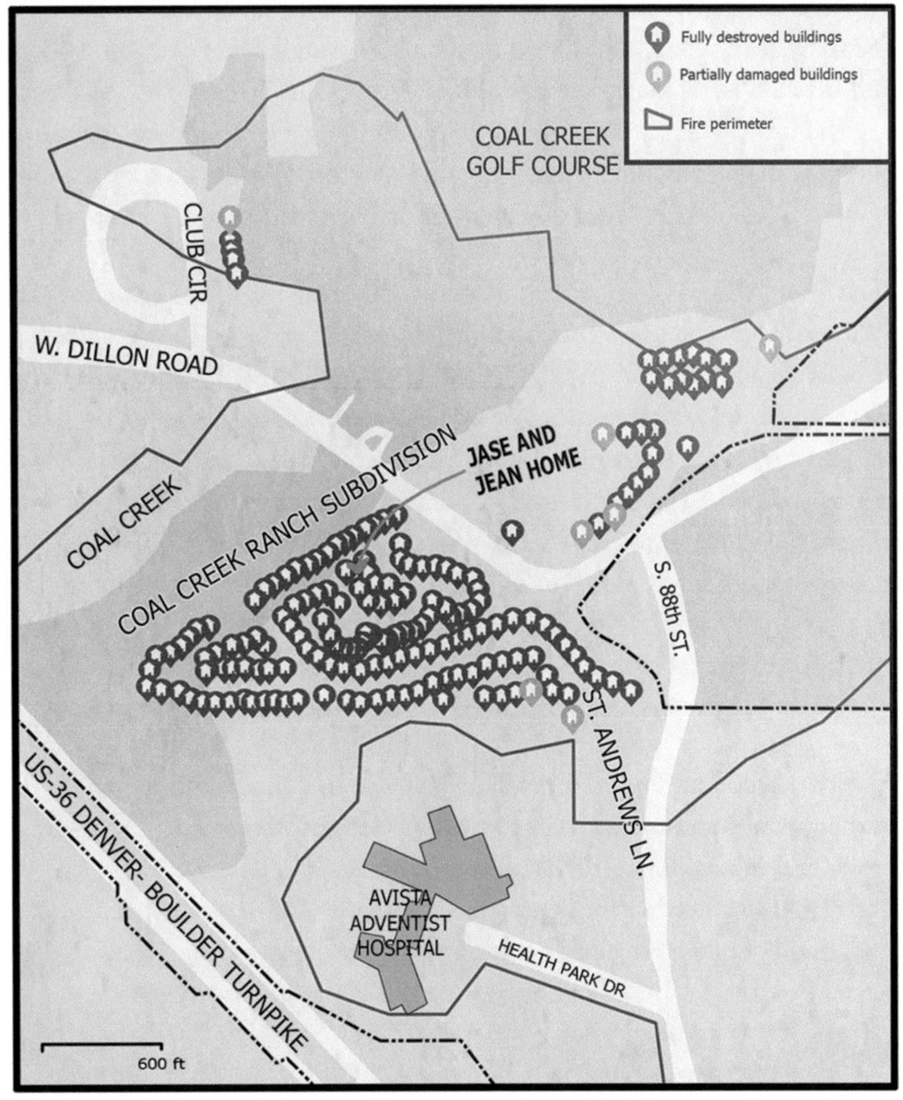

Figure 35 Coal Creek Ranch subdivision and Avista Hospital in Louisville.

As the North Fork fire was under control, the Boulder IMT Type 3 command deployed to the Marshall fire about 2:00 p.m. They met with Louisville Battalion 2760, MVFR 2262, and Sheriff Deputy 517 to assess the situation and what additional resources will be needed. Sheriff Commander Wilber joined them. At 3:40 p.m., they agreed that the IMT command would now act as overall Marshall Command. Tactical firefighting command would be split, with Louisville handling north of US-36 and MVFR directing efforts south of US-36. Much of the team was already in place at the Boulder EOC, and the remaining communications crew joined command in the old Nordstrom's department store at FlatIron Crossing Mall, while additional incoming fire crews staged outside Macy's where they had easy access to US-36 to get to the fire.

By 2:00 p.m., Davidson Mesa and Spanish Hills were fully enflamed, and structures on Spring Drive were engulfed. A wind gust of 68 mph was recorded near the Coal Creek Golf Course.[53] The fire had jumped Dillon Road in south Louisville and was burning along Coal Creek and the golf course. Dillon Road became iffy for evacuation, but Cherry Street was still open. The evacuation continued in both cities, with a call coming in at 2:07 p.m. to evacuate an elderly woman at 1669 Harris Street in southeast Superior. At 2:08 p.m., Louisville announced that it had closed all its city facilities, including Recreation & Senior Center and City Hall. A call came in at 2:10 p.m. that 943 Turnberry Circle was on fire in the Louisville Coal Creek Ranch subdivision. County Dispatch announced additional two structure fires in Old Town Superior and followed up that 820 Mulberry Street in Louisville south of the police station was now burning. The Boulder County Fairgrounds opened as an evacuation center for large animals, and the YMCA of Northern Colorado in Lafayette opened for overnight stays. COVID-positive evacuees were asked to stay at the Mount Calvary Lutheran Church in Boulder.

Louisville Fire, with a wildland engine from Sable Altura in Aurora and a Boulder Rural engine, began fighting fires in the yards of houses north on the hill above Fire Station 2 in Louisville about this time. The wind was so strong that it was difficult to stand up or open vehicle doors. They extinguished small fires in yards, on decks, fences, and trees; but the wind was too intense. With visibility near zero, crews were unsure of their location and afraid of hitting stopped vehicles. Escape routes were unclear, and water pressure dropped, so the crews backed up a block. The fire ravaged the Hillside development.

At 2:15 p.m., a frantic horse was reported galloping around the traffic circle at McCaslin and Main in Superior. Animal Control Unit 798 tried to respond but couldn't get there, and an Adams County state

[53] The National Weather Service analysis of the Marshal fire weather events with pictures, satellite loops, and explanations is at https://www.weather.gov/bou/HighWinds12_30_2021.

trooper captured the horse named Willie.[54] About fourteen years old, the horse was a familiar site in Original Superior. Holding the horse with a rope given to him by a fireman, the trooper stayed for almost four hours until Boulder County Mounted Search and Rescue Team fought their way into Old Town and transported Willie to the Boulder County Fairgrounds. Willie's only injuries were red eyes, sore from the smoke and ash. Miraculously, the state trooper witnessed the fire burn nearby while steadying the horse and stayed unscathed.

The State Highway Patrol swarmed into the area and took over traffic control for both cities around 2:15 p.m. and local police work to free up traffic on Via Appia by controlling the lights on S. Boulder Road at Via Appia and at CO-42. The fire moved so rapidly that the firemen often cut their hoses with axes and left them as the fire closed in. The fire burned the grass and homes just north of the Louisville Firehouse 2 on Via Appia. Cutup and destroyed fire hoses piled up on the west side of the fire station. At 2:17 p.m., a request went out to order the evacuation of the rest of Louisville. County Dispatch sent Boulder Engine 2501 to evacuate another elderly person at 1103 W. Enclave Circle with the fire bearing down. Another call had an eighty-seven-year-old woman still at 1053 W. Century Drive Louisville at 2:20 p.m. Unit Edward 6 handled it. The highest wind gust recorded that day was 108 mph at 2:25 p.m. in south Boulder. The fire continued to grow.

[54] Partially based on information from "Horse Photographed during Marshal Fire Is Safe after Rescue," *Denver Post* by Helen Richardson, January 13, 2022.

Figure 36 Lafayette fire in Spanish Hills at Wells Drive and Spring Drive about 2:38 p.m. Photo: Code 10 Photography.

Much of the land that was not open space west of Louisville and Superior was used to graze horses and cattle. Many smaller plots also had other farm animals like pigs and llamas. On the day of the fire, these farm animals all required evacuation. The "Horse Evacuation Boulder Fort Collins Fire" Facebook page is one social media site that successfully coordinated efforts for farmers, ranchers, and helpers. Folks from Berthoud, Parker, Bennett, and Black Forest responded with offers of stalls, gooseneck trailers, and grazing meadows. Many arrived at the FlatIron Crossing Mall staging waiting for a turn to help move animals to safety.

One story told to the *Denver Gazette*[55] is of Joan, who is wheelchair bound and runs a therapeutic riding center with fifty-five horses. Based on her Facebook Messenger request for help, many trailers came to rescue her horses. There were many successes. Barrel racer Randi Timmons posted of the problems and received $1,100 in donations from across the country for hay almost immediately. A pregnant mare named Nibbles made it successfully to the fairgrounds before dropping her fowl. Rodeo queen Megan Rickel rescued a dozen horses. Her family home in Spanish Hills South was the only one still standing on her street the next day. When the Boulder County Fairgrounds reached capacity late in the afternoon, rescued horses and farm animals were sent to the Jefferson County Fairgrounds. Other than the two horses and two goats that died at the Turnbull residence, miraculously, only nine cows were killed by the fire. All other farm animals were successfully rescued or survived the flames on their own.

Miraculously, not many residents were injured evacuating. At 2:27 p.m., McCaslin Command sent Unit 403 to treat two persons in a 2001 Toyota 4Runner stopped along S. Boulder Road and Ridgeview with burns. Louisville Police Unit 403 called in that they will transport them nonemergency to Good Sam (referring to nearby Good Samaritan SCL Hospital in Lafayette). Only six others were treated and released by area hospitals. One was a police officer injured when ash was blown into his eye.

[55] Partially based on "Social Media Groups Coordinate to Save Animals . . .," *Denver Gazette* by Carol McKinley, December 31, 2021.

Figure 37 The Louisville Police Station evacuated at 2:18 p.m. Note burning shrubs near entrance. Photo: Code 10 Photography.

Louisville Police Unit 410 assumed McCaslin Command using the Louisville Tactical channel at 2:35 p.m. to coordinate evacuations and traffic control. Two elderly evacuation requests from Regal Square and Hecla Drive (Balfour) independent living areas were called out. McCaslin Command said to leave them on the board, and they will get to them as time permitted as they were not directly threatened by the fire. Unit Edward 43 called in that he was at McCaslin and Via Appia, and the fire was rampant all around. He asked if McCaslin in Louisville was closed. Marshall Command responded that southbound McCaslin was closed at S. Boulder Road and that any stragglers should be let out. Fire Dispatch announced that there were two to four large liquid nitrogen tanks that could explode if caught in the fire at 1172 Century Drive in Louisville northwest of Lowes. As the area was not currently threatened, the call was added to the board. The "board" was the first responders' computerized tactical list of outstanding calls and who was responding. This list was extremely dynamic throughout the fire.

At 2:40 p.m., County Dispatch called out that the structure at 770 Club Circle in Louisville was on fire. The homes on Club Circle abutted the golf course north of Dillon Road and were isolated from the other fires but flying embers from the high winds swathed them in fire. The Chinook winds and mountain wave were firmly established by this time. The winds recorded near the gulf course were a steady 45 mph from the SSW with a peak gust of 68 mph. Yet near Avista Hospital less than a mile away, the winds were 46 mph but coming for the SSE, miraculously protecting the hospital from the worst of the flames.

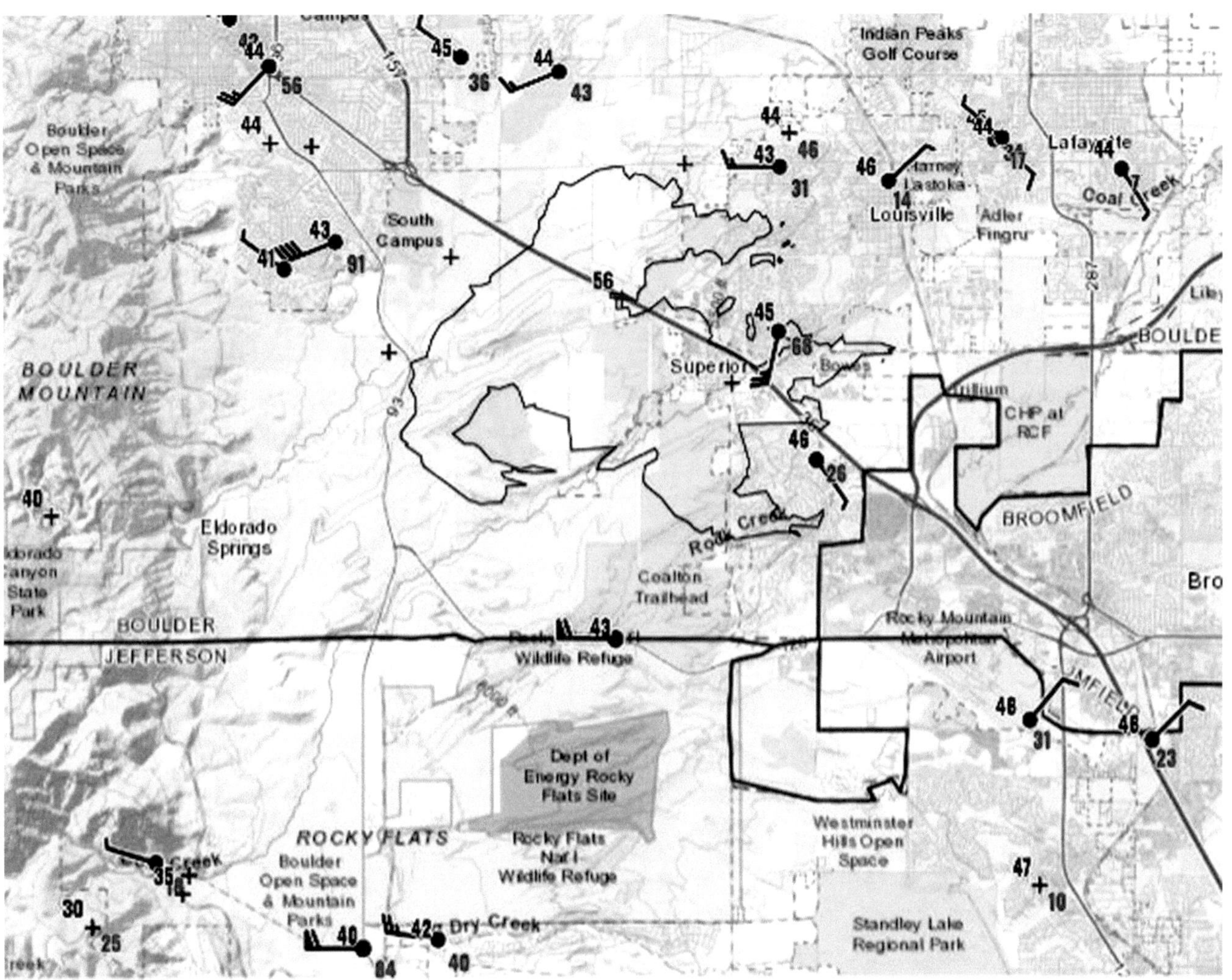

Figure 38 NOAA 2:00 p.m. Surface winds for the fire area. Courtesy of NOAA NWS-Boulder.

A minute later, County Dispatch called out fire alarms at 404 Marshall Drive in Superior and 333 Centennial Parkway in Louisville. They were put on the board. At 2:45 p.m., McCaslin northbound from Via Appia was declared impassable due to fire and smoke. The fire was now invading the neighborhoods south of Harper Lake in Louisville. Dillon Road eastbound was also gridlocked east of Ninety-fifth Street at that time. An ambulance trying to get to Avista to help with the evacuation was stuck in traffic westbound at 10051 Dillon Road. A minute later, County Dispatch sent a unit to 1206 Amherst Way in southeast Superior for a man having difficulty breathing. At 2:48 p.m., County Dispatch sent a unit to 1009 Turnberry Circle in Coal Creek Ranch Louisville for a structure fire that may be occupied. State Patrol escorted four ambulances on Ninety-sixth Street and on Dillon Road to help with the Avista evacuation at 2:49 p.m. At that time, County Dispatch called out a fire alarm at 1119 W. Enclave Circle as the fire raged south and west of Harper Lake Louisville.

Edward 6 reported to McCaslin Command that homes on Cypress Lane in Louisville had not been notified to evacuate even as structures burned on Cherrywood a block away. With siren wailing, he started door-to-door notifications. Fire Dispatch sent Marshall Command to Eldorado Lane and Larkspur Lane area north of Via Appia and the police station as the homes there were fully engulfed. The rest of Louisville was ordered to evacuate with evacuation order 8 at 2:51 p.m. This notice reached 4,806 contacts and instructed evacuees to head north on CO-42 if possible. Unluckily, many homes that were covered by this notice were already on fire off McCaslin. Traffic in Louisville was bumper-to-bumper in most areas. Via Appia and S. Boulder Road became congested. At 2:58 p.m., parts of Broomfield, Arvada, Westminster, and north of S. Boulder Road were placed on pre-evacuation notice with the final evacuation order 9. This notification reached 2,217 contacts. S. Boulder Road was closed from Plaza Drive west at that time.

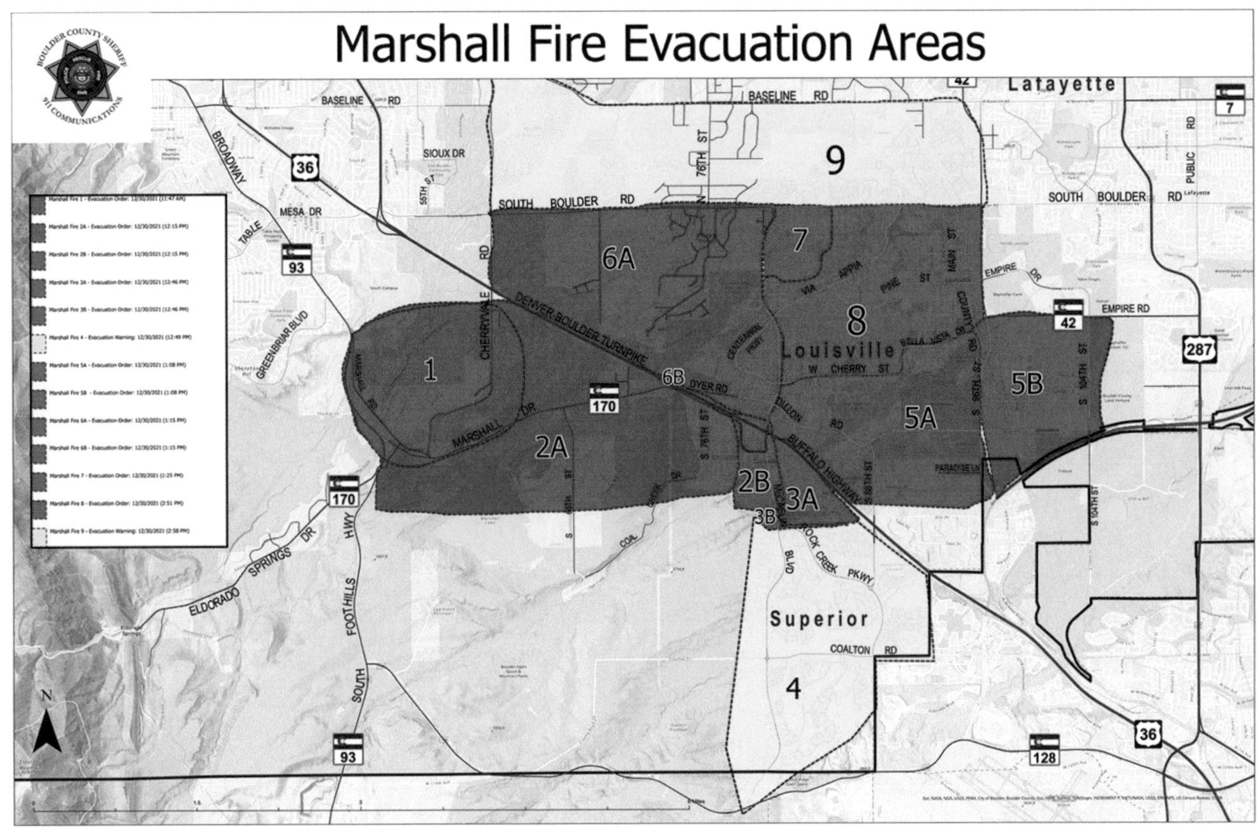

Figure 39 List of Boulder County Marshall fire evacuation orders. Courtesy of Boulder Co. Sheriff.

Balfour received another reverse 911 call before 3:00 p.m. saying that the entire city of Louisville south of Boulder Road was to evacuate. Becki Siemers commented that with that call, "It was the scariest day of my life." The two-hundred-plus employees and residents of Balfour needed to be evacuated quickly, and she was responsible. The Boulder Office of Emergency Management called right afterward and asked what Balfour needed. She told the OEM that she needed buses to move the staff and residents with handicap lifts for the wheelchair-bound skilled nursing patients.

The evacuation plan now became critical. The standard plan called for moving the residents to Cherrywood if possible and Balfour Longmont if that was not available. Since Cherrywood was evacuating to Longmont, both locations were out of the question. The staff continued to call other nearby facilities asking if they had rooms available. So far, they had only identified a couple of locations that could accept patients—four here, five there, and none with the capabilities to handle the skilled nursing patients. Evacuating piecemeal meant spreading the residents and staff far and wide and was not acceptable. Siemers asked the staff to keep calling other facilities and prayed for a miracle.

Balfour sent out an announcement to the relatives of the residents telling them of the evacuation order and asking them to pick up their resident if possible. The staff then went door-to-door to each assisted living resident asking them to pack an overnight bag with at least one change of clothes and any necessary items, leave it outside their room door, and then come downstairs to the lobby. At least one resident slipped in a bottle of wine into her "to go" bag.

Finally, Frasier Meadows in Boulder about seven miles west confirmed they had enough available rooms to handle all the assisted living residents. These residents were ambulatory and can walk and ride with assistance. Moving them to Frasier Meadows in one location will keep them together and be easier for the staff to ensure their safety. It will also be comforting for the residents. They did state that additional beds will be needed, so now the search became one for equipment.

The skilled nursing residents required the staff to prepare their overnight bags. Most can't walk, and many were incapable of deciding what was needed. They also required additional medical equipment, such as oxygen, feeding tubes, and medicines that the staff must gather and keep available for each patient. Finally, the Gardens on Quail facility in Arvada about fifteen miles south answered they had available space for the skilled nursing residents, though again facilities will be sparse and additional equipment will be needed. Incredibly, Balfour identified two locations to move its residents and employees with plenty of time to evacuate.

With the fire raging, staff homes threatened, operating during the holidays, with a blizzard expected the next day, miraculously, Balfour had two evacuation sites identified that could keep all the residents together and only needed to move them.

Louisville, December 30, 2021, 2:58 p.m., Wind W 32 mph, Gusting to 68 mph 48°F

Katie Bender[56] was an eight-year veteran firefighter with Adams County Fire and Rescue who was assigned to Type 6 Brush Truck 11 out of Adams County Station 11. A brush truck is a four-wheel-drive upscale flatbed pickup (like an F450) that has been outfitted with firefighting equipment. It doesn't carry much water but is effective fighting wildland fires with its four-man crew putting out hot spots, cutting brush and setting back fires. On Brush Truck 11, Bender worked for Brandon Donner, who was having lunch with his wife at the Old Santa Fe Restaurant in Louisville off Dillon Road just east of McCaslin on this fateful day. When it got dark outside from the smoke, Donner and his wife left the restaurant with ash falling all around. They could barely see and had a hard time getting oriented to leave the restaurant. Sensing that this might be bad, Donner called Bender and the rest of his crew and told them to get ready. Brush Truck 11 was called to help before 3:00 p.m., staging at Macy's at FlatIron Crossing Mall.

[56] All Adams County firefighter discussion is based from the January 21, 2022, Episode 14, "The Firelife—A Podcast by Adams County Fire Rescue," https://podcasts.apple.com/us/podcast/a-first-hand-look-back-at-the-marshall-fire/id1529809927?i=1000548624041.

Figure 40 Adams County Station 11 with fire trucks. Courtesy of the Adams County Fire Protection District.

Adam County Station 11 is located south of US-36 on N. Pecos Street. When Brush Truck 11 was put into service, it headed north on Pecos and joined US-36 westbound toward the fire. They drove code 1 with lights flashing and sirens wailing through the autos and trucks still on US-36 until the traffic evaporated where the highway was closed at Sheridan. They maneuvered past the roadblock and continued the twelve miles to the mall with the smoke thickening overhead. They drove to Macy's parking lot where command was located. While there, Bender called her father who lived in Broomfield and learned that he had already been evacuated. She worried about what he will do. There they were assigned to Division Zulu, fighting the eastern flank of the fire. They left the mall onto US-36 and headed west toward the McCaslin exit. As Katie Bender described it, "Insane. First thing I saw was the Element Hotel fully engulfed in flame. Then across McCaslin, all these commercial buildings completely engulfed in flames. And that's when I think we realized this was really bad."

At this time, Zulu Command was located at the Louisville Recreation Center across from Louisville Fire Station 2. Exiting US-36, Brush Truck 11 turned north on McCaslin past the Old Santa Fe restaurant where Donner just ate. They saw burnt cars in the parking lot and nearby stores consumed by fire. They drove north to Via Appia and turned northeast to the rec center. The smoke was intense, and the fire was burning hotly to the west and north. Once there, they were assigned structure protection. They were dressed to fight wildland fires and not structure fires, and their truck cannot hold much water. They turned south back down McCaslin across US-36 through burning Original Superior and set up off High Plains Drive on the west side of the ridge overlooking Rock Creek in an area of mostly townhomes.

When they drove up, the wind was howling, and they can't see a thing due to the smoke and ash. Said Donner, "As I got out of the truck, I couldn't hold the door, and it slams so hard that it cut the back of my calf." The only other fire engine nearby was a Type 1 from Denver with hoses tied into a fireplug. One or two firemen manned each hose aiming water at whatever burning building they can reach. The wind blew the burn and embers at their exposed faces as they joined in. Stated Bender, "We just grabbed a line and shoot it at a fire." Later, as the wind settled, they became more effective, driving the brush truck through the surrounding backyards and open space and stopping fires in bushes, decks, and soffits.

They spent all night fighting the fire in the townhome development, only seeing their small part of the damage. All the townhome balconies on the west side of the complex caught on fire at one point or another, and a good part of their time was putting them out before they spread to the rest of the building. Being a brush truck, they used chain saws (instead of the large circular saw common on Type 1 trucks) to cut open metal garage doors to get into units to fight the fire. Of the seventy-eight town houses in the development, only three were destroyed and fourteen damaged. Miraculously, a single Denver Type 1 fire truck and an Adams County brush truck saved sixty-one townhomes from the maelstrom. They received texts from friends and other firemen saying how bad the fire was, but they could not relate to the devastation until they saw it themselves when they left at dawn the next morning.

Sheriff Commander Wilber, with the help of Sergeant Badge 517, set up police strategic command next to Marshall Command inside the old Nordstrom store at FlatIron Crossing Mall. Radio Technician Chris Rodgers brought them additional radio equipment. They were quickly joined by additional resources from Boulder IMT Type 3. Police officers and law enforcement came into the mall from all over the surrounding area to help. As there were limited tactical channels available, they divided them into teams of about ten members each, usually led by a sergeant. Each team was assigned an alphabetic designator and sent out to perform specific tasks—evacuation notifications in a geographic area, traffic control, or priority evacuations. As they worked through assignments during the day, they ended up sending out sixteen teams through alpha designator "P." The Boulder Sheriff SWAT team, joined by Longmont SWAT, tackled evacuations in Louisville, staging from Centaurus High School. At least thirty-two roadblocks were set up to control traffic and access into the area.

Even during a major event like the Marshall fire, tactical channels were limited. Law enforcement used a maximum of six channels during the fire to track the sixteen teams. Commented Commander Wilber, "Even though we had these sixteen mixed teams of ten officers from different jurisdictions scattered throughout the area, there was little chatter on the radio. The experienced sergeants deserve all the credit. They kept the new deputies in line and on task." He estimated that three hundred officers came through Nordstrom's during the day and rotated in and out of the teams and performed other duties as needed. Though there were many jurisdictions involved, there were no major conflicts or authority battles. Everyone just wanted to help.

About 3:00 p.m., the Colorado Division of Fire Prevention and Control staff started arriving at FlatIron Crossing Mall to support Marshall Command. They brought with them additional communications equipment, allowing firefighters to further split up responsibilities and supervision. Instead of fighting the fire with just MVFR south of US-36 and Louisville north, seven teams divided up firefighting, surrounding the fire in all areas. Division Zulu has the east side of Louisville north of US-36. Tango got the heart of Louisville and Harper Lake. Foxtrot took Spanish Hills and west past Cherryvale. Alpha had the heart of Superior. Delta got the southern grasslands and Marshall Lake. And Echo fought the fire on the west side. Each of these seven commands had their own tactical channel and can talk with Marshall Command, requesting resources and providing updates. Arriving firefighting equipment can now be distributed based on need and equipment type to meet that need. But the flames and wind were still the enemy, and the firefighters will need time and a break in the weather to beat back the inferno. It was obvious that this will be a long-term battle with a long recovery afterward, so the Rocky Mountain Incident Management Team Type 1 was ordered. They will arrive on Sunday, January 2, to assume command.

At 3:00 p.m., County Dispatch informed Marshall Command that they had a call that 559 Discovery Parkway east of Old Town Superior was on fire. MVFR Truck 2201 called in right afterward that they had finally made it to the Element Hotel, but it was engulfed in flames and will be a total loss. They asked for another assignment. Marshall Command asked that 2201 be assigned to them. After playing a tone, County Dispatch sent MVFR Tower 2215 to 318 Diamond Circle off Cherry Street in Louisville to help with an evacuation. County Dispatch also called out another house fire at 1159 W. Enclave Circle, Louisville, confirming the fire was raging south of Harper Lake. At 3:04 p.m., County Dispatch called out a fire alarm at 7481 Spring Drive, Louisville. This will turn out to be a false alarm probably caused by the smoke. Marshall Command also tried to reassign the Regal Square evacuation request to Louisville Police, but McCaslin Command commented that they should wait as Regal had not started evacuations yet. County Dispatch called Marshall Command that the homeowner at 896 Larkspur Court south and west of Harper Lake had a fire on his fence and in the grass and he was fighting it himself at 3:10 p.m. Unluckily, this home and all of the others nearby were consumed by the flames.

At this same time, County Dispatch tried to send Louisville Bus 2722 to Regal Square to help with evacuations. It became obvious that Command and County Dispatch were overlapping, with County Dispatch sending units across US-36 between Louisville and Superior and not aware of decisions that the commands were making. Edward 7 called Police Dispatch for reassignment, and Police Dispatch responded, "We're pretty overwhelmed right now, and I don't even know where to start." At 3:14 p.m., County Dispatch called out a fire in the front yard at 792 Nighthawk Circle, Louisville, south of Via Appia. Luckily, this fire did not spread, and this area was spared. Unit 595 called in that he was trying to rescue horses at 753 Paragon Circle in Spanish Hills and asked for help.[57] A minute later, an unidentified unit confirmed that there were multiple structures burning in the 800 block of Mulberry, south of Nighthawk Circle. Fire Dispatch called out that 7580 Skyway Court in Spanish Hills had a fire alarm. A unit responded that the homeowner had already evacuated, and other structures were on fire on Skyway Court. A minute later, Edward 6 called in that he was still making door-to-door evacuation requests and was finding many homeowners unaware that they were to be evacuated. He asked for additional police help canvassing the neighborhoods that were on fire. Police Dispatch responded that all units were currently tasked. County Dispatch announced a call at 3:18 p.m. that homes along S. Boulder Road between Sixty-eighth and Seventy-sixth Streets were on fire and asked for a unit to confirm. Though the fire did reach S. Boulder Road west of Spanish Hills, luckily, it never crossed it to the north. Miraculously, unlike the 6-lane wide natural firebreak of US-36, narrower 4-lane S. Boulder Road remained a steadfast firebreak throughout the fire.

At 3:19 p.m., County Dispatch called out that the home at 548 Donn Court was on fire. These homes were well west of Spanish Hills between the Goodhue and Marshallville ditches north of US-36. The fire jumped US-36 a third time. Police Dispatch responded that the priority currently was still evacuation and not

[57] Numerous Sheriff Deputy body camera views are posted. The horse rescue is at https://www.youtube.com/watch?v=oucis6vkUGY.

announcing or fighting fires. Eight Larimer County police units were spotted southbound on Ninety-fifth. Police Unit 446 commented that Boulder SWAT told them to stage at Monarch High School in Lafayette. Police Dispatch broadcast he was unaware of any command center at Monarch and that Unified Command was located at FlatIron Crossing Mall in front of Macy's. Boulder SWAT established an incident command center at Monarch High School to better coordinate police evacuations around that time. Police Dispatch at 3:25 p.m. asked for any animal control officer to check on a loose horse at 7390 Empire Road near Spanish Hills. County Dispatch asked Nederland Rescue 5621 and Louisville Bus 2723 to assist evacuating a bedridden male at 340 County Road in eastern Louisville. Calls were coming fast and furious for all regions—Original Marshall, Spanish Hills, Louisville, and Superior.

At 3:20 p.m., Louisville Bus 2722 broadcast that new evacuation centers were now open at the YMCA of Lafayette, the South Boulder Recreation Center, the Longmont Senior Center, and the Boulder County Fairgrounds for large animals. At that same time, Gov. Jared Polis declared a state of emergency existed due to grass fires created by high winds across the Front Range. This allowed the state to access emergency funds and deploy the Colorado National Guard, the State Emergency Operations Center, and the Colorado Division of Fire Prevention. Though not immediately helpful, this declaration will mean needed resources will become available.

Firefighting in Louisville started in 1885 when each coal mine manned its own firefighting crew. The City of Louisville purchased its first hose cart ten years later in 1895. This hand-drawn cart had five-and-a-half-foot wheels and five hundred feet of Boston fire jacket hose. It cost a whopping $125 and was drawn to each fire by human volunteers.[58] In the early 1910s, three of these carts were stationed strategically around town. When the fire bell rang, ten men responded—seven to pull the cart, one to tug off the hose, one to connect it to a fireplug, and one to turn on and operate the water nozzle. Spirited competitions developed between the different hose cart teams, both in Louisville and between towns. Timed events included the "Wet," the "Hub to Hub," and the "Replacement." The Louisville team won the coveted Governor Shoup Cup[59] event in 1920, 1921, and 1922.

Though there was always a waiting list for new equipment, by the 1950s the town had three modern fire trucks, a 1952 International "rural fire truck," a 1932 Chevy, and a 1952 GMC. Early on, a large bell rang to

[58] Derived partially from information in the *Louisville Historian*, no. 82, Spring 2009.

[59] Oliver Henry Shoup was the twenty-second governor of Colorado from 1919 to 1923 and sponsored these contests.

alert crews of a pending disaster. This bell has survived and now sits in front of the Main Street Fire Station 1. Then later, a blaring town-wide alarm sounded three times for problems in town, four for rural, and only twice for other emergencies. Today, alarms are broadcast to cell phone applications for volunteers.

Figure 41 1926 Downtown Louisville fire rubble on Main Street. Courtesy of the Louisville Historical Society.

Prior to the Marshall fire, Louisville's largest fire threatened Old Downtown. On a cold November night in 1926, an unidentified passenger getting off the Interurban train from Denver about 12:30 a.m. raised the alarm. The fire started behind the Perrella Garage at 808 Main Street near the old telephone exchange building and today's Zucca Restaurant. The hose cart team quickly responded, but by then the fire was well entrenched and all downtown Louisville was at risk. The Boulder Fire Department was called in to help. Catherine Curtan, manager of the telephone exchange, barely escaped with her children before the building collapsed. The fire destroyed the Perrella Garage and the telephone exchange and severely damaged the Hub Store and First State Bank for a total loss downtown estimated to be $75,000 (about $1,200,000 today).

Two other fires of note in Louisville include the September 1974 fire that destroyed the original Steinbaugh Hardware store that stood north of the Old Louisville Inn on Front Street. The second is the State Mercantile Building fire in the late 1990s. Sitting at the corner of Main and Spruce, the Mercantile fire started in the basement and quickly spread to inside the walls. With traditional firefighting methods inadequate, the Louisville crew quickly requested firefighting foam from nearby Rocky Flats. This did the trick, and the building still stands today. Another famous fire is the 1988 Blue Parrot fire. This iconic fire damaged the famous restaurant, but it was quickly rebuilt.

The Louisville Fire Protection District today operates three fire stations, one on north Main Street across from Louisville Middle School, a second on Via Appia across from the police station and recreation center, and the training center on Boxelder Street near the Northwest Parkway southeast of town. The Louisville fire motto is

Our Family Serving Your Family,[60] and they strive to maintain motivated and empowered firefighters capable of delivering quality service no matter what—a simple lockout assist or a fire/medical emergency. The district mission is "to be a professional organization focusing on the safety and well-being of its community. We are driven by passion, innovation, and serving the needs of all."

According to John Willson, Fire Chief,[61] Louisville Fire has thirty-six career firemen, plus ten volunteers and additional administrative staff. The full-time firemen work forty-eight hours on, then ninety-six hours off. They have two "type 1" ladder trucks (2702 and 2703), three "busses" (2721, 2722, and 2723) for EMT and medical emergencies, and two brush trucks (whose 27xx identifiers change depending upon application and crew). Though pagers were used to notify volunteers of a fire and their need to respond, today all calls are sent out by County Dispatch using a phone application by Active911. This application allows dispatch and management to see who is responding to a call. It also allows responders to see a current map with critical and pre-staged information loaded to help them get to the scene quicker and be more effective when they arrive. Like the "board," the application also keeps all open calls listed with its status. Louisville firefighters all fought the fire on December 30, including those on Trucks 2702 and 2703, who spent the night fighting the fire with Division Tango.

Typically, Louisville deploys twenty-four firefighters and three trucks to fight a single house fire. Lamented Chief Willson, "With over five hundred buildings burning in Louisville alone during the Marshall fire, there were not enough firefighters in the whole state to keep it from spreading." Chief Willson lets his brigade leaders orchestrate how they fight a fire and doesn't second-guess their decisions. Even during this maelstrom, he spent the day from noon onward moving between strategic viewpoints and command sites to ensure that resources got deployed timely and effectively. He then camped out at the Louisville Recreation Center with Division Tango from about midnight on responding to calls from worried city officials, staff, and residents. He also coordinated with Louisville Water during the night, directing them to safe areas to turn off water supplies to destroyed buildings. He finally gave up about 6:00 a.m. He couldn't go home, as he lived in Superior. Miraculously, the fire stopped about two blocks from his house.

60 https://www.louisvillefire.com/about/district/.

61 Based on interviews conducted with Chief Willson on February 24, 2022, and May 13, 2022.

Figure 42 Louisville Fire Station 2 on Via Appia.

Figure 43 Louisville Fire Station 2 early afternoon during the fire. Photo: Code 10 Photography.

The West Side Task Force, Division Tango,[62] set up south of the Louisville Police Station off W. Mulberry Street and Cherrywood Lane, just east of McCaslin Boulevard. Tango was initially commanded by Capt. Brendan Finnegan on West Metro Wildland 1 and Capt. Dan Wenger. They deployed with West Metro Brush Trucks 9 and 17, Golden Brush 21, and Arvada Truck 56. Division Tango was tasked to cover approximately 105 acres in Louisville, including 21 streets, 384 structures, and Fireside Elementary School. West Metro deployed from Macy's at FlatIron Crossing Mall. As they came into Louisville, Wenger wondered, "Where do we fit in? Where do we make a stand?" against the raging inferno all around.

[62] Partially based on West Metro Fire Rescue's "On the Front Line—The Marshall Fire," January 20, 2022.

When West Metro arrived, the west side of Cherrywood Lane was already engulfed. Arvada Truck 56 had attached to a fire hydrant, and a West Metro brush truck set up across from him. They decided that the fire will go no further. One truck tackled the fires on one side of the street, and the other truck fought it on the opposite. The remaining two trucks positioned on different streets and tried to keep the fire from spreading to new structures. But the wind was still howling, and the fire jumped from home to home eastbound. Most of W. Mulberry Street was already an inferno. The brush trucks found many homes with outside hoses and discovered that these were as effective fighting the ember storm as the big hoses off their trucks. They did the best that they could, but the fire was intense and continued to march down the street.

As the day wore on, Command sent additional resources to Division Tango to help fight the blaze. Big Elk Meadows Brush Truck 4934 joined them. Westminster 2 came in. So did Lafayette 2601, Mountain View 2202, and Fairmount 34. And Louisville Trucks 2702 and 2703 joined in later, fighting the fires just south of their fire station 2, across the arboretum and park surrounding the recreation center. At the height of the battle, eleven trucks fought the fire with Division Tango, sometimes keeping a structure from being consumed by the blaze and sometimes losing one. But they won more than they lost, and by morning, miraculously, 322 structures of the 384 they were tasked to guard were still standing, and no one was hurt.

Lincoln 40 asked at 3:28 p.m. if Community Park in Superior was still being used as a rendezvous location for displaced people. Police Dispatch responded the park was directly in the path of the flames and recommended that everyone flee east or north if possible. The fire did burn through and around Community Park, but everyone meeting there evacuated safely. The Boulder OEM also announced that the area north of S. Boulder Road between Cherryvale and Seventy-sixth Street to Arapahoe Road was under pre-evacuation alert at 3:30 p.m. They were never ordered to evacuate as miraculously, S. Boulder Road maintained its stand as a natural fire break as the fire reached the south side of this road but never breached it.

Fire Dispatch called out another alarm at 1017 Turnberry Circle at 3:30 p.m. as the fire continued to burn in the Coal Creek Ranch subdivision in Louisville. Unit 415 announced that the fire was just about to cross Dillon Road in that area and recommended that Dillon Road be closed at Coal Creek Circle. As he was speaking, County Dispatch announced that the fire alarm had gone off at Premier Members Credit Union at 800 Coal Creek Circle, confirming that the fire was intense nearby. Police Dispatch stated McCaslin was closed both north and south. He asked how anyone in western Louisville could evacuate if Dillon closed. US-36 eastbound? Another police unit chimed in that Pine Street was still open eastbound for the interior of Louisville, and Cherry Street can be joined from Dillon if Dillon closed. He stated the fire had crossed

Dillon five times or so already. Fire Dispatch announced another smoke alarm at 977 Arapahoe Circle in Louisville at 3:34 p.m. as the fire continued to ravage southwest of Harper Lake.

At 3:40 p.m., County Dispatch directed MVFR Tower 2215 to 1561 S. Foothills Highway, a trailer park just north of where the fire began as the roof had blown off and there was a natural gas leak. Many units in the Sans Souci Community at 1561 S. Foothills Highway received wind damage covered under the Marshall fire emergency umbrella. Police Dispatch also directed Edward 6 to check on a twenty-six-year-old male at 199 S. Tyler between Cherry and Via Appia in Louisville who just had surgery and needed assistance evacuating. The fire was about six blocks away at that time. Unit 410 also commented that he had arrived at Monarch High School and was checking in with the units congregating there. Not hearing from Unit 2215, County Dispatch directed MVFR Engine 2204 to check on the natural gas leak at the Sans Souci Community at 3:42 p.m. Edward 7 took the call for 199 S. Tyler at 3:44 p.m., but no one responded at the door. Surprisingly, the dispatch radio was quiet around this time, but activities continued on the tactical channels. Fire Dispatch toned Lafayette Engine 2602 to 710 Copper Lane to help evacuate a woman whose garage door won't open with the power out. The OEM posted two emergency announcements later on how to open a garage door if the power was off.[63] Edward 6 cleared 199 S. Tyler and found no one on-site at 3:48 p.m. At 3:49 p.m., the OEM announced that the North Boulder Recreation Center was now opened for evacuees and the South Boulder Recreation Center closed due to continuing electrical outages in south Boulder due to the high winds.

At 3:52 p.m., Lincoln 40 relayed information asking for an available trailer to help transport additional farm animals. They were directed to Seventy-sixth and Barcelona west of Spanish Hills. Many ranchers staged at Macy's with their trailers to help. Horse evacuations continued even as the grass fires raged. At 3:55 p.m., Nederland Rescue 5621 called in that the bedridden patient at 340 County Line in eastern Louisville refused to be evacuated unless assured that there would be a bed available for him at the YMCA Lafayette. Around this time, calls from Fire Dispatch to Marshall Command went unanswered.

[63] How to open a garage door messages are at https://www.boulderoem.com/use-red-level-inside-garage-doors-to-open-if-no-power/ and https://www.boulderoem.com/manually-open-garage-doors/.

Louisville, December 30, 2021, 3:46 p.m., Wind E 12 mph, Gusting to 17 mph 46°F

Brian Melzer was a new fireman with Adams County, having joined a month earlier in November 2021. During his first two months, he fought two house fires, two car fires, and a couple of car accidents where the autos ran into structures that required stabilization. He was assigned to Engine 11, a Type 1 fire truck, at Station 11 with two other firemen. They told him not to expect to see another house fire for at least eight or nine months. Their engine tone sounded, and they deployed around 3:00 p.m., heading toward Macy's at the FlatIron Crossing Mall for assignment. When they arrived, Command put them on standby to answer other 911 calls, and they sat around for the next two hours watching the smoke billow and blow from the west. Finally, after 5:30 p.m., Command sent them to Division Zulu to help with the fires south of Harper Lake in Louisville. They left FlatIron Crossing Mall and headed west on US-36. Stated Melzer,

> The closer we got, the more we realized how bad it was. It was a really strange scene, going from Adams County, seeing all the smoke, and then going west on Highway 36 and seeing all the flames. Then getting closer and seeing the ash. Then we saw one burnt house, and then we saw a burnt street, and then we saw a burnt community. It was almost like we were going into Armageddon. It was dark, too, and flame was just everywhere . . . one of the weirdest things we came across was a car that was just in the middle of the road with no fire around us and the car was completely burned, 100 percent gone, and it was so bizarre and there was no fire around.

They also started out at the Louisville Recreation Center on Via Appia for tactical assignment. From there, they headed up the hillside above Louisville Fire Station 2 to help save structures. They arrived at a street of houses where the first house was completely engulfed and the second was starting to smoke from the radiant heat. The wind was still intense. Their job was to join up with a "Westy" (West Metro) engine and a Fairmount engine and do exposure protection to keep the fire from spreading. There was fire everywhere—behind them, across from them, all around them. Not only did they have to fight the fire, but they also must watch their back and be ready to flee. Luckily, the wind subsided sufficiently to allow them to stay. Then the fire hydrants started to dry up due to the high demand and all the open water lines. The three trucks went through water like crazy. Miraculously, a water tender from Big Elk Mountain arrived just in time, shuttling water between the three engines, keeping them productive fighting the fire. Melzer and Truck 11 stayed south of Harper Lake above Louisville Fire Station 2 all night.

Melzer summed up his experience,

> It's so insane to see just hundreds and hundreds of homes just leveled so quickly . . . I picture how hot the fire had to be and how brutal the wind had to be to hop not only from house to house, but from community to community to community, wiping it all out.

The fickle nature of the wind determined what stood and what was burnt. Later, debris from the fire would be discovered as far as thirty miles to the northeast.

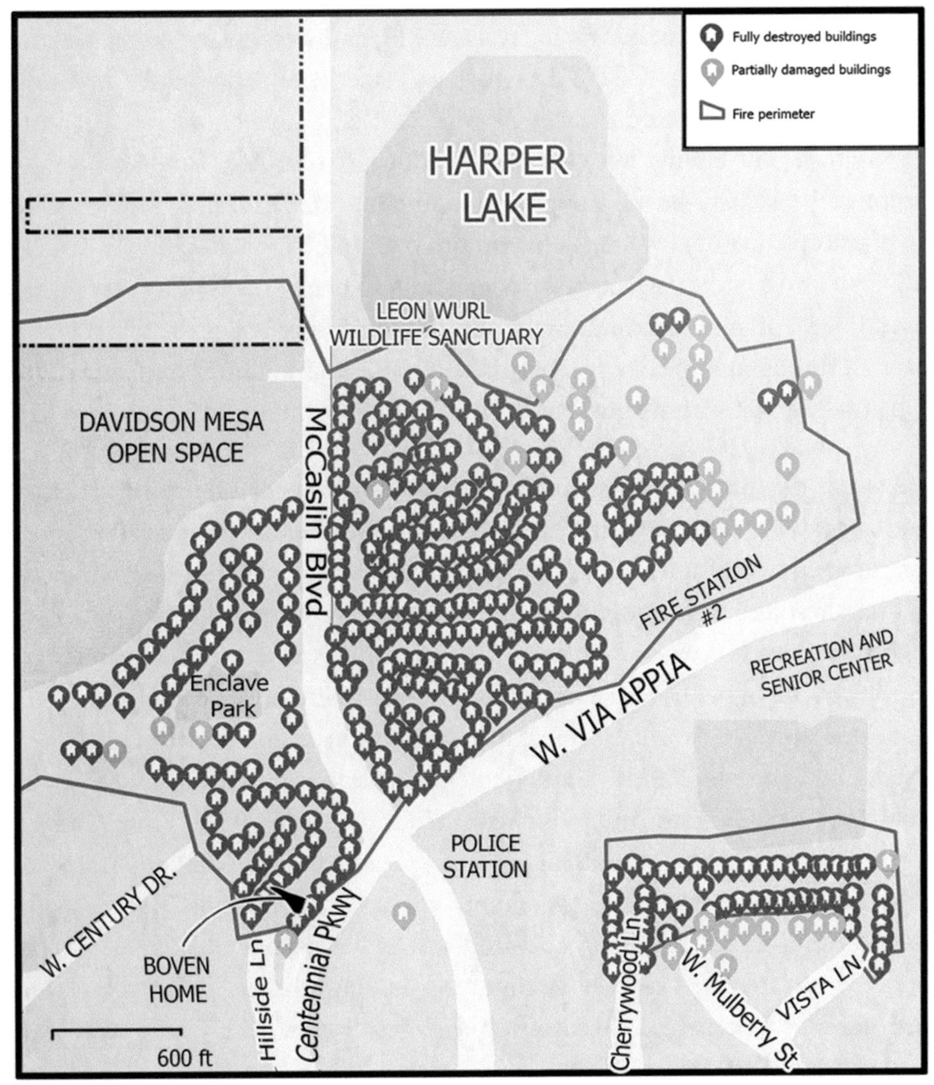

Figure 44 Louisville Harper Lake area showing Boven home, police station, fire station, and recreation center.

PWS Weather[64] logs wind speeds and temperature data from personal, commercial, and government weather stations throughout the United States. Though there were many stations within and near the burn area, most stopped reporting data for at least part of the day due to lost power, no internet, or being consumed by the flames. Station CO167 near the Louisville Water Treatment Plant 2 west of Costco on Marshall Road stopped recording at 12:30 p.m. BRIGGSPLACEPWS on Briggs Place in Superior, three houses from the Bristol Street destruction, recorded a maximum gust of 27 mph at 12:50 p.m. but stopped reporting at 1:10 p.m. 420PONDEROSA in the Spanish Hills, just west of McCaslin and south of S. Boulder Road, similarly reported a top gust of 67 mph at 12:40 p.m. before stopping at 1:30 p.m. F0288 located on Club Circle in Louisville, four houses north of the destruction, recorded a maximum blast of 68 mph at 2:00 p.m. and left the air at 3:15 p.m. KCOLOUIS77 sat north of the golf course on Manorwood Lane in Louisville, just two blocks from F0288 and the fire, and recorded a 38 mph maximum gust at 1:12 p.m. It was one of the few stations in the area that continued to broadcast throughout the day. It reported wind speeds less than 13 mph after 2:00 p.m., dropping to less than 5 mph at 6:00 p.m., with no gusts over 31 mph and most under 10 mph from 2:00 p.m. on.

By 4:00 p.m., the winds diminished and switched direction in parts of Louisville. Though still blowing a steady 12 mph with gusts to 17 mph in most places, they were coming from the east in some areas. The worst of the Chinook was over. According to the National Weather Service,[65] the strong winds that developed in the midmorning hours resulted in a mountain wave. Mountain waves appear like a sine wave when viewed from the side and can oscillate for two or even three sine wave forms after the mountains if the wind is strong enough. Usually, they occur high above the surface, but today the winds reached the ground. A mountain wave of this magnitude only forms under the right combination of meteorological parameters, including stability, wind shear, and wind magnitude. Lenticular clouds often form within the "trough" in a mountain wave but didn't on this particular day. Strong westerly winds dived down the Front Range Mountains and Foothills and accelerated to the base. From there, they spread east into the Superior and Louisville area before suddenly weakening in what is called the "jump" region. In this region, the winds oscillated upward or "jump." In the morning hours, this zone occurred east of Louisville and Superior, near Lafayette and Broomfield. Easterly winds may be observed at times in these jump areas as the wind formed a rotor and actual wind direction reversal occurred. This jump zone shifted westward toward Louisville and Superior as the Chinook lessened around 4:00 p.m.

---

[64] Logs for different weather stations can be searched at https://www.pwsweather.com.

[65] Interesting analysis on the weather during fire is at https://www.weather.gov/bou/HighWinds12_30_2021.

Due to the Chinooks, winds gusted to 81 mph in south Boulder and up to 99 mph near the intersection of CO-93 and CO-72 at 11:00 a.m. By noon, a peak gust of 115 mph was recorded near the same intersection, an 85 mph gust in south Boulder, and a 100 mph gust south along CO-93 close to Rocky Flats. These high wind speeds may be compared to a Category 2 hurricane. But they lacked the intensity, as hurricanes occur at sea level where the air is 80 percent denser. Thus, the high-speed winds at Boulder's altitude lacked the punch to do the physical damage of a hurricane but were sufficient to drive fire at high speed. Between noon and 2:00 p.m., the stronger winds shifted east, through all Superior and most of Louisville. As noted, the fire spread through Superior and was attacking Louisville as the peak Louisville gust of 68 mph was recorded near the Coal Creek Golf Course at 2:00 p.m. This Thursday, the mountain wave was visible in the smoke and cloud structure when viewed from the north and south. A short video taken around 2:00 p.m. clearly showed the smoke oscillating three times as it streamed to the east with moisture clouds forming on the crests of the waves even on this extremely dry day. A 2:45 p.m., a weather radar loop showed the smoke and ash already blowing far out over Denver International Airport and the eastern Colorado plains. The GOES-16 East geosynchronous satellite captured images of the smoke plume from 22,236 miles in space. It recorded the peak fire temperature reaching at least 2500°F and the fire power rated at 1848.94 megawatts.[66] Winds by 6:00 p.m. had slowed dramatically, but pictures still showed the smoke blowing east from Louisville at altitude. And a weather satellite image taken at 8:00 p.m. from 22,200 miles up clearly showed how hot the fire still burned. At 4:00 p.m., the fire still had plenty more hours to be destructive even as the wind abated.

Edward 6 and Unit 658 went house-to-house ordering evacuations around Cleveland Avenue and Buckthorn Way in Louisville at 4:00 p.m. as the fire was only a few blocks to the west. Edward 7 worked S. Washington Avenue south of Via Appia at the same time. Police Dispatch asked him to check on 166 S. Washington to ensure they had evacuated as the fire was only a block away. Fire Dispatch toned Lafayette Truck 2602 to 509 Ridgeview Drive north of Dillon in Louisville as a person named Daniel may still be asleep in the basement and unaware of the evacuation. Fire Dispatch then announced that there was a structure fire at 569 Canary Lane in Superior east of McCaslin with animals inside. Meanwhile, a call went out that traffic was still entering Louisville from CO-42 northbound. Police Dispatch asked for a unit to respond to shut down traffic northbound on CO-42 at Empire Road. Lincoln 9 responded she will work traffic there. A minute or so later, Edward 7 responded on 166 S. Washington that the lights were out, no one responded, and it appeared

[66] View of the smoke plume from space is at https://www.nesdis.noaa.gov/news/seen-space-the-colorado-marshall-fire.

vacant. He asked if there were any other locations that needed to be checked in the area. Police Dispatch responded that 821 W. Mulberry west of his location near the fire was still listed on the board but should have already vacated. He also asked that 105 Vista Lane in the Centennial Heights subdivision of Louisville be checked as earlier an eleven-year-old was listed being there alone. These homes all were destroyed by the fire.

About 4:05 p.m., County Dispatch announced that they cannot reach the YMCA to confirm whether a bed could be guaranteed for the patient at 340 County Line. About 4:03 p.m., Unit 2594 called in that they had three fire trucks from Longmont available. Fire Dispatch sent them to Macy's at FlatIron Mall. At 4:05 p.m., Marshall Command announced that Rocky Mountain IMT had assumed command of the Marshall fire. During the transition in management, Marshall Command stayed off the air which is why County Dispatch did not receive any replies from them earlier. County Dispatch acknowledged and responded that 363 Troon Court in Coal Creek Ranch, Louisville, and 567 Canary Lane west of McCaslin in Superior were the only additional structure fires posted while Marshall Command was unavailable. At 4:07 p.m., County Dispatch sent units MVFR 2222 and Lafayette Engine 2602 to a two-car accident at Arapahoe Road and Westview Drive just north of the fire. At 4:08 p.m., Police Dispatch asked if Edward 7 could check on a person on Longs Peak Drive. Edward 7 responded that they were still clearing 105 Vista Lane though no one appeared to be there. A minute later, Edward 7 said they were available as the home was empty. Eight homes on Vista Lane including 105 as well as many more on W. Mulberry Street were burned in the Centennial Heights subdivision.

Fire Dispatch toned Louisville Medic 2723 to the Erie Airport to transport emergency medical personnel to the Broomfield Rocky Mountain Metropolitan Airport at 4:10 p.m. Flights from Erie to Broomfield were impossible due to the smoke plume and ash. Police Dispatch then directed Edward 7 and Edward 43 to Quail Circle north of S. Boulder Road in Louisville to help evacuate a seventy-five-year-old woman who was blind and had multiple sclerosis. State Highway Patrol handled the two-car accident, and MFVR Medic 2222 and Lafayette Engine 2602 canceled at 4:11 p.m. County Dispatch sent Louisville Medic 2723 to Dogwood Circle north of S. Boulder Road in Louisville to help evacuate an elderly woman who needed oxygen at 4:13 p.m. Edward 32 called in asking for a medical evacuation for a diabetic at 1609 Sunset Drive south of S. Boulder Road in Louisville at 4:16 p.m. Fire Dispatch rang tones for Louisville Bus 2722 and MVFR Engine 2204 to respond to the request. Police Dispatch directed Edward 7 and Edward 43 to Sunnyside Street north of S. Boulder Road where a husband was prohibiting his wife from evacuating at 4:20 p.m. He also notified Unit 410 that they may be needed if it turned into a domestic dispute. At 4:24 p.m., Edward 7 stated that it was not a domestic dispute, and the woman was now free to leave, and no other units will be needed.

Also, at 4:20 p.m., Edward 6 stated that he was helping to evacuate several patients at Flatirons Health and Rehab[67] at 1170 W. Century Drive west of McCaslin in Louisville. Flatirons is a skilled nursing facility providing short-term rehabilitation, extended care services, and respite care. They had forty-two patients in their forty-five available beds, four who just tested positive for COVID. He asked Dispatch which direction to take the patients through the fire. Police Dispatch responded north and south McCaslin were impassable, but Cherry Street and possibly Via Appia may still be open. Edward 6 stated that he will try Via Appia to S. Boulder Road and that about twenty vehicles were following him in a caravan with the patients. Neighboring facilities including Elms Haven, Ridgeview, Boulder Canyon, and Sunrise at Flatirons all sent vans and buses to help evacuate Flatirons. While they were leaving, the remaining staff used fire extinguishers and buckets of water outside the facility to put out nearby small grass and shrub fires caused by the blowing embers. A call came in right afterward asking for help evacuating the center, and Fire Dispatch toned Lafayette Medic 2622 and Engine 2602 to help with the evacuation. Edward 6 commented the fire was just to the west of the facility, and he thought all the patients were in the convoy, but a few staff were still there and getting ready to leave. The facility was fully evacuated by 4:45 p.m. Miraculously, it will be one of eighteen nursing homes, hospitals, and medical facilities safely evacuated during the crisis with no loss of life or injury.

At 4:25 p.m., County Dispatch toned MVFR Truck 2216 to 1307 N. Franklin Avenue north of Via Appia in Louisville to help with an evacuation of a male parent and paraplegic son. Fire Dispatch also called out another commercial fire alarm at 920 St. Andrews Lane as the fire continued to ravage the Coal Creek Ranch development in Louisville. At 4:32 p.m., County Dispatch informed Marshall Command of a fire at 2011 Emerson Lane in Superior. The fire was starting its burn further south along McCaslin. MVFR Truck 2216 responded that they were engaged and asked Dispatch to reassign the paraplegic evacuation request. Fire Dispatch then toned MVFR Bus 2621 to assist with the evacuation at 4:35 p.m. A minute later, 2621 said that they were taking one patient and rider to Longmont United. At this time, a police unit confirmed that McCaslin was still impassable between S. Boulder Road and Via Appia and S. Boulder Road was open for emergency traffic only in Louisville.

At 4:39 p.m., County Dispatch toned MVFR Engine 2204 to the Legacy Assisted Living at 225 Wanaka Parkway in Lafayette to help with their evacuation as their lift broke and they needed help moving wheelchair patients. This facility was over two miles from the fire and not in its direct path but decided to evacuate due to the risk and time

[67] The fire advanced toward Flatirons Health and Rehab, but it only received smoke damage. It reopened three weeks after the fire.

it took to move its residents. Police Dispatch asked for any additional Lafayette units to help with traffic at US-287 and Empire Road. Lincoln 65 responded they will cover traffic delayed response. Fire Dispatch toned MVFR Truck 2216 to Tri-County Airport at 395 Airport Drive, Erie, to transport another medivac team and equipment. MVFR Bus 2223 responded that they will cover the medivac team. If the fire was not enough, Police Dispatch then announced at 4:39 p.m. that a train had derailed, blocking traffic at Fifty-fifth and Arapahoe in east Boulder just a few miles northwest of the fire. Miraculously, the train wreck was not an emergency, just an inconvenience.

Mines bring prosperity and people to Colorado, trains transport the riches, and coal fires the trains.[68] The first commercial trains operated in England in 1825, and by 1827, the Baltimore & Ohio Railroad operated the longest stretch of track in the world with 133 miles from Charleston to Hamburg, South Carolina. By 1840, over 3,300 miles of track extended throughout the Atlantic states, surpassing canals and rivers as the major means of transportation. Talk of a transcontinental railroad spanning from the Atlantic Ocean to the Pacific Ocean started in the late 1840s and exploded after the Spanish-American War when America received the lands west of the Rockies.

Train boosters in Denver and Gold City (now Golden) promoted a route through Colorado. Senator Thomas Hart Benton backed them as such a route would originate in his home state of Missouri; and his son-in-law, John C. Fremont, surveyed possible routes. In 1855, the U.S. Army provided Congress with ten volumes of possible train routes through the west. Unlucky for Colorado, these surveys all showed that paralleling the Overland Trail along the North Platte River in southern Wyoming would have much gentler grades than the steep and torturous routes needed to traverse through the Colorado mountains. Then the Pikes Peak gold rush started in the summer of 1858 in what was then the western Kansas territory. With the cry "Pikes Peak or Bust," prospectors flocked to the region in droves. By February 1859, four railroad companies formed to bring the railroads to Denver. All four petered out within a year. Colorado City near Pikes Peak was declared the territorial capital with the creation of the Colorado Territory in February 1861 as gold miners poured in. By 1862, Gold City usurped Colorado City and became the provisional territorial capital. But in 1863, the Union Pacific Railroad started laying track from Omaha following the Overland Route, bypassing Colorado. Then the Civil War intervened, and Union Pacific only laid forty miles of track from 1863 to 1865. Colorado took

[68] Most of the following railroad discussion adapted from "Railroads in Colorado 1858–1948," by Clayton Fraser and Jennifer Strand, August 31, 1997, US Department of the Interior.

the opportunity to persuade Union Pacific to reconsider routing further south to gain access to the mining riches. No suitable route could be found that did not involve significant tunneling and steep grades. And the promised gold mining riches dwindled from $3.5 million per year as the easy gold placer ore was extracted. Union Pacific stayed with the Overland Route.

But Colorado did get part of the transcontinental railroad. In June 1867, Union Pacific ran nine miles of track along Lone Tree Creek into the Colorado Territory past the small farming town of Julesberg (now Julesburg). For the next two years, it alone had access to rail service back east. If the rest of the territory wanted rail, they needed to determine a way to finance it on their own. Competing companies emerged in Denver and Gold City to do just that. Meantime, Denver claimed the final title as the territorial capital in 1867 by a single vote.

Denver promoters convinced the Kansas Pacific (KP) Railway Company to build a line from Kansas City to Denver. In the spring of 1866, KP announced that they would use the Smoky Hills route to reach Denver within three years. This turned out to be an empty promise as its key representative, Gen. William Palmer, surveyed two routes through New Mexico to reach the Pacific, bypassing the Colorado mountains.

A group from Gold City in 1865 formed the Colorado Central (CC) rail line. Headed by W. A. H. Loveland, E. L. Berthoud, and Henry Teller, the CC intended to extend tracks north from Gold City to the Union Pacific, west over Berthoud Pass to Utah, and southeast to the future Denver Pacific terminus and points east. In 1867, Loveland struck a deal with Union Pacific that complied with congressional restrictions on spurs where CC would grade the road from Gold City to Wyoming and UP would lay the tracks and provide rolling stock. Unluckily, none of the towns along the way pledged the bond money necessary to complete the grading, and the deal dissolved, and the CC slipped into a period of inactivity.

Figure 45 Colorado Central train above Boulder in Wallstreet. Courtesy of the Carnegie Library for Local History / Museum of Boulder Collection.

In November 1867, the Denver Pacific (DP) Railway & Telegraph Company incorporated to link the city with the Union Pacific. Organized by ex-governor John Evans and businessmen Bela Hughes and David Moffat, they began their first surveys in December. Evans, a medical doctor, was appointed territorial governor in 1862 by Abraham Lincoln and firmly believed that adequate, efficient, and cheap rail transportation to be the future. Moffat opened a stationery store with D. G. Woolworth, which prospered by hauling eastern newspapers to Denver faster than the mail and selling them for a premium. He knew speed made things worth more and believed in railroads. DP approached Union Pacific and reached a deal similar to Colorado Central's—the UP would build a railroad from Cheyenne to Denver for majority control, if DP could obtain a congressional land grant. By March 1869, DP had its land grant and by May had graded a line from Denver to Cheyenne. But due to lack of financing, the UP reneged, and no rails were laid.

In frustration, DP merged with Kansas Pacific, and together they began building rails south from Cheyenne and west from Kansas City in 1869. Though the famous golden spike was pounded in at Promontory, Utah, in May 1869, commemorating the linking of the Union Pacific with the Central Pacific, that railway only connected the Missouri River with the Sacramento River. Passengers and freight transferred by horse and wagon to other railways to go the entire distance across the country. It was not until the silver spike (from silver mined in Georgetown) was laid near Strasburg, Colorado, at the completion of the Cheyenne to Denver to Kansas City railway, that the United States had a continuous transcontinental track reaching from the Atlantic Ocean all the way to the Pacific Ocean.

With the first line complete, additional rail spurs and runs started. Denver Pacific created a subsidiary called the Denver & Boulder Valley Railroad and ran a line from Hughes (now Brighton) to the coalfields at Erie in late 1870. Union Pacific helped the Colorado Central complete a line from Gold City (now Golden) to Denver also in 1870. The great railway race began with lines reaching throughout the state, including to the northern coalfields in Boulder and Weld Counties.

Most of these new lines were considered "placer railroads" where the roads were built cheaply and expected to last less than ten years. When possible, new lines shaved costs in materials and construction to stretch limited capital funding. Bridges were made of wood (and lined with barrels of water to fight fires) instead of metal or stone. Buildings were also wooden instead of brick. Operating profits were expected to fund subsequent upgrades and replacement costs. Knowing this, directors often took their profits during construction and left the railway with little or no capital and exposed to bankruptcy and takeover. Passengers and freight were at risk to derailments and train wrecks. But trains still brought prosperity to the new Colorado Territory.

During the 1870s, counties with railroads tripled in appraised values while counties without increased by 70 percent. Colorado population exploded fivefold during this time, and most newcomers lived in towns served by railroads. Colorado Springs, Castle Rock, and Manitou Springs were all settled because railroads passed through them.

In 1881, the Union Pacific started building spurs up nearly every canyon along the Front Range, including rugged Boulder Canyon. Grading for this effort was led by W. H. Cox, a contentious southern subcontractor, who hired two hundred African Americans from Kansas at half the going wages. When workers walked off the job, he jailed them for breach of contract. Order was kept by the point of a shotgun. But the workers charged him with assault, and a Boulder judge found him guilty. The line building continued, and instead of rock blasting and digging tunnels, sixty-six wooden bridges spanned Boulder Creek and Four Mile Creek, making it one of the worst placer lines in the state. The line stopped after fifteen miles up the canyon at Sunset (now a ghost town), but it did reach the Caribou mine, where the silver boom started (and later the home of Caribou Ranch, a renowned recording location used by Elton John, Amy Grant, and the '70s band Chicago for five consecutive albums).

Figure 46 1898 day trip up Boulder Canyon by train to Mont Alto Park. Courtesy of the Carnegie Library for Local History / Museum of Boulder Collection.

A flood wiped out miles of track and trestles and dumped Engine No. 155 into the creek in 1893. The UP subsidiary declared bankruptcy, and the line lay dormant until 1898 when the Colorado & Northwestern Railway acquired the right-of-way and extended the tracks to Ward. They also built a tourist destination just past Sunset called Mont Alto Park that included a dancing pavilion, picnic tables, and a white quartz fountain. The scenery was spectacular, and the route became known as the Switzerland Trail. Tourism and tungsten kept the line open through 1913 with Stanley Steamers bringing additional tourists from Estes Park.

Deputy 581 called in that another semitruck had blown over at 2200 Foothills Highway CO-93 near the Community Ditch just south of the initial fire at 4:40 p.m. A minute later, Deputy 516 called in that Foothills Highway near Marshall can be reopened as the fire had moved on and the wind slowed. Fire Dispatch called out another smoke alarm at 7574 Spring Drive north of Dillon Road in Louisville. Traffic had been turning off S. Boulder Road southbound on Washington back into Louisville, and Edward 7 said he can send a unit to stop it. As southbound McCaslin at S. Boulder Road was now blocked off by city workers, Unit 416 said they can move to Washington so that the Erie police can continue to roam and keep the evacuation running smoothly. Unit 446 also requested that southbound Ninety-sixth Street be blocked off south of CO-42 as the smoke was becoming too dense to transit at 4:43 p.m. Lincoln 58 called in at 4:44 p.m. that an individual asked to check on a house on Longs Peak Drive south of S. Boulder Road in Louisville as one of the inhabitants was disabled and may need assistance evacuating. Edward 32 broadcast that they were just at Longs Peak, and the residents expected family to help them. Lincoln 58 responded that it was the family that contacted him, and they cannot make it to Longs Peak. Edward 32 stated at 4:49 p.m. he will return to Longs Peak until they were evacuated. Ten minutes later, the family arrived to help evacuate, and the medical call was canceled.

At 4:50 p.m., County Dispatch toned Boulder Mountain Brush 4332, Lafayette Engine 2602, and MVFR Battalion 2260 to respond to a grass fire at 3351 S. Indiana Street in south Superior near the Eldorado K-8 elementary school.[69] Miraculously, with schools out for the holidays, no schools were threatened or destroyed by the fire. Simultaneously, Edward 6 asked if any units had been dispatched to Owl Drive and W. Pinyon Way in Louisville south of Via Appia as the condominiums there were on fire and no fire trucks were visible on-site. Blowing embers from the large fires on Mulberry and above Via Appia caused numerous outbreaks on Night Hawk Circle, Fillmore Court, and Owl Drive. These fires will eventually be addressed by Division Tango. Fire Dispatch toned MVFR Medic 2224 and Engine 2204 to 1450 Lincoln Avenue south of S. Boulder Road in Louisville to aid an elderly woman who fell at 4:43 p.m. Engine 2204 responded that they cannot go to the Lincoln Avenue call as they were attempting to rescue three parties trapped by the wildfire near Boulder Valley Christian Church on S. Boulder Road west of Spanish Hills.

Lincoln 90 called in a three-car accident on Empire Road and CO-42 at 4:54 p.m. where at least one of the vehicles was disabled. Lincoln 65 responded that they will cover the accident. Lincoln 59 arrived at the

[69] This area is south of the Marshall fire and listed as part of the damage area, probably caused by embers tossed by the swirling winds.

accident within a minute. One of the cars took off eastbound and turned onto US-287 with Lincoln 59 in hot pursuit. She stated the fleeing vehicle was an SUV and was trailing smoke headed north. The smoking SUV pulled into Blue Federal Credit Union near Good Samaritan Hospital, and State Highway Patrol Unit 1851 detained the occupants who left the scene of the accident.

Louisville, December 30, 2021, 4:59 p.m., Wind NNE 9 mph, Gusting to 19 mph 43°F

Flanked by Gov. Jared Polis, Boulder County sheriff Joe Pelle held the first news conference on the Marshall and Middle Fork fires at 5:00 p.m. He stated that the fire had grown to at least 1,600 acres and had likely destroyed at least 580 homes, along with the Element Hotel, Target, and other businesses. Early indications were that a downed power line ignited the blaze.

The official OEM summary from the briefing follows:[70]

> The two fires, Middle Fork fire and Marshall fire, started in the late morning. The first fire, called the Middle Fork fire, was reported just before 10:30 a.m. near the intersection of North Foothills Highway and Middle Fork Road. Crews were able to contain the Middle Fork Fire later in the day, and resources were reallocated to the Marshall Fire.
>
> The Marshall Fire was reported just after 11 a.m. at South Foothills Highway and Marshall Road. Over the course of the day, the fire grew exponentially due to extreme wind conditions and spread east. It spread through Superior and parts of Louisville. Avista Hospital and many care facilities in the area were evacuated. At the time of the press briefing at 5 p.m., the fire was estimated to be approximately 1600 acres in size. It was estimated that more than 560 homes were destroyed at the time of the press briefing, including the Sagamore neighborhood and homes in Old Town Superior.
>
> At this point, we only have one report of an injury, a minor injury to an officer's eye from wind-blown debris. It is too early to tell if we have any fire-related casualties, but there is potential for casualties given the vast destruction that occurred in a short frame of time. At the time of the press briefing, there were no reported fatalities or missing persons.

[70] The full briefing is at https://www.boulderoem.com/emergency-status/page/12/.

There are three Boulder County evacuation centers open:

- North Boulder Recreation Center, 3170 Broadway, Boulder, CO 80304
- Lafayette YMCA, 2800 Dagny Way Lafayette, CO
- Rocky Mtn Christian Church, 9447 Niwot Rd., Longmont (Niwot)
- **If you are COVID-positive** and must evacuate, please evacuate to the COVID Recovery Center at Mt. Calvary Lutheran Church, 3485 Stanford Ct, Boulder, CO

A community call center has been established. This call center has information concerning the fires' impact on Boulder County and can be reached at 303-413-7730. Any community members with questions or needs are encouraged to call here instead of 911.

The fire activity is constantly changing and highly impacted by the weather. We are hopeful the winds will decrease through the evening, but forecasters are anticipating continued, occasional gusts.

Individuals should not attempt to return to their neighborhoods until they receive official word that it is safe to do so. This may not be for several days.

We wish to thank the many agencies that are responding to this emergency with us.

Sheriff Pelle commented, "I'd like to emphasize that due to the magnitude of this fire, the intensity of this fire, and its presence in such a heavily populated area, we would not be surprised if there are injuries or fatalities." Governor Polis added that firefighting aircraft had been unable to engage due to the high winds.

It was also announced that FEMA approved a federal Fire Management Assistance Grant (FMAG) request, which will pay for 75 percent of Colorado's firefighting costs. Governor Polis urged President Biden to declare a major disaster declaration, and he did so on December 31. DR4634 was issued by President Biden for relief from the Marshall fire and straight line winds. A follow-on briefing was scheduled for December 31 at 10:00 a.m.

Fire Dispatch sent MVFR Command 2262 to Springs Drive south of Cherry in Louisville for an evacuation assist at 5:00 p.m. Fire Dispatch asked Marshall Command to direct a unit to 1724 Steel Street to help evacuate a wheelchair-bound elderly woman at 5:03 p.m. A minute later, County Dispatch announced a fire alarm at 895 Paragon Drive west of Spanish Hills along the Goodhue Ditch. This home survived the fire with damage. At 5:05 p.m., County Dispatch announced that one of the cars from the three-car accident had caught on fire. A minute later, County Dispatch toned MVFR Bus 2227 and Truck 2216 to 1577 Holman Drive in Erie for a three-year-old male seizing. Simultaneously, Unit 436 was conversing with Police Dispatch on how to enter the Louisville Harper Lake area to evacuate an elderly lady. The smoke and fire were intense in that region. Unit 797 requested animal control to help evacuate additional horses at 5:08 p.m. Edward 23 responded to the toddler seizure on-site at 5:09 p.m. At the same time, County Dispatch toned MVFR Engine 2208 to 11900 block of S. Boulder Road in Lafayette for a thirty-five-year-old male who had passed out from alcohol consumption. At 5:12 p.m., County Dispatch called out a smoke alarm at 333 Centennial Parkway in Louisville behind Lowes. This area survived the fire.

At 5:14 p.m., County Dispatch told Marshall Command that a grass fire had been called in at Safeway at 1601 Coalton Road in Superior heading east. The grass fire here was following the vegetation along Rock Creek and burned nine homes on Eldorado Drive. It also followed the Community Ditch to the south but stopped at Community Park. It is interesting to note that the fire burned through the Coal Creek Ranch development north of US-36 three and a half hours earlier. Fire Dispatch also reported a call about a grass fire at 7999 Coalton Road south across from Safeway. At 5:17 p.m., Tri-County Fire announced to Marshall Command that they received a call that the fire jumped Coalton Road past Safeway in Superior and was heading toward FlatIron Crossing Mall. This call will turn out to be an exaggeration.

Worried about the possibility of the fire heading east, Broomfield County announced a mandatory evacuation south of US-36 to 112th Avenue and west of Wadsworth Avenue, including the Interlocken development area and the FlatIron Crossing Mall, which had already closed to help ease traffic concerns. The Broomfield Detention Center at 11600 Ridge Parkway south of 120th was evacuated as a precaution. The 1stBank Center opened as an evacuation point for Broomfield, and about 150 residents gathered there. The Lafayette YMCA, the North Boulder Recreation Center, and the Rocky Mountain Christian Church in Niwot all became overnight shelters while COVID-positive evacuees headed to Mt. Calvary Lutheran Church in Boulder. The American Red Cross operated the center at Rocky Mountain Christian. Authorities arranged for meals, and cots were brought in for sleeping. Out of an estimated 37,500 evacuated, less than 200 spent the night in shelters. Miraculously, the remainder found their own accommodations. The OEM announced at 5:40 p.m.

that the Boulder Community Foundation will collect and distribute financial aid to those affected by the Marshall fire. The Boulder County Fairgrounds also filled up to capacity for large animals by 5:45 p.m., and the Jefferson County Fairgrounds opened to accommodate additional evacuated large animals.

At 5:19 p.m., County Dispatch directed MVFR Medic 2224 and Boulder Rural Engine 2302 to 107th and Mineral Road in Longmont for a woman having cramps and difficulty breathing. This was not related to the fire but still must be addressed. Lafayette Engine 2602 also called in to cancel the smoking car at Blue Credit Union as it was out. A Longmont unit announced that a house was on fire near Polk Avenue and Owl Drive in Louisville at 5:20 p.m. (this was confirmed later to be 457 Fillmore Court, which was destroyed). Fire Dispatch also informed Marshall Command of a call that the fire was approaching the houses at 6988 S. Boulder Road west of Spanish Hills. Dispatch continued that the fire was approaching the Eldorado Corner Market at 1805 S. Foothills Highway (CO-93) west of the original call at the RTD Park-n-Ride and against the original direction of the wind[71]. At 5:24 p.m., Nederland Wagon 5621 said it was available, and County Dispatch sent it to 1724 Steel Street north of S. Boulder Road in Louisville to help with the elderly wheelchair evacuation from earlier.

Edward 6 announced that King Soopers in Louisville at the old Hecla Mine site was now closed to the public but open for first responders needing food or drink. He said that he was available to deliver. Police Dispatch changed shift around 5:30 p.m., and a female voice assumed dispatch radio. County Dispatch announced that Boulder Community Hospital was only receiving critical patients and Longmont United Hospital was on advisory at 5:30 p.m. Due to the extent of the fire and the closing of both Avista and Good Sam hospitals, these hospitals instituted restrictions. Miraculously, the anticipated flood of injured persons from the fire never materialized. Police Dispatch announced a possible DUI at Dillon and Ninety-sixth as someone upset at being evacuated was seen drinking vodka while driving. County Dispatch toned Louisville Medic 2722 to 725 Meridian Lane in Superior to help a fall victim. This was about a block from the homes blazing on Canary Lane. At 5:32 p.m., Lincoln 14 called Police Dispatch that two Boulder Valley School buses were at his roadblock wanting to go to Monarch High School for evacuation assistance. Police Dispatch told Lincoln 14 to hold, and she will check on where the school buses were needed. At 5:34 p.m., Lafayette police tweeted that there were no evacuations in Lafayette at this time, but residents east of US-287 between Arapahoe and Dillon were encouraged to be prepared to evacuate if conditions worsened. Lafayette Bus 2621 took the

[71] It is possible that the wind was swirling by this time in the afternoon. It may explain some of the burn patterns observed later.

Meridian Drive fall victim as they were now free and closer than 2722 at 5:35 p.m. Edward 7 headed toward 855 W. Dillon in Louisville to help with an evacuation.

County Dispatch toned Lafayette Engine 2602 and the now-free Louisville Medic 2722 to 1995 E. Coalton Road in Superior to help evacuate a woman with a broken back at 5:36 p.m. This was near Autrey Reservoir and was directly in line with the fire. Though it received a lot of smoke, the fire did not cross S. Rock Creek Parkway a couple of blocks west. Police Dispatch informed Lincoln 65 that there was a report of stolen vehicles at 610 S. Public Road in Lafayette. Lincoln 65 asked her to hold it for now. At 5:38 p.m., Police Dispatch called Lincoln 14 that the two school buses were supposed to be going to Centennial Peaks Behavior Health Hospital off Eighty-eighth Street in Louisville near Avista to help with the evacuation of patients. Lincoln 14 directed the buses past his roadblock onto Dillon to the facility. At 5:39 p.m., Police Dispatch called out an intrusion alarm in the basement of 2011 Emerson Lane in Superior east of McCaslin beside the green space and the Community Ditch. The fire set off this intrusion alarm as this home was destroyed, along with six of its neighbors.

Other calls were still coming in as Police Dispatch asked County Unit 7 to respond code 1 for a stuck-in-the-snow gray Toyota Corolla on County Road 102J (Spring Gulch Road) in Ward high in the mountains. Unit 584 signed off for the evening, and Unit 587 signed on and joined Law 3 tactical communications at 5:40 p.m. Another grass fire was reported north of Oxford Road in Longmont at 5:40 p.m. Also at that time, Unit 581 responded that they will take the intrusion alarm on Emerson if they can get there. At 5:41 p.m., Police Dispatch announced a domestic disturbance in the 1100 block of Centaur Circle in Lafayette where a male was acting aggressive, and a female was screaming. Lincoln 59 responded he was enroute.

Police Dispatch announced that a Larimer County unit was reporting an eighty-year-old was refusing to evacuate on Raymer Lane in Superior at 5:43 p.m. This area was just south and east of the fire near US-36. Unit 468 called Police Dispatch at 5:44 p.m. that they were just north and east of Harper Lake in Louisville and were going door-to-door to get residents to evacuate. The fire dispatch radio changed employees around then. At 5:44 p.m., County Dispatch toned MVFR Medic 2223 to the domestic disturbance in the 1100 block of Centaur Circle in Lafayette. Police Dispatch announced at that time that the Home Depot in Louisville near US-36 west of McCaslin now had flames on the south and west sides. Eight buildings on Dyer Road just west of the Home Depot were destroyed, and several businesses just east of it were also damaged or destroyed, but the Home Depot had slight external damage and miraculously reopened the next day. Lincoln 59 updated on the domestic disturbance on Centaur Circle at 5:45 p.m.

At that same time, Edward 7 stated he was evacuating residents on the north side of Dillon Road at 855 W. Dillon in Louisville. Police Dispatch conversed back and forth about whether relatives were coming to help. Two units announced that they were going to the Oxford Road grass fire at 5:46 p.m. Fire Dispatch also announced to Marshall Command that the garden center at the Home Depot in Louisville may be on fire. At 5:49 p.m., Lincoln 58 said that he had the relatives at Ninety-sixth and Dillon Road who were trying to pick up the person at 855 W. Dillon, and Edward 7 said he will take them there. Police Dispatch announced that residents at 517 W. Lois in Louisville needed help evacuating at 5:51 p.m. Unit 435 responded they will cover.

Unit 585 called in that they were at Sixty-third and Oxford south of Longmont and cannot find any fire. Police Dispatch announced that a party at 256 S. McCaslin in Louisville needed help evacuating. Edward 6 responded he will help. Fire Dispatch toned Louisville Medic 2722 to the Lafayette YMCA evacuation center at 5:55 p.m. to help an eighty-year-old lady whose oxygen tank was low and needed refilled. Louisville Medic 2723 responded that he will cover the YMCA so that 2722 can stay in service.

Meanwhile, fire trucks from all over Colorado deployed to help fight the fire. As the sun set, the wind include a vertical component over much of the fire, and citizens from all the surrounding towns photographed the bright-orange flames against the darkening smoke clouds and wondered if the fire would keep spreading toward their homes.

Figure 47 Fire as seen from 111th and Arapahoe in Erie at 5:42 p.m. six miles northeast. Courtesy of W. Lerch.

Louisville Manorwood, December 30, 2021, 5:53 p.m., Wind NW 5 mph, Gusting 6 mph 43°F

Balfour's evacuation, though hectic, was organized and methodical. Based on the OEM request, St. Vrain School District sent a school bus to help vacate the residents. Balfour facilities in Central Park and Riverfront Park in Denver both sent their vehicles to help load the residents and equipment. Balfour Littleton also sent their transports, but they arrived later and were used for equipment. Unluckily, none of these vehicles included a handicap lift for wheelchairs.

The Villa residents were all ambulatory. Though slow, they all climbed into the vehicles without incident. Their overnight bags followed separately. Once loaded, they proceeded north and then west to Boulder to spend the night at Frasier Meadows. Frasier Meadows graciously helped them move into their temporary quarters and provided a meal. Unfortunately, many of the name tags fell off the overnight bags, and it took a while to sort them out. But with the staff working hard, all the assisted living residents were safe for the night, wondering when they would return to Balfour.

With no handicap lifts, the skilled nursing residents had to be carefully hand-lifted one by one into the vehicles for transport. It was a struggle with some of the residents and several caregivers later complaining of back injuries. The weather was still in the forties, so the bus heaters kept everyone mostly warm. By 6:45 p.m., all the residents were loaded and on their way. Once they made it to Gardens on Quail, they took a rapid COVID test to allow them to enter. Though all the residents came up negative, one staff member tested positive and was not allowed to enter the building.

Though Gardens on Quail in Arvada had space, they were missing beds. The staff kept calling facilities, and finally Saint Paul Health Center in Denver said they could send twenty beds for the skilled nursing residents. It took a while to load, but they were finally delivered, and all were installed by midnight. Though a bit late, the skilled nursing residents were all safe for the night. The Balfour late staff stayed the night, and the early crew headed home, wondering if they would have a house when they arrived.

Meanwhile, the staff continued working on transporting the remaining equipment and supplies needed for skilled nursing. Extra oxygen, feeding tubes, ostomy bags—everything needed to be checked and loaded onto buses or trucks and taken to Gardens on Quail. It took until after 2:00 a.m. to get it all loaded into the trucks and buses and sent to Arvada and Boulder. Then the Balfour buildings themselves had to be properly locked down. Three times the buildings were checked room by room to ensure that everyone had evacuated and nothing important was left behind. The third time, the fire department also cleared the buildings. Finally, all the air intakes were shut down to minimize smoke damage. Becki Siemers made it home by 3:15 a.m. and prayed that all the residents stayed safe and the facility survived.

At 5:58 p.m., Unit 581 called in that Police Dispatch can clear the intrusion alarm on Emerson Lane in Superior as the house was engulfed in flame. The homes on the southwest side of that street were all destroyed. At that time, Police Dispatch also called in a three-car collision at US-287 and S. Boulder Road in Lafayette. There were no injuries. Lincoln 65 responded. Edward 7 called in at 6:00 p.m. that he had delivered the evacuee to his relatives on Dillon Road in Louisville and was available. Many units checked out after a long day around this time, and others called in service. Many who left didn't know if they still had a home.

At 6:02 p.m., Police Dispatch asked for officers to clear the "lookie-loos" at Washington and McCaslin by Harper Lake who were watching the fire. This was the Leon Wurl Animal Sanctuary south of Harper Lake where the Bovens stopped after evacuating. Unit 434 responded he would move them along. At 6:04 p.m., MVFR Tactical Tender 2242 called County Dispatch to say that a woman had parked on S. Boulder Road and returned to 940 Paragon Drive in Spanish Hills to fight the fire herself and asked that officers escort her out. That home will only be damaged by the fire. Concurrently, Lincoln 53 called in that she had a civilian passenger on board at the roadblock at 104th and Dillon east of Louisville.

Edward 6 called in at 6:06 p.m. that one of the large doors at the Home Depot was wide open and asked if someone can confirm if the store had been evacuated. He added that it was not currently on fire. Police Dispatch called Edward 7 to respond. At that time, the Home Depot had been evacuated and was empty. The high winds opened the large garage door due to the air pressure difference caused by internal fans that had been turned off to keep the smoke out. Miraculously, the store only suffered a few damaged items outside its south side and opened for service the next day (though only two customers called due to road closures). Simultaneously, County Dispatch called Marshall Command that they had a thirdhand report that there was a structure fire at Lincoln and Lafayette northwest of downtown Louisville. This will turn out to be false. Unit 446 called in that she had a report of two elderly persons stuck in an apartment at 2600 S. Rock Creek Parkway in Superior. This was just east of the fire burning in Community Park. Edward 7 responded to this request at 6:07 p.m. Fire Dispatch then called Marshall Command to report a house fire near the eighth hole of the Louisville Coal Creek Golf Course at 6:11 p.m. These were the homes burning on Pinehurst Court north of St. Andrews Lane. Twelve homes were destroyed in this area.

Figure 48 Marshall fire as seen from the air about 6:00 p.m. Courtesy of Amy Leedham tweet KRDO.

Fire Dispatch toned MVFR Medic 2223 to 245 N. Ninety-sixth Street in Louisville to aid an incapacitated male in the parking lot who can't get up. Edward 32 stated that he was close to Rock Creek Parkway and will cover the elderly evacuation. Edward 7 canceled. At 6:14 p.m., Unit 561 called County Dispatch to ask if anyone cleared 935 El Dorado Lane north of Via Appia. Unit 412 responded that there was no access to that area as the entire neighborhood was gone. A minute later, Police Dispatch called Unit 581 to 1955 El Dorado[72] in Superior as a party in New York claimed a female there was not being permitted to evacuate. Edward 6 called in that he was clear at 6:16 p.m. Unit 410 also announced at 6:18 p.m. that all evacuation requests should now be routed through Unified Command. Police Dispatch asked how to contact them as she needed an evacuation at 711 Walnut Street in Louisville. Lincoln 40 requested an ambulance at Ninety-sixth Street and Highway 42 in east Louisville for a male having difficulty breathing. Estes Park fire trucks called County Dispatch that they were just coming into Boulder at Twenty-eighth and Kalmia and were now available where needed.

At 6:20 p.m., Police Dispatch directed Edward 23 and 54 to Highway 52 for a gold Lexus with Virginia plates where a male was hitting a female. Simultaneously, County Dispatch toned Louisville Medic 2723 to respond to the man having difficulty breathing. Edward 6 called in that they were available to help with evacuations. Unit 410 informed Police Dispatch that Unified Command was directing evacuation requests using tactical channel Law 3 and asked that Edward 6 continue roaming at 6:23 p.m. Edward 8 called in on duty. Unit 416 called in at 6:25 p.m. that the home at 1050 Meadow Court just south of Harper Lake in Louisville was just beginning to burn and might be salvageable if units respond quickly. Lincoln 14 called in that the flames were intense within one hundred yards of his position. Edward 7 called in that he was transporting two elderly persons from 2600 S. Rock Creek in Superior at 6:26 p.m. Fire Dispatch simultaneously announced that 1050 Meadow Court below Harper Lake in Louisville was now on fire. Marshall Command acknowledged.

[72] Louisville's El Dorado Lane was destroyed by the fire. El Dorado Drive in Superior was the northern boundary of the southern tongue of the fire and El Dorado Circle was untouched.

Figure 49 Firefighters engaged at Imperial Lane and Eldorado Drive in Superior at 6:21 p.m. Photo: Code 10 Photography.

At 6:27 p.m., County Dispatch called out a grass fire at N. Ninety-fifth St. Courtesy Road and Summit View Drive in Louisville. This was just north of Balfour and probably caused by flying embers. Luckily, it was small and quickly extinguished. Police Dispatch called out a hit-and-run by a Gold Lexus with Virginia license plates off SR-7 Arapahoe Road. Edward 22 responded. At 6:28 p.m., MVFR Medic 2223 told County Dispatch that they will be helping to transport independent living residents from Balfour. Balfour was only responsible for transporting assisted and nursing residents and not independent living. Independent living residents were on their own to evacuate.

At 6:30 p.m., Edward 22 updated that there were two cars involved in the hit-and-run at the side of the road. Edward 32 called in at 6:31 p.m. that they were also transporting evacuees. Unit 1768 called County Dispatch asking to be relieved at the Foothills onramp roadblock to US-36 in Boulder. Fire Dispatch responded that they were unable to contact Boulder police as they cannot get an outside phone line. Unit 1736 indicated she would call Boulder direct. At 6:34 p.m., Police Dispatch sent Unit 435 to an apartment at 855 W. Dillon Road in Louisville to check on a male refusing to evacuate who may be suicidal. This was in the middle of the fire area, but no structure fires were currently nearby. Unit 435 was occupied, but Unit 438 covered.

Louisville Medic 2723 called County Dispatch that they were clear of the man having difficulty breathing at 6:35 p.m. and asked where they were needed next. Unit 416 called Police Dispatch that there was still a large gathering of people at the south end of Harper Lake and that he was trying to disperse them. Around this time, a special dispatcher was assigned to the Law 3 tactical channel to help keep evacuation communications flowing smoothly. At 6:46 p.m., Unit 416 called Police Dispatch that he had cleared all the vehicle traffic from around Harper Lake, but there were still several pedestrians walking the trails. He planned to pursue on foot. At this time, no additional 911 calls came in, and County Dispatch did not play any tones. Most of the activity was now coordinated on the tactical channels, and both police and fire dispatch radio channels were quiet.

At 6:50 p.m., Nederland Rescue 5621 called County Dispatch that they were now clear and available for assignment. Fire Dispatch asked them to stay on standby as resources were still scarce. At 6:52 p.m., both County Dispatch and Police Dispatch called out a small spot fire near the Louisville Cemetery off Empire Road. With the wind shift causing more of an uplift in the Louisville area, hot ash was blowing farther, and small fires cropped up away from the general conflagration. Fire Dispatch called Marshall Command that a structure was now burning near 518 Meridian Lane in Superior at 6:52 p.m. Though several homes burned on nearby Discovery Parkway and Canary Lane, firefighters contained the spread; and buildings on Meridian Lane, Promenade Drive, and Superior Drive a couple of blocks east were only damaged and not destroyed. Edward 20 and Edward 31 checked out at 6:53 p.m. Longmont units Paul 211 and Paul 225 called Police Dispatch that they were now available for coverage. After a long, hard day, units started changing.

Figure 50 Looking north toward Louisville from south Superior in thirty-second exposure at 6:50 p.m. Note wind blowing west. Photo: Code 10 Photography.

Louisville operates two drinking water treatment facilities, the North plant at 1955 Washington Avenue and the South Howard Berry plant at 7000 Marshall Road about a half mile west of Costco. Water to be treated comes from South Boulder Creek and the Northern Colorado Conservation District. South Boulder Creek supplies most of the untreated water. It is stored in Marshall Lake, Harper Lake, and Louisville Reservoir, which together hold about five thousand acre-feet of water. Louisville can also obtain additional water from Northern Water during times of drought and high demand. Northern Water obtains its water from west of the continental divide through the 1937 Colorado Big Thompson Project, which diverts water from Lake

Granby on the Colorado River via the Adams Tunnel to Mary's Lake, Lake Estes, and Carter Lake. A series of pipes, intermediate reservoirs, and canals then shuttle the water to where it is needed. Superior in turn has its water treatment plant at 1300 McCaslin Boulevard just south of Old Town. Water for Superior is obtained from Northern Water and stored in Terminal reservoir, next to the treatment plant. Terminal reservoir holds about 400 acre-feet or 130 million gallons of water, and Superior processes about 2 million gallons per day.

Sometime around noon, as the fire raced eastward, both the Louisville South Howard Berry plant and the Superior plant evacuated, lost electrical power, and were in the direct line of the fire. From that time forward, based on gravity feed, the previously treated water in their storage tanks was the only water available for firefighting in Superior and western Louisville. The Louisville North plant continued to supply additional treated water, but it could only maintain pressure for several additional hours as water consumption far exceeded its treatment capacity.

As water pressure dropped, Louisville Chief Water Plant Operator Greg Venette and Water Plant Operator Jeff Owens decided to connect Superior's water supply to Louisville's to maintain Superior's water pressure.[73] Driving against the evacuation traffic, they left the North plant and wound their way through the fires in Louisville and Superior to make it to the interconnect point at the South Howard Berry plant. Though surrounded by fires and nearby burning buildings, the plant was untouched by the fire. Arriving just after 1:00 p.m., Owens climbed to the top of a twenty-five-foot water tower. The wind was hurricane strength, and he physically crawled against it to visually check the water level at the center of the tank. They were low and dropping fast. The height of the water in the tank was now what supplied pressure for the hydrants as the electricity for the pumps was out.

Meanwhile, Kurt Kowar, the director of Louisville's Public Works, coordinated with the Town of Superior and Xcel Energy to prioritize turning electrical power back on to Superior's water plant. The power lines and gas lines were down going to the Louisville South plant, so he worked with the Boulder County OEM and Xcel Energy to arrange for portable natural gas tanks for the electric generators at Louisville's South plant. Kowar—along with Cory Peterson, Deputy Director of Utilities; Chris DePalma, Water Plant Operator; and Matt Fromandi, Water Plant Operator—took city trucks and drove to meet Xcel. There they hitched up to large natural gas tank trailers to attach to the electrical generators at the South plant. At high risk to themselves, they drove these trucks with explosive trailers attached through the fire zone against evacuating

[73] Based partly on the information posted at https://www.louisvilleco.gov/Home/Components/News/News/5679/17.

traffic to the South plant on Marshall Road. Once they arrived, they hooked the tanks to the generators, and started them to run the pumps and equipment needed to make the plant operational.

But the water pressure continued to drop, and the fire was still burning fiercely. Venette made the difficult decision to allow untreated water to enter the water system from Marshall Reservoir in the burn zone sometime after 6:00 p.m. He started the process of opening the series of bypass valves that allowed untreated water to fill the storage tanks and restore water pressure. A "boil water advisory" was issued at 7:38 p.m. for all of Louisville and for Superior the following day.

During the day, the Operations group of Ben Francisco, Assistant Manager of Operations; Shane Mahan, Operations Technician I; and Tom Czajka, Operations Technician II, evacuated city equipment from danger areas and assisted with traffic management by placing barricades. With traffic management under control, they headed over to the South plant late that night around 1:00 a.m. to check on Owens, Kowar, and Peterson, who were keeping the generator running and the plant providing water. But the water pressure continued to drop. More water was being consumed than could be pumped into the tanks, even using untreated water. Strategizing why, Francisco hypothesized that the lost water was draining out of open pipes in the hundreds of destroyed buildings. Water must be turned off individually at each ruined property to raise the pressure back up to fight the fire.

Kowar contacted Louisville Fire Chief Willson and explained their theory of why the water pressure was not increasing. Kowar told Willson his team would follow firefighters into the burn areas and turn off water at destroyed buildings. While Peterson and Venette stayed at the South plant to keep the generators running and maintain water levels, Kowar, Francisco, Mahan, and Czajka split up and began the tedious task of shutting off the water at each destroyed home and business. As they traveled with firefighters, they also closed off fire hydrants left open when firefighters evacuated quickly. They worked tirelessly throughout the night, turning off running water at the edge of each affected property and helping to increase pressure until 7:00 a.m. on December 31. Miraculously, the heroic efforts of these nine city employees kept the water flowing in both cities. Without them, more fire hydrants would have failed and more buildings burned.

Figure 51 Louisville Water and Operations staff who kept the water flowing. Photo courtesy of Louisville Public Works and Utilities.

At 6:57 p.m., Unit 524 called in to Police Dispatch that he cannot find any spot fires at the Louisville cemetery. At the same time, Police Dispatch called Unit 581 for a welfare check at the 1900 block of E. Coalton Drive in Superior as the residents had been drinking alcohol and did not feel safe driving to evacuate. A minute later, Unit 524 also informed Marshall Command that there was no fire at the cemetery. At 6:58 p.m., Unit 416 called in that car after car was turning onto S. Boulder Road from Roosevelt and causing traffic problems and asked for a police unit to close it. At 7:02 p.m., Unit 412 responded that Longmont law enforcement units Paul 204, 211, 225, and 304 were available to assist Louisville. Police Dispatch asked if Paul 211 could work traffic at S. Boulder and Roosevelt. Several units called in good night around this time. Paul 211 said he would head to S. Boulder Road, but his map didn't show Roosevelt intersecting.

Figure 52 Fire consuming homes along Eldorado Drive Superior. Photo: Code 10 Photography.

NREL, December 30, 2021, 7:00 p.m., Wind WSW 35 mph, Gusting to 47 mph 41°F

Numerous top national research laboratories are located near Boulder, and many of the employees and scientists who work there live in Superior and Louisville. The Marshall fire is personal to them. The National Center for Atmospheric Research (NCAR), National Oceanic and Atmospheric Administration (NOAA), and National Institute of Standards and Technology (NIST) all have research facilities located in Boulder. The National Renewable Energy Laboratory (NREL) is located along CO-128 just south of the start of the fire. And the University of Colorado (CU) has six institutes related to atmospheric and environmental science, including the Cooperative Institute for Research in the Environmental Sciences (CIRES), Lab for Atmospheric and Space Physics (LASP), Renewable and Sustainable Energy Institute (RASEI), and Sustainability, Energy, and Environment Complex (SEEC). Almost one hundred scientists discovered their homes were threatened by the fire, and many lost them.

The National Center for Atmospheric Research (NCAR) is nestled at the base of the Flatirons foothills above south Boulder. Established in 1960 by the National Science Foundation, NCAR's mission is:[74]

- To understand the behavior of the atmosphere and related Earth and geospace systems
- To support, enhance, and extend the capabilities of the university community and the broader scientific community, nationally and internationally
- To foster the transfer of knowledge and technology for the betterment of life on Earth

NCAR also undertakes wildfire research, including improving models of wildfire behavior; exploring air quality impacts of smoke plumes by using aircraft, drones, and other tools; and calculating the impact of climate change on wildfires. NCAR is trying to help firefighters by developing actionable tools to better predict weather, fire spread, smoke concentration, heat release, and fire-generated updrafts and downdrafts to deploy firefighting resources safely to protect lives and property.

[74] Adapted from https://ncar.ucar.edu/who-we-are.

One of the scientists working at NCAR is Dr. Janice Coen, who is a project scientist for the Mesoscale and Microscale Meteorology Laboratory. Dr. Coen uses advanced weather-fire computer models and other means to determine the factors leading to such events as megafires, fire whirls, and pyrocumulus. Her latest work concentrates on predicting fire growth and fire dynamics and ember spread in the wildland-urban interface. Having the Marshall and Middle Fork fires so near her home, Dr. Coen quickly developed a Coupled Atmosphere-Wildland Fire-Environment (CAWFE) model of the Marshall fire.[75] This model is based on a macro scale and does not provide sufficient granularity to identify why one building burns and another doesn't, but it does provide visualization of how the fire spreads. She also includes a model of what could have happened had the earlier Middle Fork fire north of Boulder not been contained.

Dr. Coen studies many wind-driven fires, both here in Colorado and in California. The Marshall fire occurred during a particularly heavy Chinook wind with gusts approaching one hundred miles per hour. She commented on what happened with the fire and wind in the Marshall fire[76]:

> The wind event is characterized by stable stratification of the air near the surface—i.e. it resists being lifted over topographic features and if it does, cools, and experiences a restoring force (gravity) pulling it back to its elevation of neutral buoyancy. As such, it is driven from behind by the wind but resists going over topographic features. I noted many tendrils of fire spread within drainages (such as Hwy 170 out of Marshall toward Superior), creeks, ditches next to sidewalks. Some of these are quite subtle (like the bike path through the riparian zone from Hwy 36 into the Coal Creek homes) and others I'd never taken note of (like the drainage and green belt up into Spanish Hills). Fire will (and did) climb the walls of the drainages channeling it, but it seems like the cold heavy air driving the fire made its way through many of these subtle topographic dips. (Evidence being the hardwoods in these narrow riparian zones along the creeks were incinerated in a downwind path while a short distance to either side was left untouched.) It was remarkable.

Dr. Coen has access to images from many different satellites. Most satellites have low-resolution images of the fire. But the Suomi NPP and NOAA-20 satellites carry the Visible Infrared Imaging Radiometer Suite (VIIRS) that provides fire and heat details in both daylight and nighttime. These two satellites transit over Colorado twice daily. On December 30 and 31, their crossings occurred six times during the major fire burn. The

[75] Dr. Janice Coen CAWFE models are at https://www2.mmm.ucar.edu/people/coen/files/newpage_m.html.

[76] Email from Dr. Janice Coen to author on March 26, 2022.

first VIIRS image was taken at 12:19 p.m. and clearly showed the fire burning hotly west, north, and east of the Costco shopping center in Superior and up to US-36. The second image at 1:07 p.m., forty-eight minutes later, showed the Costco shopping center surrounded by fire with Original Superior burning and the fire entrenched across US-36 behind the Home Depot in Louisville. The third, fourth, and fifth images taken just over twelve hours later, at 12:38 a.m., 1:26 a.m., and 2:18 a.m., showed the intense flames as buildings burned in both towns with residual heat still emanating from earlier fires in the burn zone. It is interesting to note that there was still a hot spot near where the fire originated in Marshall on images 3 and 4. And the last image, from 2:00 p.m. on December 31, only showed residual heat as the major fire had stopped spreading as snow moved into the area.

Fire Progression: Satellite Active Fire Detection Data from VIIRS
I-Band – 370 m pixels 2x daily (12:30-3 p.m. and a.m.) from each of 2 instruments

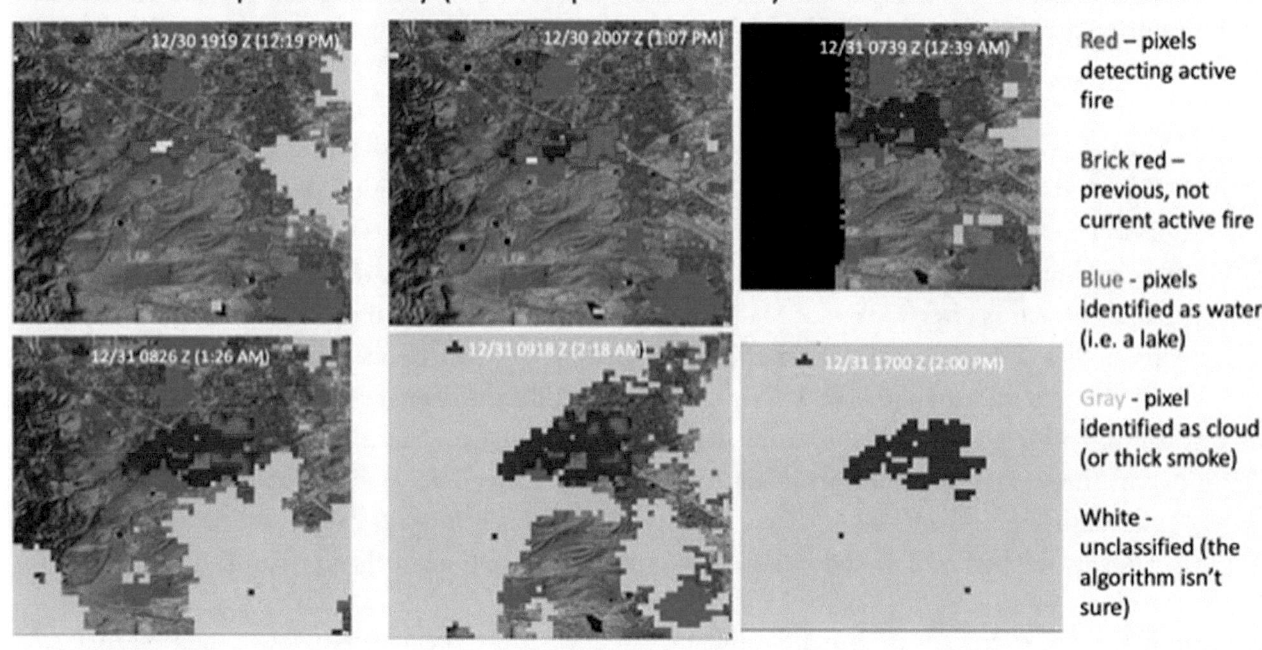

Figure 53 VIIRS Satellite images by Dr. Janice Coen. © University Corporation for Atmospheric Research.

Said Dr. Coen of the images,[77] "So much red indicates it moved so fast that even light fuels had some burning. Pockets of active burning at later times, which stay bright red, likely indicate housing, where fuels may burn for several hours."

The National Science Foundation (NSF) doesn't fund wildland fire research, but one University of Colorado scientist received an emergency grant from them as he was evacuating his Louisville home. He used it to send a drone aloft over the burn zone the next day, December 31, before the snow set in to gather important video of how the fire moved from open space to burn several nearby homes. He was on a team examining the relative flammability of different kinds of construction and used the drone to explore the surrounding landscape. Part of the NSF funding is also paying for a survey of four hundred people who lived in the perimeter of the fire to get a better sense of what started it and the damages it caused.

The National Oceanic and Atmospheric Administration (NOAA) and the University of Colorado's Cooperative Institute for Research in the Environmental Sciences (CIRES) partnered on air quality research after the fire.[78] They fielded the NOAA Chemical Sciences Laboratory's sophisticated mobile lab throughout Louisville and Superior. Mounted in a white cargo van, these scientists measured minute quantities of pollutants and air particles. Their analysis aimed to determine how atmospheric chemistry changes depending upon proximity to the fire, time of day, wind, and other factors. Miraculously, even when the winds were gusty like on the morning of January 11, the fire-caused emissions outdoors in Louisville and Superior were no worse than normal daytime air pollution. The previous snow and moisture dampened the ash sufficiently to minimize pollutant spread.

But what about homes that survived the fire but were exposed to long-term smoke and soot from burnt buildings? Very little scientific research exists on the effects to surviving buildings after a large urban fire like Marshall. With a rapid grant from the CIRES Innovative Research Program, scientists installed detailed instruments into one Superior home near the fire and lower-cost instruments in ten other homes throughout both communities. The data from these instruments identified the chemical composition of the air and dust left behind and allowed the team to evaluate the outcomes of various cleanup and mitigation techniques. Preliminary results are inconclusive, and only additional time will provide answers as to what cleanup techniques are the most effective and what the long-term health effects might be on returning to a surviving home.

---

[77] Email from Dr. Janice Coen to author, March 28, 2022.

[78] Adapted from CIRES Communications https://csl.noaa.gov/news/2022/340_0113.html.

Boulder County Public Health installed twenty-five air quality monitors throughout the Marshall fire burn area. These monitors track the volume of ultrafine pollutants and particulates that are 2.5 microns or less in width (PM2.5) and report the results per the EPA's US Air Quality Index (AQI). The AQI provides a value between 0 and 500 where less than 50 is good, less than 100 moderate, less than 150 unhealthy for sensitive persons, and less than 200 unhealthy for all. Each monitor is solar powered and reports results continuously that are then available on a map at the county website.[79] Current results show snow and moisture kept particulates low, which increased as areas dried out and during wind.

As 2021 was a La Niña year, 2022 was expected to be a transition year, or even an El Niño. However, by June it was apparent that La Niña was still entrenched in the ocean currents, and the winds were expected remain high and rain scarce. La Niña weather patterns have been occurring more frequently in the past twenty-odd years, which may account for the extended drought occurring in the west. Additional fires may be fueled by these stronger winds and continued drought. However, by July the monsoon began and Colorado received normal or above normal precipitation in most areas during 2022. Even though August and the summer itself were among the top five hottest ever, the monsoons kept the grasses green and the few forest fires minor. Of course, with only +150-years of tracking climate in Denver, "hottest ever" doesn't mean much.

[79] Boulder County air quality updates are at https://www.bouldercounty.org/disasters/wildfires/marshallfireaq/.

Figure 54 Fire burning Eldorado Drive in Superior around 7:00 p.m. Photo: Code 10 Photography.

At 7:09 p.m., Unit 524 called in that he was assisting an evacuation at 2390 Coalton Road in Superior. Unit 412 asked Unit 435 to relieve Unit 416 on traffic duty on S. Boulder Road at 7:11 p.m. At 7:15 p.m., Unit 527 radioed Police Dispatch that remaining day shift units should check out. Sufficient police units were now available from other jurisdictions to cover without extending the day shift further. Fire Dispatch called Marshall Command at 7:17 p.m. that an RV was reporting a thirty-by-thirty spot fire near the mesa trailhead at Eldorado Springs Drive and Foothills Highway. This was very near the site where the first fire was reported and may be related to a coal seam fire. At 7:18 p.m., Unit 435 called in that he was blocking Washington and McCaslin Boulevard in Louisville. Unit 527 asked Police Dispatch to direct Deputy 643 to the Foothills Highway call to assist at 7:19 p.m. Unit 643 acknowledged.

At 7:20 p.m., Lincoln 18 called Police Dispatch that they received a page to go to the county lot. Police Dispatch responded that they did not have a record of such a page. Lincoln 18 responded that they will ignore it and stay engaged on the tactical channel. Additional day units checked out for the evening. Dispatch announced very few new calls during this time as all units were coordinating firefighting on tactical channels and police units were also monitoring them for assistance and evacuations. At 7:31 p.m., Police Dispatch called out a fire in the backyard of 773 W. Fir Court south of the major burn area of W. Mulberry St. in Louisville. Fire Dispatch forwarded the backyard fire to Marshall Command two minutes later. The Fir Court fire was confined to shrubs and bushes, and the house was not damaged by the flames. Unit 581 called in code 2 at McCaslin and Marshall Road in Superior at 7:35 p.m. This area is between the major fires in Original Superior and the Element Hotel. As the Louisville Water Department bypassed the water treatment plant to increase water pressure, the city issued a "boil water" notice for all residents at 7:38 p.m.

At 7:41 p.m., County Dispatch toned Lafayette Medic 2621 and Engine 2602 to US-287 and Baseline Road for a two-car accident. Police Dispatch simultaneously informed Lincoln 61 that one party reported a back injury, and the other party refused to provide their contact and insurance information. Lincoln 15 and Lincoln 52 both responded. Lincoln 15 arrived first and announced that the crash had no injuries at 7:42 p.m. Fire Dispatch canceled 2621 and 2602. Lincoln 15 called in that he was moving the vehicles to the gas station nearby.

At 7:45 p.m., Unit 4733 called County Dispatch and asked if anyone else had lost fire hydrant pressure in Louisville. Fire Dispatch responded that they were the first to report it. Marshall Command then reported that Louisville hydrant pressure was dropping in other areas as well. Water pressure at the time hit a low of about a third of normal. Louisville Public Works desperately tried to bypass filtration and connect untreated water directly from Marshall Lake to Louisville's water supply to boost pressure. Fire Dispatch acknowledged the water pressure drop and informed Marshall Command that the fire was flaring up around the Home Depot in Louisville for a fourth time.

Figure 55 Firefighters battled flames along Discovery Parkway in Superior about 8:30 p.m. Photo: Code 10 Photography

At 7:51 p.m., County Dispatch toned Lafayette Engine 2602 to the 1078 S. Eighty-eighth Street living complex to help with a call for a missing evacuee. This was just east of Avista Hospital in Louisville, and the fire was burning both northwest and southwest of the address. The missing person was an eighty-five-year-old nonambulatory female, and the building supervisor could not locate her among the other evacuees and was afraid that she was still in the building. Lafayette Medic 2622 responded that they would respond, and Unit 2602 stayed available.

At 8:05 p.m., County Dispatch toned Lafayette Engine 2602 and Louisville Medic 2722 to Seventy-fifth and Arapahoe north of the fire zone for a multicar accident. Police Unit 831 also responded. A few seconds later, County Dispatch toned Hygiene Units 2802 and 589 to an address on Sixty-third Street near the same location for an eighty-year-old unconscious party at an Airbnb. Police Dispatch provided Unit 589 additional instructions for accessing the property. A minute later, Lafayette Medic 2622 called County Dispatch for the access code to the building on Eighty-eighth Street to look for the missing person. They also asked for a Louisville law officer to help search. Fire Dispatch responded at 8:07 p.m. that they did not have the door access code, but Unit 2622 replied that they had found an open window and were inside. At that time, Police Dispatch called out a fire alarm at the industrial bakery at 185 S. 104th Street in Louisville. This will prove to be just smoke and was cleared by 8:23 p.m.

Louisville Middle School, December 30, 2021, 8:08 p.m., Wind E 1 mph, Gusting to 12 mph 42°F

At 8:10 p.m., Lincoln 42 called in that there was a lot of traffic southbound on SR-42 coming from downtown Louisville and asked if the road reopened. Lincoln 59 responded that the road was still closed at Empire Road, but the traffic may be coming from late evacuees leaving. Police Unit 831 called Police Dispatch to ask if there were additional directions to the multicar accident as he cannot locate anything at Seventy-fifth and Arapahoe. Police Dispatch replied negative and 831 said he will keep looking. Lafayette Engine 2602 also asked where the accident was located. Unit 831 stated it was west of Seventy-fifth on Arapahoe and no parties were injured. Lafayette Engine 2602 was waved off. Hygiene Unit 2802 called in at 8:12 p.m. that they were on-site for the elderly unconscious person and started CPR.

Police Dispatch called out at 8:15 p.m. that the fire was ten feet away from the home at 145 Barcelona Drive in Paragon Estates just south of S. Boulder Road. This home survived, but the house next to it will be destroyed. An additional unconscious elderly female and two ambulatory evacuee calls will be announced in the next few minutes that Paramedic 430 will cover. At 8:28 p.m., County Dispatch informed Marshall Command that they received a call that the owners of 85 Barcelona near Spanish Hills left a large box of fireworks in the backyard for New Year's Eve celebrations that might explode. Luckily, the fire stopped two houses south of this address, and the fireworks were saved for later theatrics.

Figure 56 Close-up view off Discovery Parkway in Superior. Photo: Code 10 Photography.

Also at 8:28 p.m., Police Dispatch sent Unit 104 to an apartment at 750 Copper Lane in Louisville for a possible female evacuation assist. And again at 8:32 p.m., County Dispatch requested Lafayette Medic 2622 and Nederland Rescue 5621 to help with another nonambulatory female evacuation at a trailer at 400 W. South Boulder Road in Louisville. Even though the fire had been raging for over eight hours and evacuation posted for five hours, calls for help evacuating continued to come in and were handled as a priority. At 8:34 p.m., Unit 104 called in that the evacuee on Copper Lane was awaiting a ride from a relative. Police Dispatch called back that the ride was at the roadblock guarded by Unit 1-David-25. Unit 104 stated he would take the evacuee to the roadblock. At 8:42 p.m., Lafayette Medic 2622 called in that they were taking their evacuee to the Lafayette YMCA evacuation center.

At 8:43 p.m., Unit 412 called Police Dispatch asking for relief for Unit 416 performing traffic control at south Boulder and Washington in Louisville. Police Dispatch asked if a Longmont unit could assist, and Longmont Unit 225 responded she will head there. At 8:46 p.m., Louisville Bus 2722 called in that they were deploying to Trail Ridge and Washington in Louisville for a medical situation. The fire was burning fiercely a block or so away. Numerous other law enforcement units called in with new location updates.

Fire Dispatch toned Louisville Medic 2723 to Grant Avenue in Louisville to help with a blind evacuee at 8:48 p.m. At that same time, Lafayette Medic 2622 called in that they were at the YMCA and were back available. At 8:51 p.m., County Dispatch called Marshall Command to send a unit to the Superior city water plant at 1300 McCaslin as a generator there had caught fire. Power was still off in Superior, and generators were the only way to pump water into the treatment center and out to the hydrants to fight the fire. Police Dispatch also requested a law enforcement unit to go to the water plant. At 8:52 p.m., Louisville Medic 2722 reported clear, and Longmont 225 reported on-site. Unit 420 called County Dispatch at 8:54 p.m. that the evacuee they were trying to help was in a motorized wheelchair and refused to evacuate without it. They requested another unit with a wheelchair lift to help. Louisville Medic 2723 called at 8:55 p.m. that the blind party on Grant refused to leave with them and requested law enforcement be called in. They also reported out of service. Police Dispatch called Paul 204 to Grant Avenue to assist with the blind evacuee at 8:56 p.m. Numerous units called in around this time as end of shift and out of service.

Figure 57 Burning homes along Canary Lane in Superior about 8:30 p.m. Photo: Code 10 Photography.

As the wind shifted around, the fire spread back westward. Pictures showed it burning back down Marshall Mesa toward Eldorado Springs around 9:00 p.m. Other pictures showed the conflagration still burning hotly in the Coal Creek Ranch subdivision in Louisville and burning along Dillon Road the furthest to the east that it will reach.

Paul 204 arrived at Grant Avenue in Louisville at 9:02 p.m. and asked how to find fire (Louisville Medic 2723). Through several communications, County Dispatch and Police Dispatch assured 204 that she was at the correct address. Paul 204 responded she will talk with the person and try to convince them to evacuate. At 9:06 p.m., she called in that she was talking with him. By 9:16 p.m., she called in that he was evacuating.

At 9:04 p.m., Police Dispatch called Unit 412 that a party at the Ninety-sixth and Dillon roadblock would like an escort to Ridgeview Drive in Louisville to pick up chemo medications. Unit 412 responded that he needed to check on fires in the area before responding. MVFR Medic 2224 called in at that time that they were on Longs Peak Drive in Louisville nonemergency. Longmont 225 called in at 9:09 p.m. that numerous cars were sneaking back into Louisville at Linden off Washington and asked to relocate there. A Louisville unit responded that they would cover it.

Several units including Nederland Fire reported that they were clear for the evening at 9:15 p.m. Fire Dispatch thanked them for their help and said that they were caught up for now. With the winds abating, the fire was not spreading as rapidly, and firefighters were effective in keeping the fire contained. Water pressure was still an issue, but water tenders kept all engines active in the battle against the blaze.

Unit 441 called into Police Dispatch at 9:17 p.m. requesting help with a hurt cow at Sixty-sixth and Marshall Road in unincorporated Boulder County. Unit 631 responded they will come. At 9:22 p.m., Unit 631 asked for a city ranger to help with the request as he was unclear whether the cow was on city or private land. A minute later, Police Dispatch responded that a ranger was on the way.

Figure 58 Firefighters tackled the flames along Canary Lane in Superior about 8:30 p.m. Photo: Code 10 Photography.

At 9:20 p.m., Police Dispatch called Paul 204 that Community Care Health Alliance had an ambulance to help evacuate a resident in an apartment at 1130 S. Kestrel Lane in Louisville, but the resident wasn't answering the door. They asked for police assistance to gain entrance. At 9:26 p.m., Paul 204 responded he was on-site at Kestrel Lane looking for the ambulance. At 9:43 p.m., Paul 204 called clear at the Kestrel address, and Wagon 435 called in that they were in transit to the YMCA with the Kestrel evacuee. At 9:50 p.m., Unit 435 announced arrival at the YMCA.

At 9:25 p.m., Police Dispatch called out a fire at the BCH Urgent Care at 3 Superior Drive. This address was in central Superior, south of Rock Creek and just west across US-36 from the burning Rock Creek Ranch subdivision in Louisville. Two police units responded along with fire, but the facility was damaged and remained closed for three months. The Boulder OEM issued a release to avoid evacuation zones, saying that no one will be allowed into the evacuation area overnight. Even firefighters didn't know the status of their own homes in the burn zone as they fought the fire, protecting others. Natural gas was turned off throughout most of Louisville and Superior, and electricity was off in many areas.

At 9:28 p.m., Police Dispatch announced that a 911 caller from Longmont claimed to see a large fire in Niwot and asked Police Unit 589 to check it out. Deputy Units 643 and 631 responded that they were in Niwot, and they will handle the call. They didn't find any blaze in Niwot and suspected the Longmont caller saw the Marshall fire at 9:33 p.m. With the winds subsiding and the darkness full on, the glow from the fire could be seen for miles around, even in Longmont fifteen miles to the north.

Unit 412 called Police Dispatch at 9:37 p.m. asking her to redirect the Ridgeview Drive chemo medication escort to Paul 304. He further stated that, though there was fire in the area, they should be safe if they used W. Cherry Street to transit from Ninety-sixth and Dillon. Paul 304 confirmed. Several additional units called in good night, including Nederland Wagon 5621 and Lincoln 24 at 9:40 p.m. At 9:49 p.m., Paul 304 arrived at Ninety-sixth and Dillon and asked Police Dispatch who they were to meet. Paul 304 confirmed that she had the party on board at 9:52 p.m., and they were in transit to Ridgeview Drive to pick up the medication. They arrived at Ridgeview Drive successfully at 9:56 p.m. and made it back safely to Ninety-sixth and Dillon by 10:00 p.m. They witnessed the fire's extreme devastation during their transits.

At 11:05 p.m., the Boulder OEM announced that a media briefing will be held the next day at the sheriff's office at 10:00 a.m. The briefing will include remarks from Sheriff Joe Pelle, Gov. Jared Polis, and various fire officials. No members of the public were permitted, and all were invited to watch on local news or the live internet stream.

Firefighters and law officials toiled tirelessly through the night battling the blaze. The wind calmed, and burning ash was no longer flying blocks away causing additional carnage. Most remaining daytime law enforcement officers and deputies checked out for the evening around ten. Commander Wilber stayed at the command post at Nordstrom's until about 1:30 a.m. He was really concerned about possible missing officers and residents caught by the fast-moving fire. In all his twenty-plus years of experience, this was the fastest-moving, craziest fire he had ever seen. Miraculously, at midnight, only four persons were officially listed as missing, and all officers and firefighters were accounted for. He left for the night knowing that he would be back in the morning and the next few days working through how to get residents back home and to a sense of normalcy.

The task for those staying through the rest of the night was to save as many buildings as possible.

Louisville Manorwood Lane, December 31, 2021, 8:01 a.m., Wind Calm 29°F

After spending the night with his daughter's family in Loveland, Paul Williamson drove back to Louisville before 8:00 a.m. on Friday, December 31. He cut past the roadblocks and wound through town, finally taking Cherry Street west to McCaslin. There he saw firsthand the devastation from the fire. Burned-out businesses and trees intermixed with perfect buildings to the west of the street. A torched SUV sat just east of McCaslin on Dillon Road seemingly isolated from other devastation. Buildings still smoldered. The power was out, so the stoplights were strangely blank. He parked his car and hiked past the roadblocked onto McCaslin bridge over US-36 tying Louisville to Superior. From the far side, his worst fears were confirmed. His home for the past seven years was gone. The Element Hotel was gone. The Tesla dealership was damaged but still standing. The museum was gone. His whole neighborhood had been devastated and mostly was just a smoldering morass of twisted metal.

Additional firefighters and police officers continued to arrive from throughout the state on the second day to help control the blaze. Trucks from as far away as Durango came to Boulder County. They staged at Macy's and were directed to one of the seven firefighting commands from there. Sheriff Commander Wilber also returned to the command center to coordinate police efforts. Xcel Energy assigned employees to work at Nordstrom's with command to help manage utility repairs with firefighters and law enforcement. Utility workers converged there from companies like LG&E in Louisville, Kentucky, and KS Energy Services of New Berlin, Wisconsin. They drove all night and arrived the next day to help restore electrical and gas services to the stricken communities. These employees worked tirelessly to turn off services to the destroyed buildings, isolate them, and then restart services to the unaffected buildings.

At 8:32 a.m., the Boulder OEM posted a notice that all evacuation areas were to be avoided by civilians. Active hot spots still existed, downed power lines may still be hot, and burned trees were a risk of falling.

First responders were diligently working to secure each area to allow residents to check on their properties. Residents entering the area took resources away from emergency responders and hindered efforts to extinguish hot spots, search the area, assess damage, and conduct fire investigation. The OEM also announced that all trails were closed in the burn area, and US-36 remained closed.

Nearby areas not evacuated were also affected by power outages. At 10:15 a.m., the OEM announced that Xcel Energy had restored electrical power to many neighborhoods and was working on additional. Residents without power were asked to keep their refrigerator and freezer doors closed to minimize temperature fluctuations as outages may continue into New Year's Eve. If possible, frozen meat should be transferred to iced coolers if power outages extended beyond eight hours. A single light can be turned on in the home to alert residents when power was restored. As gas stoves and ovens should never be used for home heating, residents without power were urged to use an external generator to power electrical heat.

Sheriff Pelle hosted a 10:00 a.m. news conference that included an updated map[80] of the fire zone. This map illustrated that the fire had consumed over 6,000 acres so far. Over 1,700 houses were located within the burn zone, and 580 houses were confirmed destroyed. Sheriff Pelle commented that he will not be surprised if that number exceeded 1,000 homes burned. The map included the seven tactical zones used to battle the fire. Sheriff Pelle and Governor Polis shared that they flew over the burn area and witnessed the devastation earlier. With the wind abating and significant snow forecast, the fire was not expected to spread. But firefighters stressed that the fire remained uncontained, many hot spots still burned fiercely, and residents will not be permitted into the closed area until the fire was under control.

[80] The OEM December 31, 2021, press conference summary is at https://www.boulderoem.com/press-conference-summary-12-31-21-at-10-a-m/.

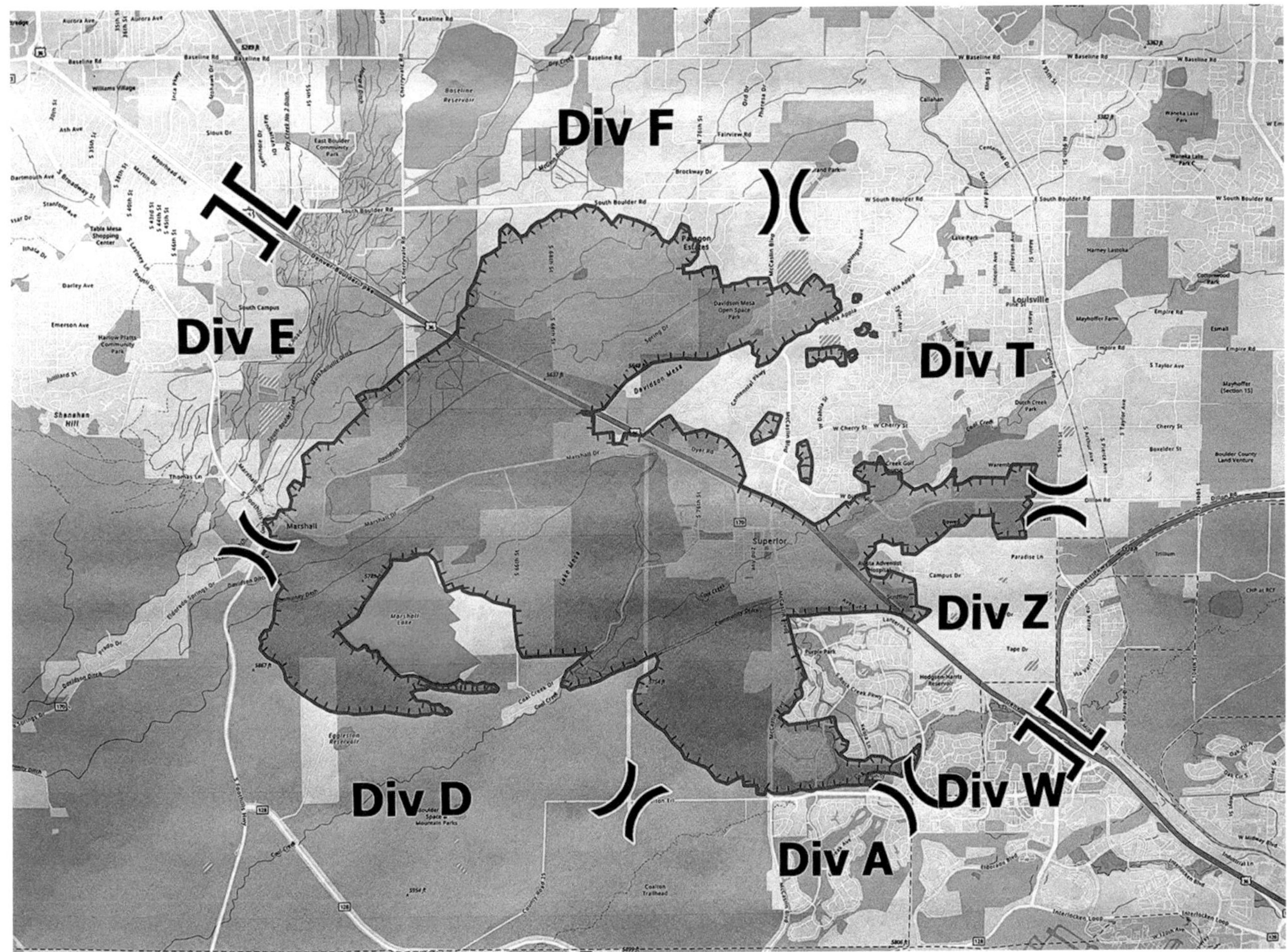

Figure 59 December 31, 2021, 6:00 a.m. map of burn area including firefighting resource allocation. Courtesy of the Boulder OEM.

Miraculously, less than 200 residents out of 37,500 evacuated stayed in the opened shelters overnight. All the remaining evacuees found other places to stay. With no real demand, the North Boulder Recreation Center shelter closed by noon on December 31, 2021. The Lafayette YMCA and Rocky Mountain Christian Church in Niwot stayed open to handle the few evacuees who still need a place to stay the second night, New Year's Eve.

Xcel Energy reported to the OEM that they had examined their equipment in Marshall near where the fire started. They found no downed power lines in that area. They did locate compromised low-voltage communication lines that may have been mistaken by residents reporting the fire as power lines. The OEM reported this at 1:04 p.m. and commented that communication lines such as telephone, cable TV, and internet typically cannot start a fire. The OEM stated fire investigation was ongoing.

At 1:55 p.m., Louisville mayor Ashley Stolzmann announced that electrical power had been restored to most of the non-evacuated city residents, but 15,000 residents remained without power. All Louisville evacuation orders remained in effect, and only those in Old Town and north of S. Boulder Road were permitted to return home. A boil water order also stayed in effect for Louisville.

Town officials wanted to reopen evacuated areas as quickly as possible so that homeowners could return and stave off additional damage from freezing pipes from the frigid weather expected that night. But firefights still needed to put out hot spots, and utility workers must review gas and electric equipment. Police controlled access and roadblocks appropriately to prioritize these needs. Commander Wilber and the command team at Nordstrom's worked tirelessly to balance these conflicting objectives and created a plan to safely open as many areas as possible as soon as possible. They will direct utility, police, and firefighting resources out of Nordstrom's for the next couple of days to meet these objectives.

At 3:00 p.m., the Town of Superior reopened the evacuated area south of Coalton Road between Highway 128 and Rock Creek Parkway to residents through screened access from Highway 128. They also opened the Bell Flatirons Apartments with access from S. Tyler Drive. Xcel expected to restore electricity to these areas soon, but natural gas would not be available. As temperatures were expected to be below freezing overnight, Xcel provided free electric space heaters at the YMCA in Boulder on Fourteenth Street and the YMCA shelter in Lafayette. Returning residents were cautioned to drive slowly and be alert to hazards and firefighting activities. Hot spots and weakened trees will exist. Once they returned, residents were asked to remain in their homes. At 3:44 p.m., the OEM posted that US-36, the Denver-Boulder Turnpike, was now open through Boulder County. However, the McCaslin Boulevard exits remained closed.

Firefighting efforts continued throughout Friday with snow arriving in the afternoon. Luckily, breezes remained light, and the fire did not spread but continued to burn hotly in many locations. Firefighting resources continued to rotate in and out, and by late afternoon, the fire was estimated to be about 35 percent contained. The snowfall lingered throughout the night. Though over eight inches of snow blanketed the fire during its second day, the blaze was not considered 100 percent contained until five days after it started. Hundreds of firefighters continued to fight spot fires and hot spots for days throughout the burn zone.

On Friday, New Year's Eve, with the snow falling, there was little news. Most residents could only wonder about the fate of their property. The University of Colorado estimated that over 1,300 of its students, faculty, and employees were affected by the evacuation. A special location was set up to help CU students and employees with emergency food, housing, financial assistance, and other support.[81] Additionally, the Boulder campus cleaned up numerous downed trees from the strong winds that also caused power outages there. Many windows were broken by the Chinook winds, and the later freezing temperatures caused pipes to burst and flood numerous buildings on campus. As a result, and with COVID still about, CU announced that the spring semester will begin fully remote.

In conjunction with Colorado State University Extension, the Boulder County OEM rushed the pamphlet "After the Disaster Guidebook—Boulder County" to press on December 31. Though in the works for some time, they completed it and sent it to print so that it would be available for the many households affected by the disaster. They knew that homeowners would need a simple booklet that includes checklists of what to do and resources on who can help once they discovered that their home was destroyed. The booklet included sections on immediate safety, communications, mental health, returning to your property, insurance and finance, and tips on handling debris and caring for animals. Based on the experiences of homeowners from the Pine Gulch and Cameron Peak fires, the booklet included many firsthand accounts. It was rushed to print to be available when the Disaster Assistance Center opened and was also quickly posted online.

On New Year's Eve, the temperature hit a high of 37° then started falling in early morning. Winds remained calm in the morning but flared to about 10 mph when the snowstorm arrived in the afternoon. The snow fell all night and coated the area with up to eight inches, hiding the devastation under a mantle of white. Firefighters breathed a sigh of relief as fire had a hard time spreading in these conditions. Even though it was only considered 35 percent contained, the worst of the conflagration was past.

Knowing his home and possessions were gone, Jase and his family drove all day on Friday, December 31. After eight hours on the road, they spent a quiet New Year's Eve at a Holiday Inn in Lubbock, Texas. They got up the next day and drove home to his folks to stay until they figured out what to do next.

---

[81] Based on a story at https://denvergazette.com/news/local/dozens-of-cu-boulder-students-and-staff-impacted-by-marshall-fire/article_7a3c977a-6dbd-11ec-9bba-1b5326d8e6bf.html.

Rocky Mountain Metro Airport, January 1, 2022, 8:45 a.m., Wind Calm 5°F

Though Larry and Mary Boven didn't know it, both of their sons snuck through the roadblocks in Louisville back to the Centennial Heights West subdivision early on New Year's Day. They couldn't believe the devastation. Not only was their parents' house gone, but the whole neighborhood was nothing but a smoldering moonscape. All the trees were burned. Only one or two houses still stood, and these were obviously damaged. They went back to Longmont to their sister's house and told Larry and Mary the bad news. Larry didn't even want to see it. He had witnessed enough burned-out buildings in his role as a fireman. He decided to find a hotel short term and then look for someplace longer term to live until they could rebuild.

Figure 60 View of Centennial Heights West subdivision taken mid-March three months after the fire.

Becki Siemers woke up in the new year and confirmed that Balfour's eastern facilities were safe. They never lost power or natural gas but were without potable water. She asked the maintenance crew to verify each building was safe and turn on the air and heat throughout. She then began the arduous task of planning the logistics needed to return the assisted and skilled nursing residents home.

First, she requested drinking water through the emergency assistance center. The response was overwhelming. Over the next two days, trucks and U-Hauls delivered cases and cases of bottled water to Balfour. Conference rooms overflowed with it. Water won't be a problem.

She then checked on her staff members. All were physically unhurt, but two had lost their homes, and one member's home had suffered damage. A few also strained backs moving the nursing residents during the evacuation. And one had COVID. She organized the rest to bring the assisted living residents back from Frasier Meadows in Boulder. They started the tedious process early that afternoon of loading up the residents with their overnight bags and returning them to their rooms. The returning residents were relieved to find that everything at Balfour looked normal—the lights all worked, the heat was on, and there was little smoke smell. Her staff cautioned each that the tap water was contaminated and to use the provided bottles of water for drinking and brushing teeth. But with the exposure to COVID during the moves, Siemers made the difficult decision to quarantine everyone to their rooms. As one resident[82] put it, "After being evacuated, we got to celebrate the New Year locked in our rooms with a cold hot dog for dinner."

Moving the skilled nursing residents home took more effort. With time available, Siemers coordinated with other Balfour facilities to obtain additional vehicles with handicap lifts to move the nonambulatory patients back to the nursing facility. Nursing staff accompanied each vehicle and ensured each resident was comfortable during the transfer home. Though it took time, they were all moved and returned to the first-floor facilities safely.

Siemers commented that though the evacuation was stressful, all the residents did very well. None were physically injured during the moves. The biggest problems encountered involved emotional issues and maintaining sugar levels. Five nursing patients under hospice care did pass away soon afterward and may have lived longer had they not been evacuated. And over sixty cases of COVID spread throughout the facilities and staff during the following week. Miraculously, none were life threatening.

---

[82] Based on telephone conversation between author's mother and resident friend on January 1, 2022.

And all the remaining cases of water? Siemers laughed. "Right after the city turned the drinking water back on, Balfour Riverfront lost their potable water. So we packed up truckloads of our remaining cases and sent it to them." Had Louisville not been evacuated, Riverfront would be searching for water for its residents, another miracle.

After spending a quiet night putting out spot fires and hosing down hot spots, firefighting crews rotated, and fewer were required. The Boulder OEM and tactical command at Nordstrom's remained open throughout the night, and the OEM issued an update at 2:38 a.m. January 1 that only three persons were currently missing—two from Superior, one from Marshall, and none from Louisville. Sheriff Pelle expected to look for the missing persons using search and rescue dogs later in the morning if the snow will allow it. City and county officials also started the task of recording what buildings and addresses had been damaged and destroyed by the fire. The OEM posted at 9:35 a.m. that Xcel Energy had begun the process of restarting natural gas lines in the affected areas. Residents should not contact Xcel requesting relights. With help from outside companies, Xcel will follow an established process to efficiently restore natural gas service to each area. At 10:48 a.m., the OEM posted that Superior was shutting off water in the burn area to restore pressure and keep the pipes from freezing. With natural gas and electricity shut off in many areas, freezing pipes were a major concern.

Figure 61 Hazmat crews gathered to inspect damage. Photo: Code 10 Photography.

Boulder Hazmat crews started the work of deciding how dangerous the fumes and burn residues of businesses were early that Saturday morning. With eight inches of snow on the ground, teams from around Colorado gathered in Superior and started at the skeleton of the Element Hotel. Only twisted metal and the brick elevator shaft remained of this once-proud hotel. They also checked out the nearby burned-out Tesla dealership and then moved across US-36 to the damaged businesses in Louisville's Centennial shopping area. Carefully ensuring no danger existed, they first extinguished any hot spots before starting their investigation. At each site, they took samples of ash and debris for hazardous components as well as air samples for analysis. With all the snow, miraculously most contaminants were tamped down and diluted, and very few locations required immediate remediation efforts.

On day 3, the outpouring of support from the community and nation became overwhelming. The OEM posted a notice at 12:56 p.m. requesting no additional physical donations be delivered to the evacuation centers or to Sister Carmen. They recommended making financial donations through the Community Foundation, Red Cross, and Sister Carmen, and signing up to volunteer. Donations of materials, food, water, and services could be registered on the OEM's website. Airbnb's "Open Homes" program was recommended to list available short-term housing for victims. At 1:02 p.m., the OEM announced that the Rocky Mountain Christian Church shelter had closed. The YMCA of Lafayette remained open for those few evacuees who had not yet located a place to stay. The Y also offered free electrical heaters through the Xcel program for those who needed them. They ran out of heaters by 1:20 p.m., and the YMCA in Boulder became the only location short term with heaters (additional ones were delivered to the Lafayette YMCA by 2:45 p.m.).

Figure 62 Twisted metal and elevator shaft remains of the Superior Element Hotel. Photo: Code 10 Photography.

Sheriff Pelle hosted another update at 2:00 p.m. on Saturday, January 1. During it, he reported that the confirmed number of structures destroyed now stood at 991 with another 127 damaged. He listed 553 buildings destroyed and 45 damaged in Louisville, 332 structures destroyed and 60 damaged in Superior, and 106 destroyed and 22 damaged in unincorporated Boulder County. A preliminary list and map of the affected buildings was posted to be updated as new information was received. He also noted that there were no known deaths currently, but three people remained missing. As for the cause of the fire, he verified it remained under investigation. Though low communication lines were down near where the fire started, no downed power lines were identified at the ignition location. He confirmed a search warrant had been issued.

Figure 63 House at Arapahoe Circle and Willow Place in Louisville still standing with basketball net ready to play. The adjoining houses are all gone.

The randomness of the fire is hard to understand. Touring the area, it seems one or two houses survived nearly untouched in every burned-out neighborhood. Fences and adjoining trees and shrubs may be burnt, but miraculously, a house stands with seemingly minor damage here and there. Often windows are gone, so smoke damage is an issue. But the home still stands, ready for the family to renovate and come home.

Though most of Superior and unincorporated Boulder County stayed under firm evacuations, Louisville issued "hard closure" and "soft closure" zones on Saturday afternoon.[83] No nonofficial vehicles were allowed into the hard-closure zone for any reason as the fire was still active. Residents were allowed access to soft-closure areas through checkpoints where resident IDs were verified. Those accessing the soft closure areas were asked to only drive during the day and plan to spend their time at their property only. They were cautioned that many hazards will exist, including weakened trees, smoldering fires, and exposed sharp objects. Electricity and natural gas may not be available, though Xcel was providing free space heaters for those with electricity to protect pipes from tonight's anticipated deep freeze. Potable water was also not available throughout the city, and residents should bring their own. Food in refrigerators and freezers where the electricity had been off should be considered suspect, and the city will provide dumpsters in strategic areas for food disposal. Only these dumpsters should be used as it was unclear when citywide trash service would be restored. Residents were requested not to place any electronics, fire debris, hazardous materials, or ash into these dumpsters. Other dumpsters will be provided for these items later. With this notice, Louisville residents started returning home. Many discovered their houses standing but uninhabitable due to smoke and ash accumulation.

[83] Extracted from https://www.boulderoem.com/re-entry-information-for-louisville-updated-corrected-soft-and-hard-closure-details-here/.

The OEM updated the fire status map online to reflect these closure zones. It also made the map searchable by address to allow residents to determine whether they could visit their property. During the day, the map was updated numerous times as additional areas were cleared by emergency personnel. The 7:14 p.m. appraisal included more soft and hard closures for Louisville and added two soft closure neighborhoods in Superior.

Louisville also posted at 8:00 p.m.[84] that a Disaster Assistance Center will open at 1755 S. Public Road in Lafayette on Sunday from 12:00 p.m. to 5:00 p.m. for residents who had lost their home or had severe damage. The center will be manned by representatives from FEMA and Boulder County Housing and Human Services to provide short-term assistance. Residents will be able to connect directly with DOLA, FEMA, various insurance providers, and human services to obtain mental health services, food, clothing, housing, and financial assistance. Louisville also announced that bottled water and "grab-'n'-go" meals will be available for all ages at the recreation center starting Monday. The library also opened on Sunday without heat for free access to computers, printers, and Wi-Fi. All other city services remained closed.

[84] Based partly on https://www.louisvilleco.gov/Home/Components/News/News/5530/17?arch=1&npage=2.

Superior, January 2, 2022, 8:45 a.m., Wind Calm 5°F

With the colder weather and snow, the containment numbers on the fourth day of the fire officially surpassed 62 percent. Firefighters reported flare-ups and rekindling of structures previously burned as they dried out. Some fire-weakened structures also collapsed with the weight of the snow. Firefighters methodically secured each structure to ensure that residents could return to the area.

Working tirelessly, firefighters, Xcel Energy, city officials, and county deputies structured a plan to open additional areas in Superior. As a result, the Town of Superior announced changing ten additional hard closures to soft closures by noon. These were the following:

- South Pitkin Avenue
- East Gill Way
- East Heartstrong Street
- South Elbert Court
- Vernon Lane
- Campo Way
- Masters Court
- Eldorado Circle
- Edison Place
- South Indiana Street from Rock Creek Parkway to Eldorado Circle/Drive intersection

At 6:00 p.m., Superior updated this list of soft closures to include Creekside, Circle Park, and the Ridge, including the area from the intersection of Rock Creek Parkway and McCaslin south to Coalton Road and east to the intersection with Coalton Road and Rock Creek Parkway. They also changed South Sixty-eighth south to the Davidson Ditch and all areas accessible off South Sixty-eighth as soft closures.

They cautioned residents that identification proving residency will be required to reenter the area. Gas, electricity, and water may be unavailable. Food in freezers and refrigerators should be considered as contaminated if the power was out. N95 masks were suggested due to the large amount of smoke and ash in the air. Residents should only return to their property and not wander about as this could affect fire and response operations in the area.

Firefighters and housing inspectors continued reviewing homes and structures in and near the burn area. Inspections followed recommendations made by the Applied Technology Council (ATC), a nonprofit corporation that provides advanced engineering applications for hazard mitigation. Its ATC-45 Field Manual provides advice on evaluating structural, geotechnical, and nonstructural risks for buildings affected by a disaster. Though ATC offers a Detailed Evaluation procedure, inspectors now followed the Rapid Evaluation procedures. They marked each structure inspected with a colored card based on completing the ATC-45 Rapid Evaluation form. GREEN cards indicated that the building had been inspected and was deemed safe. YELLOW cards meant the building had the issues listed on the card, and only RESTRICTED USE was advised. RED cards marked the building as UNSAFE for the listed issues. Residents returning home and finding one of these cards could call the phone number listed on the card for additional information.

Governor Jared Polis and FEMA Administrator Deanne Criswell flew over the Marshall and Middle Fork burn areas early January 2 and then hosted a news conference at noon. During the conference, Governor Polis confirmed that the FBI was investigating the cause of the fires. Said Polis, "If there was any form of deliberate or accidental arson, I fully expect that any of those responsible will be held fully responsible under the law for the utter devastation that was caused."[85] They also announced that one missing person had been found safe and unharmed. Two others remained unaccounted—one from the Marshall area and one from western Superior.

FEMA Administrator Deanne Criswell also confirmed that a unified assistance center will be running seven days a week from 9:00 a.m. to 7:00 p.m. at 1755 S. Public Road, Lafayette. Though affected residents should first notify their primary insurance company, other assistance organizations will be available with a single visit. Many insurance companies, FEMA, SBA, Boulder County Housing and Human Services, Mental Health Partners, and nonprofit relief agencies will be on-site. Rapid COVID tests will also be available.

By 1:30 p.m., the OEM posted that Animal Rescue was close to completing its list of live animal rescues from fire locations. Residents were requested to contact the Boulder Humane Society for found animals and to receive information on how to file a report for any missing animal.

---

[85] Based in part from https://www.cpr.org/2022/01/02/boulder-county-fires-fema-visits-impacted-area-press-conference-set-for-noon/.

The Colorado National Guard and Rocky Mountain Type 1 Incident Management Team moved into the Marshall fire area on January 2. The National Guard deployed twenty-four guardsmen to provide twelve roadblocks in the county rural areas. Each Guard unit was self-contained, providing its own food, restrooms, and personnel to man the roadblocks no matter the weather or conditions and stayed on-site until no longer needed. Before their arrival, law officers ran the roadblocks and had to coordinate breaks and relief schedules to ensure safety during the frigid conditions.

The Type 1 Incident Team took over coordinating all firefighting responsibilities from Boulder County and the state Division of Fire Prevention Type 2 team, fighting flare-ups, and consolidating the fire perimeter. Trained in fighting forest and urban interface fires, the Type 1 Incident Team first concentrated on keeping the uncontrolled grasslands fire from spreading again. It then focused on putting out hot spots followed by working with utility providers and city officials to isolate and fix problems. Its main task was to help conflicting organizations work together to get the stricken communities back to some semblance of normalcy as quickly as possible.

At 8:23 p.m., Dan Dallas, Incident Commander for the Rocky Mountain Type 1 Incident Management Team, posted their first update.[86] In it, he reported that the fire stood at 6,219 acres burned with 74 percent of the perimeter contained. Firefighters continued to work closely with Team Rubicon, Xcel Energy, multiple law enforcement agencies, Division of Fire Prevention and Control, and Colorado National Guard on the fire and recovery efforts. He also noted that "temporary flight restrictions" had been placed over the area prohibiting all flights, including drones. As that time, 182 personnel were listed as fighting the fire.

The Rocky Mountain Incident Management Team is one of sixteen Type 1 teams located across different regions of the United States. It is composed of members from local, state, and federal agencies from Colorado, Nebraska, Kansas, South Dakota, and Wyoming. They operate following the standards of the National Wildfire Coordinating Group. Their mission is to "meet or exceed the expectations of those who invite us to their home area to help in times of difficulty."[87] They deploy when requested to manage large, complex incidents to get life back to normal as quickly and cost-effectively as possible while doing it safely with sensitivity to the land, resources, and public interests. Typically, they are called in to natural disasters when the scope and complexity of the situation exceeds the capacity of local resources to manage.

---

[86] The first IMT1 update is at https://www.boulderoem.com/rocky-mountain-type-1-incident-management-team-marshall-fire-update-jan-2-2022/.

[87] The expired IMT1 informational website is at https://sites.google.com/site/rockymtnimt1/.

The US Fire Administration recognizes three main types of incident management teams. Type 3 teams are organized at the local, state, or tribal level and includes a designated team of ten to twenty trained personnel from differing areas of expertise. Type 3 teams usually deploy right after an incident occurs and may be replaced later by a Type 2 or Type 1 team. The Boulder County Type 3 team deployed to the Marshall fire after completing work with the Middle Fork fire. Both Type 2 and Type 1 teams operate at the state, regional, and national level. Type 2 teams have less experience than Type 1 teams and typically work smaller-scale incidents. Most operate through the US Forest Service. Type 1 teams are the most robust and experienced. They are fully equipped and self-contained and able to operate in any natural disaster situation. Type 1 teams have thirty-five to forty core members while Type 2 have twenty-five to thirty. Type 2 teams manage incidents involving less than five hundred first responders and agencies while Type 1 can handle larger incidents. Due to the size and complexity of the Marshall fire, the Rocky Mountain Type 1 (IMT1) team deployed on January 2, replacing the state-level Type 2 team, and operated using the OEM offices and FlatIron Crossing Mall facilities through January 7.

It became apparent that the normal process of reporting the fire's "percentage contained" would not adequately measure success for the Marshall fire, so the IMT1 quickly adopted an "all hazards" approach to capture the needs of the delegated authority. These included such activities as restoring gas and electricity, hazardous materials assessment, and thermal imaging. Luckily, the IMT1 equipment depot was located close by, so radios and other identified equipment needs were deployed quickly. Avista Adventist Hospital allowed IMT1 to install a portable radio repeater on its rooftop that covered communication needs throughout the burn area. IMT1 and the Boulder EOC continued to work seamlessly together during the aftermath. As the IMT1 deployed over a holiday weekend during COVID and in a major snowstorm, obtaining some resources required ingenuity. Luckily, the Boulder OEM helped and was able to meet most of their short-term needs.

Each day during their deployment, Todd Legler, Safety Officer, and Pat Seekins, Operations Section Chief of the Rocky Mountain Type 1 Team, provided a short three- to four-minute update on the status of the Marshall fire from the IMT1 perspective. The first two updates emphasized full containment and working with utilities to lock down burned structures and restore service to other areas. The fire was considered 100 percent contained on January 3. As winds were forecast for January 4, resources concentrated on hitting any flare-ups and 911 calls within the burn zone quickly. The January 5 report noted that numerous flare-ups and at least one wall collapse occurred due to the previous day's weather, but all were successfully handled. They also noted that many roads had nails and other sharp objects causing tire punctures. Snow fell overnight again and into January 6, and the number of flare-ups and 911 calls fell along with it. IMT1's final update was given on January 7, and the Type 1 team handed day-to-day operations back to Boulder County.

Flying on Air Force 1, President Joe Biden and his wife, Jill, arrived in Colorado on January 7 to visit the Marshall fire devastation in person. They were accompanied by Colorado senators Michael Bennet and John Hickenlooper and US representative from Boulder, Joe Neguse. Homeland Security Secretary Alejandro Mayorkas and FEMA Administrator Deanne Criswell also attended. They were met at the Harper Lake parking area, where the Bovens watched the fire, by many state and local officials, including Gov. Jared Polis, Sheriff Joe Pelle, the mayors and city administrators of Louisville and Superior, and various invited residents, police, and firefighters. After minor remarks and handshakes, they traveled down to the Louisville Recreation Center where the dignitaries, including Jill Biden, provided comments.

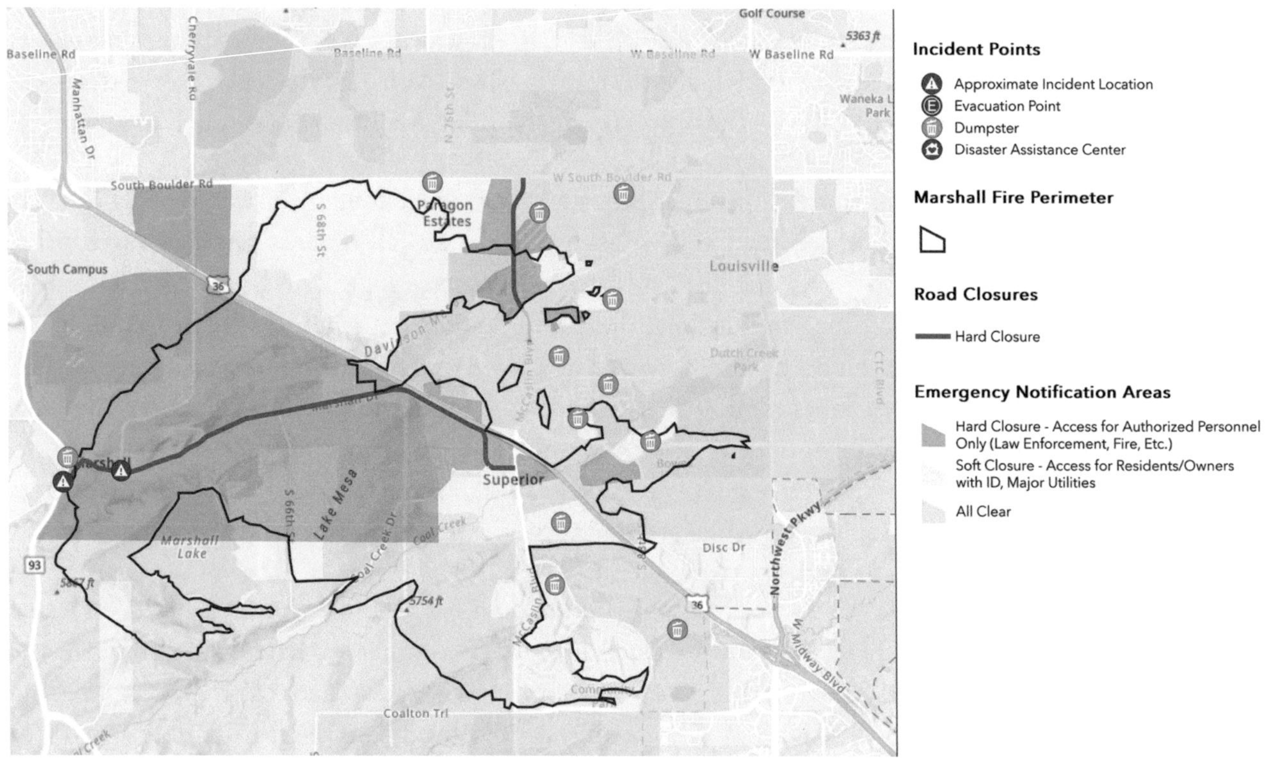

Figure 64 January 4 OEM map showing the closure zones around the Marshall fire area. Courtesy of Boulder OEM.

Sheriff Commander Wilber continued to work daily at the Nordstrom's command center with the Colorado Rocky Mountain Type 1 team, Xcel, and all the other agencies involved with opening the restricted areas in Superior, Louisville, and the county through January 7. Each morning, they reviewed the events from the previous day and set goals for the firefighters and utility teams. At noon, they met with the city officials and appraised what could and could not reopen. They then updated the plans to include when and how to change roadblocks to release these new areas. Once verified, the OEM sent out a notice announcing which areas changed from hard closure to soft closure to fully open.

Thirteen thousand customers lost natural gas service because of the Marshall fire. Utility workers from around the nation descended upon the area to help restore services. Relights required homeowners to be present, so Xcel established nine zones to effectively restart service based on the priorities set by the IMT1 team at Nordstrom's. As repairs were completed in each zone and residents were allowed in, 550 crew members contacted homeowners between 7:00 a.m. and 10:00 p.m. each day to gain permission to relight their appliances. Service was restored to about five thousand customers by the afternoon of January 3 and the remaining eight thousand within seventy-two hours. These herculean efforts helped keep many homes warm, pipes unfrozen, and ovens operating. Xcel and its employees and subcontractors did a magnificent job through very trying times and restored services throughout the area by January 4.

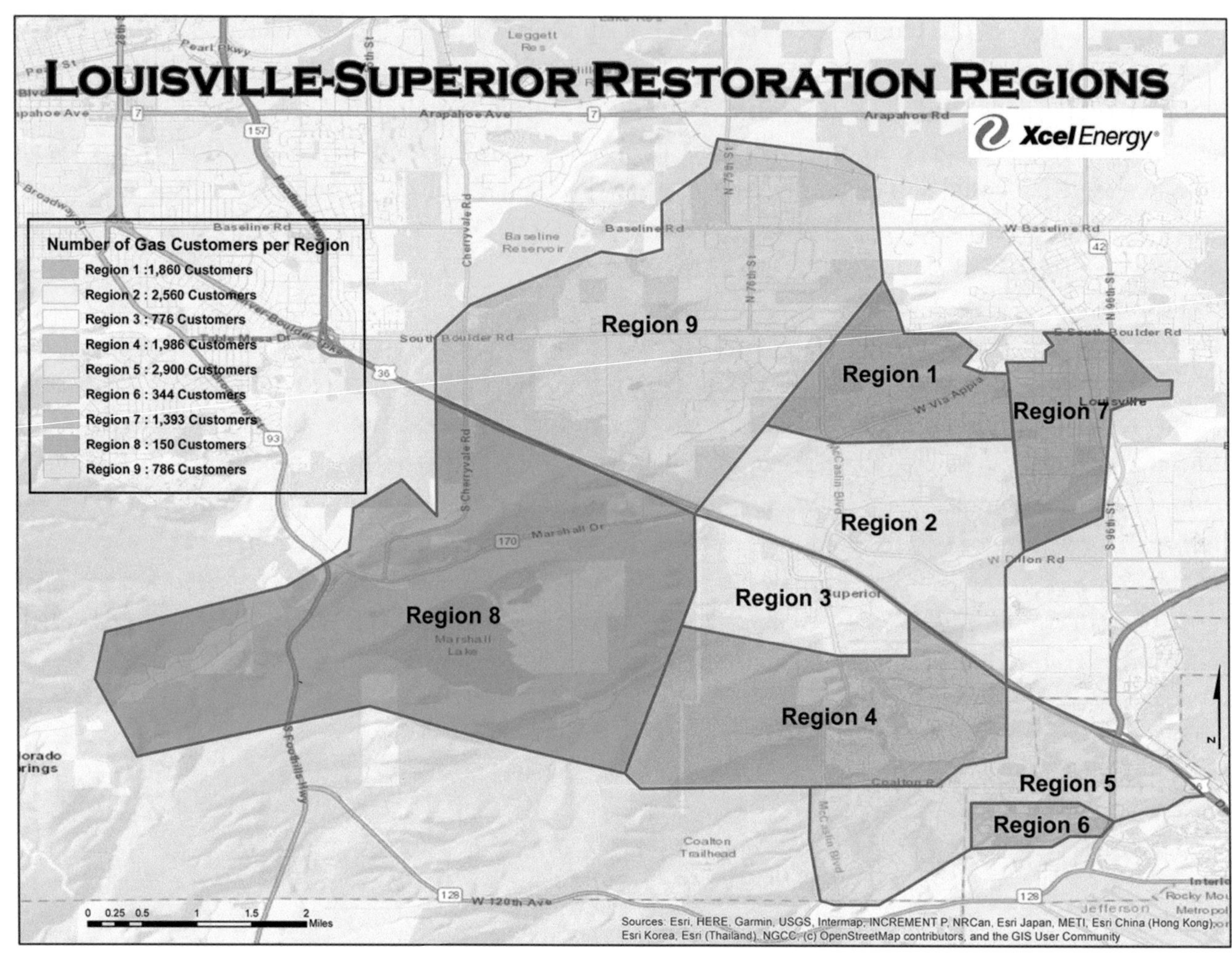

Figure 65 Xcel Energy Natural Gas Relight Regions after the fire. Courtesy of Xcel Energy and Boulder OEM.

Louisville and Superior Cleanup, Early January

Within a couple of days after the fire, Paul Williamson again returned to his home of seven years to see if anything can be salvaged. He wore what he hoped was adequate gear—protective clothing, boots, heavy gloves, an N95 mask, and glasses. He arrived at his address and still cannot believe the devastation. The ground around his home was wiped clean as if in a battle zone. Obviously, cement board and steel roofing didn't stop a firestorm. Surprisingly, a few trees and one nearby home stood unscathed by the inferno. The fickle nature of wind and flames cannot rationally be explained.

Figure 66 Remains of Paul Williamson Superior house made of cement board and steel roofing after the fire.

Paul started looking for anything that survived. He found his 2700°F-rated firesafe. In it were many of his important documents, including his Social Security card, passport, and truck title. Surprisingly, the safe opened. But the contents inside were all just ash. The fire was over 2700°F. As the remains of the metal roof covered most of the ruins, Paul started cutting it up and throwing it to the side. He will get a large dumpster to dispose of it later. He continued cutting, removing the roofing, and looking for anything salvageable. But even glass returned to sand at temperatures above 2700°. Very little survived. He found his metal belt change machine that he used as a kid delivering newspapers. He also discovered a ceramic bust of Lincoln from his office that did not shatter when the burning floor collapsed below it. Very little else made it through the maelstrom.

He surveyed his yard and garden. Anything made of wood was just gone, including his wooden arbor and large gazebo. With the wind and snow, even the ash had disappeared. Seven years of loving care gone. He decided then and there that he will clean up the mess himself and rebuild. His original contractor called and inquired how the house fared. After Paul told him it was all gone, he replied he will help. Paul also checked with the manufacturer of the preformed insulated panels in Fort Collins. They also can be remade. Paul was convinced he can rebuild. He ordered a large dumpster to dispose of the debris and planned how to restore his sustainable living home.

He moved from his daughter's home into a friend's daughter's house until he could get the yard clean enough to place a camper on-site. He started the tedious steps of cutting up the roofing and piling it into the dumpster. One dumpster full and carried away . . . two dumpsters full . . . three dumpsters full . . . four dumpsters full . . . five dumpsters full. This was going to be long, hard, back-breaking work and a bit expensive. His daughter started a GoFundMe page, and he knew that he will also get his veteran's insurance eventually. But will it be enough? He also checked to see what was available through the disaster aid center. He signed up for what he could and continued working.

Then it happened. The Town of Superior issued a "cease and desist" order on January 24. He called the city to set up a meeting to discuss why they were stopping him from cleaning up his own property. When he arrived, he was surprised to find not just a clerk, but every city department head on hand to meet with him. They explained that he didn't have the necessary city permits to be performing demolition work within city limits. He asked how he could obtain the necessary permits. They said they didn't know. Just then, the city manager came in and told him in explicit terms that the town was working with the county and FEMA, and they will be doing all the cleanup, and he should not risk doing it himself. He replied that he would continue doing the cleanup and please provide the necessary legal forms to meet the town's requirements.

Two weeks later, the town clerk called him and said that he could now obtain the permits necessary to continue working. The town wanted money and to make sure that Paul knew that he was solely responsible for any liability if something happened while he performed his own cleanup. They also emphasized how to properly dispose of the debris. Ever conscious of the environment, Paul paid the fees, posted the permits, hired a contractor to help him, and got back to work.

He got the lot sufficiently clean that he felt safe to move his daughter's camper on-site to lower his costs and commute time. He kept working until February 28 when the town slapped a parking ticket on his RV. He again approached the city, and they backed down, allowing RVs to be parked on burned-out land once the property was sufficiently cleared. He continued working.

Superior, the county, and the federal government required a mountain of paperwork to perform cleanup work. There were demolition permits, right-of-entry forms, disposal notification forms, stormwater quality permits, and city approval for right-of-way. Water and sewer service lines must be capped, and then on-site inspections and environmental testing must be completed. Paul went through all the rigmarole required by the government entities and finally completed the land reclamation process on March 19, 2022. He was the first to complete the process in Original Superior and may be the first in all of Boulder County. But it wore him out and cost him $54,000. About $15,000 of that came from the GoFundMe page his daughter set up, but the rest came out of pocket until insurance settled. Paul asked his friends, "Should I spend the next three years rebuilding or find a pretty girl and move to a beach?" He decided on the latter and posted a homemade "For Sale by Owner" sign on the now-barren double lot.

Figure 67 Paul Williamson's property after the reclamation process.

As part of Housing and Urban Development (HUD) and FEMA funding, the federal government agreed to pay 90 percent for debris cleanup of destroyed houses and businesses from the Marshall fire, the state agreed to pay 5 percent, and Superior, Louisville, and Boulder County agreed to pay the rest. To ensure a smooth cleanup, both

Louisville and Superior in January proposed Boulder County issue and coordinate the cleanup contract. Boulder County established a committee that developed cleanup specifications, and eleven companies provided bids to meet it. This committee reviewed the bids in private and scored each bid using various criteria on a scale of 1–100. Two companies scored on top at 84 and 91 and were interviewed by the committee. All the other companies were rated in the 60s or lower. Based on these interviews, the committee recommended that the county issue the cleanup contract to DRC Emergency Services of Galveston, Texas, for $52 million. Boulder County reviewed the bids and issued the contract to DRC on February 10, 2022. DRC stated that it hoped to start the cleanup by March 1.

While the contract was being negotiated, Boulder County announced that hydro-mulching would begin on February 2. Hydro-mulching is a mixture of organic substances applied by spraying that creates a semisolid blanket as it dries to seal off properties and stabilize soil. The intent was to keep potential toxins from becoming wind-blown and running into local waterways. Work was to begin only on properties already sifted for valuables and where property owners had provided permission. It would first be applied to high-density areas and locations closest to waterways. Work would then proceed to areas of decreasing home densities. The entire process was to take about ten days to complete, but valuable sifting delayed completion. Properties with orange stakes were ready for hydro-mulching, and those with numbered black-and-white signs were still awaiting sifting as of February 17. Sifting not completed by March 1 would instead be completed by the debris removal company. Once hydro-mulching was applied, the property was to be left undisturbed until cleanup.

When the contract award was announced, two of the losing companies filed appeals contesting the results. A separate nonprofit, called Demand Integrity in Government Spending (DIGS), headed by former FEMA director Michael Brown, filed a lawsuit against the County demanding that the cleanup process be rebid and requesting an injunction to stop work while the court reviewed their suit. They stated that the county officials violated open meeting laws by allowing a separate committee to review the bids in closed meetings. After losing its appeal, Ceres Environmental filed a late lawsuit on April 7, asking the court to invalidate and terminate DRC's cleanup contract as DRC exaggerated its experience in its bid. Ceres ranked third in the committee's evaluations with a score of 68 and was not asked to be interviewed by the committee.

Boulder County announced the cleanup schedule on April 1 based on consultations between each governmental authority. In a news release, Boulder County stated,[88] "Each jurisdiction prioritized the schedule for their own neighborhoods." A county committee took these priorities and created forty-eight "runways," grouping

[88] Information mostly from https://www.bouldercounty.org/disasters/wildfires/marshall/debris-removal-program/.

neighboring homes and businesses together. The forty-eight runways were then ranked into a priority sequence "based on careful analysis of several factors including:

- Imminent environmental hazards . . .
- Environmental Justice . . ., based on demographic factors of low income, people of color, and those age 64+, and
- Efficiencies of removal using input from the contractor, DRC Environmental Services, LLC."

DRC assigned thirty crews to attack these runways, with fifteen crews working in Superior, nine in Louisville, and six in unincorporated Boulder County. Each crew worked a single runway until all the addresses in it were complete. DRC contacted owners by email twenty-four to forty-eight hours before starting work to inform the owner of the work commencing and to allow the owner the opportunity to attend the walk-through of the work planned.

Each crew began by performing a 360-degree walk-around of the property to ensure that the plan for the address was correct. A water truck then drenched the site to minimize dust emissions. All metals, including any vehicles, were removed first and taken for recycling. Other ash and debris were then removed, including any incidental and contaminated soil. Reusable items, such as stone blocks and pavers, were piled on a corner of the lot. Starting with folding in basement walls, concrete was removed. A pre-inspection by the monitoring contractor was performed to ensure all glass, nails, and other debris had been removed. The site was then rough graded to promote positive drainage and eliminate tripping hazards. Soil samples were collected to test for any residual contamination. After sample verification, government inspectors performed a final walk-through, and a safety fence was installed, if required.

Per the review meeting,[89] owners could expect the following:

1. Removal of the ash footprint, including incidental soil.
2. Removal of foundations, including concrete slab floor and structural support piers.
3. Removal of driveways that were damaged by the fire/heat.
4. Homeowners could elect to have their non-damaged/destroyed driveways and other concrete flatwork (patios, private sidewalks) removed.
5. Removal of accessory buildings (sheds, detached garages, etc.) that were damaged or destroyed.

[89] Based from https://assets.bouldercounty.org/wp-content/uploads/2022/03/PPDR-Town-Hall-March-29-2022-FINAL.pdf.

6. Utility locates and confirmation of capping/disconnecting.
7. Removal of trees deemed hazardous by a certified arborist.
8. Natural grading of the debris site if homeowner did not plan to rebuild right away, or sluffing of basement holes with installation of OSHA compliant safety fencing if homeowner intended to rebuild right away.
9. Proper separation, handling, and disposal of all materials.
10. Community air monitoring to confirm engineering controls were effective. Erosion control measures installed in accordance with Stormwater Pollution Protection Plans.
11. DOT inspections for all vehicles operating on the project to ensure local roads are as safe as possible.

The total cost of the debris removal was expected to be $60 million to cleanup 862 homes. Participating property owners contributed their homeowner's insurance amount dedicated to debris removal to help defray the local cost not covered by federal moneys. Uninsured and underinsured owners' costs were covered by the cities and county.

At least thirty homeowners in Rock Creek in Superior dropped out of the FEMA-funded cleanup immediately. Rock Creek was one of the last areas scheduled, and completion could be as late as September, too late to start digging and pouring foundations for most contractors. With the late Ceres lawsuit, these homeowners hired a contractor to complete the cleanup without FEMA funding.

When the court received the DIGS lawsuit, it denied the stop-work injunction, and the county allowed the cleanup to start. The court also did not stop work based on the later Ceres lawsuit. DRC sent out subcontractor bids. They also announced all workers would wear protective hazmat garments throughout the cleanup as environmental hazards were unknown. DRC continued with right-of-way cleanup of debris along and in roadways in the area while the judge deliberated. Finally on March 28, 2022, the judge dismissed the first lawsuit, stating that DIGS and its founder had no connection to the area and thus could not benefit or suffer any harm based on the outcome of the bid award. Eight hundred sixty-two households agreed to the FEMA-funded cleanup at the end of March when the process and timeline were announced. That number dropped to around 750 a week later as homeowners assessed the process and to 696 by April 16. Though a few others joined back in later, many, like Paul Williamson, chose to complete the cleanup on their own. After the court announcement with no comment on why the contract had increased, Boulder County declared that DRC would begin the cleanup process by the middle of April and targeted completion by July 1 for a total contract price of $60 million. DRC started digging on the first lots in the Sagamore subdivision on April 18 even as the court reviewed the Ceres lawsuit.[90]

Boulder County planned to issue demolition and cleanup permits through June 30. Louisville committed to its residents to have all demolition and debris removal complete by August 1. Of the 550 residences and buildings destroyed, Louisville issued 493 debris permits, had 93 lots cleared, and released 2 building permits by May 30. For Superior, the statistics were 293 active debris permits for the 391 buildings destroyed, 25 lots cleared, and 1 building permit issued by the end of May. Boulder Public Works reported that of the final 588 properties opting into the FEMA-funded program, 316 were being cleared, 105 were in final inspection, and 60 were awaiting the final erosion control step by the end of May. No statistics were available for rebuilding permits issued in unincorporated Boulder County for Marshall and Spanish Hills, but the first rebuilding permit[91] was issued to Pam and Dan Decker on Marshall Road by mid-May. Groundbreaking for the first house to be rebuilt in Louisville occurred on June 6. DRC made good progress but did not meet its target completion date of July 1.

By the end of July, 352 lots in Louisville were cleared of the 550 destroyed. The city issued 549 debris removal permits and 16 rebuilding permits. For Superior, 264 lots were cleared of 385 destroyed by the end of July. The town issued 20 rebuilding permits. For unincorporated Boulder County, of the 206 buildings impacted, 57 lots were cleared, 2 in process, and an additional 104 had permits issued by the end of July. Surprisingly, 43 had no cleanup permit applications. The county issued 7 rebuilding permits, and 5 were in process at that time.

DRC finally completed clearing debris the week of August 22, eight months after the fire. Though $60 million was allocated for the cleanup, final DRC costs ended up in the low-$30 million range. Private lot clearing was still underway at the end of August with 124 lots in Louisville and 23 lots in Superior sitting untouched and covered in burned-out remains. County records report 106,662 tons of ashen debris removed, 64,658 tons of brick and concrete recycled, and 2403 tons of metal recycled during the clearing process. Rebuilding continued throughout the burn area and the Target store reopened on August 30.

[90] The court dismissed the Ceres lawsuit May 27, 2022, ruling Ceres failed to make a claim under Colorado law.

[91] Based in part on an article at KDVR.COM titled *Boulder County grants first permit to rebuild after Marshall Fire.*

Jase and Jean settled into a house in Texas that Jase's parents used as a rental that was miraculously vacant. The youngsters loved to be close to Grandma and didn't realize what they had lost. Jase's parents contacted the parish priest, and the Catholic Relief Services brought toys and clothes for the kids the second day after their arrival. Jase and Jean shopped for clothes and at least felt safe. They tried not to think about what happened but knew that they would have to replace the important papers and documents that they lost. With Jase's parents watching the kids, they had their first date night since the birth of their youngest two years ago. Maybe they would just stay in Texas and not return to the bad memories in Colorado.

But Jase needed to visit his elder son and reassured him that everything was fine. He also wanted to see for himself what happened to their home and possibly look for any sign of their dog, Violet. He made reservations at an Airbnb and flew back to Colorado for a long weekend in mid-January. His elder son was excited to see Dad and loved the Airbnb. They had a wonderful quiet weekend together, then his son returned to his mother and school. Jase drove over to see the remains of their home. He hoped that he could salvage something, and maybe his truck and Violet survived the maelstrom.

He commuted the few miles from the Airbnb to Louisville and could still smell the smoke in the air as he arrived three weeks after the fire. When he got to Dillon Road, it looked like a bomb had gone off. The Coal Creek Ranch neighborhood was gone. Nothing was left but snow-covered rubble. He showed his ID to the police guarding the entrance to St. Andrews Lane and slowly crawled to his old home. No, the truck did not survive. It was a burned-out hulk sitting just where he left it. The house and everything around and in it were all gone. Miraculously, two houses still stood as sentinels guarding the outside of the burned-out neighborhood.

Figure 68 The remains of Jase and Jean's home in the Louisville Coal Creek Ranch subdivision with his destroyed truck in front.

Just two weeks before the fire, Jase had opened the moving boxes containing his childhood memories. His dad worked in IT, and Jase was born in Saudi Arabia during one of his dad's work deployments. There he and his dad searched the desert and found pieces of Libyan desert glass that were in the moving boxes in the basement. Though everything else might be destroyed, surely, they will have survived the inferno. He wondered how he can find them.

While he was there poking around the ruins, Justice Takes Flight personnel came into the development with a bloodhound. One walked over and talked to Jase. Jase told them about Violet, and he asked if maybe the bloodhound could look for some sign of her. Jase had one of Violet's toys and let the team work Violet's scent from it. The bloodhound took off on a trail from the back of the house baying. Miraculously, Violet survived the fire and had come back to the remains of the house enough times that the bloodhound had a recent scent trail. She must have gone out the doggie door before the fire became too intense and took off through the downed fence in the backyard. Jase was beside himself and did not know what to do. Violet had been a large part of his and Jean's life. He called Jean, and they decided Jase should stay longer to see if he could find her. He made seventy-five posters showing Violet's picture with a $1,000 reward for information and placed them all over the burned-out neighborhood and surrounding areas. He distributed another three hundred before he left. He put out her favorite food, the toy, a blanket, and a dirty sock with his scent on it, hoping Violet would stay and know that Jase was in the area. He also positioned a game camera that triggered when any animal approached the food and blanket. He hoped it will capture a picture of Violet.

Figure 69 The fire at Jase and Jean's house was hot enough to warp the central support girder.

While back in Colorado, he also visited the Disaster Assistance Center (DAC) on Public Road in Lafayette. Jean's sister set up a GoFundMe page for them, and Jase did have renter's insurance, but he knew that wouldn't be enough to restore everything. He was surprised by the breadth of support available at the DAC. The first floor housed the intake registration area and included documentation on what was available and how to do many things. It also had FEMA personnel. He started with FEMA registration and began the process of getting important documents like Social Security cards and passports restored. He knew it will take a long time to get just these documents replaced. He also spent time with the Boulder County Humane Society and told them about Violet. They took her information and assured him they would contact him when they heard anything about her. Unluckily, most of the resources were aimed at families staying in the area and not those who had moved away. After grabbing food and drink, he headed up to the second floor. This area was mostly dedicated to family support and volunteer organizations like Samaritan's Purse, ARC Thrift, and the American Red Cross. In some ways, he wished Jean and the kids had come with him so that they could see the help available. As he left the DAC, he saw several insurance companies in the parking lot working claims.

He stayed in Colorado another couple of days and returned to the ruins of his home each morning. He poked around but really couldn't get into the foundation to look for anything of value. Two local TV news crews interviewed him about the bloodhounds and his losses. But the game camera and the posters didn't lead to any additional information about Violet. Dejected, he returned to Texas to Jean and the kids.

Jase came back to Colorado in late February to meet with his elder son again. The original Airbnb was booked, so they stayed at another, but it was not as nice. He contacted the Humane Society, but there was no new information about Violet. The game camera also had no pictures of interest. On his last day, he went back to the DAC and signed up with Samaritan's Purse to sift through the foundation during his next visit in March. He hoped they could at least find the desert glass.

In late March, he returned to the original Airbnb with his son. He confirmed with Samaritan's Purse to start sifting the foundation for anything of value the next day. He knew where the desert glass should be located and was confident that they would be able to find it. But when he arrived at the ruins the next day, he was shocked to see the Samaritan's Purse crew just standing around. The property had already been hydro-mulched, and they were prohibited from disturbing it by entering the grounds. Jase and Jean had lost everything and now could not even look through the remains for anything that might have survived. Jase gave up hope of ever finding Violet or anything of value from their home.

Assistance and Aid

Miraculously, the outpouring of support from the surrounding community overwhelmed the ability of the evacuation centers to handle physical donations within two days after the fire. The OEM posted the following announcement January 1 at 1:56 p.m.:

> We have been overwhelmed by the community's generosity (but we cannot accept) any more physical donation drop-offs at this time. Please DO NOT bring donations to any of the evacuation centers or Sister Carmen. If you would like to help victims impacted by the fire, please consider a financial donation through the Community Foundation serving Boulder County, Red Cross or Sister Carmen, or sign up to volunteer. There will be many opportunities to volunteer in the days ahead as we continue to recover from this catastrophic event. If you have materials, food, water and services to donate, you can register online through a form on Boulder OEM's website. Also, if you have housing you want to offer to victims, please register your home through the Airbnb's Open Homes Program.

The Community Foundation Boulder County[92] is a community catalyst to inspire ideas and actions to improve the quality of life in Boulder County. It makes informed decisions to respond to immediate needs and anticipate future challenges. Immediately following the Marshall fire, the foundation sprang into action and became the local focal point for monetary contributions and disbursements. The state organization Colorado Gives[93] directed all donations through the Community Foundation. They engaged with government, business, nonprofit, and community partners to find innovative solutions to meet community needs and honor the donor intent during this unprecedented philanthropic effort. By January 20, the Community Foundation distributed $5.5M to 2,200 households affected by the fire and started distributing an additional $1.5M to those whose livelihoods were affected.[94] By February 8, the Community Foundation raised over $27M for

[92] Based on information from https://www.commfound.org/wildfirefund.

[93] Based on information from https://www.coloradogives.org

[94] See https://www.commfound.org/news/media-releases for more information.

fire victims. By May 9, the foundation raised over $40M from more than 77,000 donors worldwide. They distributed $8,165,000 (20 percent):

- $5.5 million in direct financial assistance to damaged and destroyed households
- $1.5 million in direct financial assistance for lost wages or livelihood equipment
- $150,000 to United Policyholders for insurance policy navigation
- $265,000 to Impact on Education to ensure adequate mental health advocates at the most fire-affected schools
- $250,000 to Boulder Jewish Family Service to provide crisis counseling
- $500,000 in direct assistance to wind-damaged mobile and manufactured homes

The remaining +$32,000,000 was allocated as follows:

- Up to $20 million to support rebuilding efforts
- Up to $2.5 million for unmet basic needs through disaster case management
- Up to $750,000 for mental health support
- Up to $1 million assistance with smoke/ash remediation
- Up to $500,000 for social infrastructure / community resilience through entities like Marshall Together, Superior Rising, and/or their fiscal sponsors
- Up to $750,000 supporting other nonprofits assisting disaster response
- Up to $2 million for debris removal for uninsured/underinsured through Boulder County

The Marshall Together[95] movement is a self-organized group of community members who are collectively working toward supporting neighbors to heal and rebuild. Their rebuilding website of Marshall Together serves Louisville, Superior, and unincorporated Boulder. It serves as a central hub for resources, announcements, and events. They publish a newsletter on information of interest to persons affected by the fire at least biweekly.

Superior Rising[96] is a grassroots movement of Marshall fire survivors and community leaders from the public and private sectors who are dedicated to serving the long-term needs of the Town of Superior's disaster-affected residents, businesses, and workforce. Founded in January of 2022, under the mentorship of Colorado Springs Together, the nonprofit foundation provides access to resources to help lower barriers to entry for

[95] Based on information from https://marshalltogether.com.

[96] Based on information from https://www.superiorrising.org/about/.

those repopulating the disaster-affected areas. Its website maintains information pertinent to the 437 homes destroyed and damaged during the fire in the Town of Superior. It includes links and references to available resources, rebuilding information, and progress being made toward rebuilding. It cooperates with other nonprofits and governmental agencies to help Superior residents get the most current information on the fire.

In late May, Superior Rising and Marshall Together asked government agencies to waive "use fees" for rebuilding efforts. Use taxes are collected by the city, county, and state, plus RTD, for construction, including those rebuilding from the Marshall fire. These groups argued homeowners have paid these taxes already when they first built their destroyed properties and should not have to pay them again. The organizations estimated that the average rebuilding effort would pay $30,000 in use fees if they were not rescinded. And according to the Colorado Department of Insurance, 92 percent of Marshall fire victims were underinsured, and such costs would be out of pocket. The government agencies did not budget these fees coming in and therefore should have no need for them. By June, Superior agreed and waived rebuilding use fees.

Collaborating with Energy Smart, Boulder County, Superior, and Louisville established a new website[97] aimed at homeowners who are rebuilding after the Marshall fire. The stated purpose of the website is to provide "resources for planning, designing, and constructing high-performance homes that are more resilient to future climate crises." Sections of the website address such topics as building a healthy and comfortable home; building a more resilient home; identifying incentives, discounts, and financing; finding a design and construction team; choosing materials and equipment; and implementing appropriate landscaping. Rebates and incentives will be added. The intent is to encourage net-zero energy home rebuilding with little or no incremental expense resulting in lower utility costs, thus saving the homeowner for years to come.

Sister Carmen Community Center of Lafayette[98] started in 1970 by Sister Carmen Ptacnik of the First Daughters of Charity at the Catholic Immaculate Conception Parish. The church operated it as a food bank, thrift store, and charity support organization. It moved into a new facility built by the City of Lafayette on W. Baseline Road in April 2002 on land donated by the Masonic Lodge. As it continued to expand its mission, it acquired warehousing space on Aspen Ridge Drive in 2011. It became secular and part of the Family Resource Center Association in 2012.

[97] Based in part from https://rebuildingbetter.org.

[98] Based on information from https://sistercarmen.org.

Sister Carmen provided direct financial aid to over 115 families after the Marshall fire for rent, mortgage, storage, auto, and babysitting expenses. They also provided 20,000 pounds of food, hygiene, and baby items to affected families, as well as $450,000 in gift certificates to their thrift store, to gas stations, and to local groceries. Numerous one-on-one support and guidance from trauma-informed advocates were offered as well.

Besides these secular organizations, numerous religious organizations pitched in to help survivors. The United Methodist Committee on Relief (UMCOR) provided money to the Rocky Mountain District to distribute to local Methodist churches for relief efforts. Larry and Mary Boven took advantage of this as it paid for their stay at Edgewater UMC in Denver. Even in Texas, Jase and Jean H. received help from the Catholic Relief Services with almost immediate toys and clothing for the children.

Figure 70 Colorado Baptist Disaster Relief provided meals on December 31. Courtesy of Dennis Belz, CBDR State Director.

The Southern Baptist Disaster Relief[99] was on the ground by December 31 providing meals to displaced persons and first responders. They later paired up with Samaritan's Purse in the Disaster Assistance Center to offer free sifting of property ashes for burn victims. Volunteers joined with them to help recover lost items in burned-out foundations and cars. Team leaders were first trained, credentialed, and passed through a background check. Morning and afternoon training sessions taught volunteers how to shift through the ash. Coming from all over the world to help, many volunteers stayed for long periods at local churches, including the Boulder Valley

[99] Based on https://www.baptistpress.com article *Colorado Baptists respond to wind-driven fire destruction.*

Christian Church on S. Boulder Road at the edge of the burn zone just west of Spanish Hills. They suited up in special protective gear and spent hours scouring through ash and debris looking for the smallest personal items that survived the decimation. Miraculously, many items were recovered. Sadly, more were lost forever.

Roger Wilt[100] helped Samaritan's Purse sift foundations eight times during February 2022. Roger explained each volunteer first attended a quick training session and was issued a bright-orange T-shirt that the police guarding the destroyed neighborhoods recognized and allowed entry without proof of address. They met at the site to be sifted where Samaritan's Purse would already have a truck and trailer parked. There they donned white Tyvek one-piece protective suits with built-in booties and received waterproof gloves, N95 masks, and eye protection. The team lead walked the property with the homeowner and identified three or four locations to sift, assuming possible valuables would fall straight down from their location in the house prior to the fire. Eighteen-inch by twenty-four-inch frames with one-fourth-inch screens were set up on sawhorses near each sift site. The volunteers first cleared off any large debris, like metal roofing or sheet metal, and then started shoveling the ash onto the screen frames. With all the snow and the water from the fire hoses, the ash was like mush. The screens were shaken and scraped to reveal anything of value. Usually, three or four volunteers worked a site location, placing anything useful into a five-gallon bucket and calling out if they discovered something that the homeowner wanted.

One foundation sifted was for an older couple who moved here in the 1960s from Czechoslovakia. They were heartbroken at the loss of their home. Hardly anything survived the fire. Aluminum melted in most cases. Roger found what looked like a roll of quarters, but the fire was so hot that they fused together. Roger's team miraculously found several of her missing rings, some from her original homeland.

The work shoveling ash was backbreaking, and sifting was not much easier. As the ash was like mush and the air temperature often just above freezing, most ignored the provided eye protection as they steamed up, and some even dropped the N95 masks. Very little was salvageable—some rings, occasional silverware, parts of an antique shotgun, the head and hands of a ceramic doll. Everything else was ash or a melted blob of metal. Nothing made of wood or cloth remained. After the shift finished, the Tyvek suit, gloves, masks, and eye protection were all placed in garbage bags and left on-site as they were considered toxic, and even Samaritan's Purse could not transport them without special permits. Each volunteer signed a special Billy Graham edition Bible that was presented to the homeowner when they finished. When asked if he would

[100] Based on a phone interview with Roger Wilt and author on June 7, 2022.

volunteer with Samaritan's Purse again, Roger Wilt replied, "I would gladly do it again as the homeowners are so appreciative. But the Tyvek suits and protective gear get uncomfortable. I figure at my age, something else will get me before the toxins from the ash can."

No schools or churches were consumed by the fire. Ascent Church in the old Sam's Club building off McCaslin in Louisville was within one hundred feet of the spreading flames but survived intact with minor smoke damage. Many of their members were not so fortunate, and the church provided resources to help them through the ordeal. They paired families for long-term support. They provided prayer, financial, and meal support. Even though the church met remotely for a few weeks after the fire to allow the church's smoke damage to be repaired, they continued to spread hope and support to their members and the community. One of the cutest items they shared is the children's book *Trinka and Sam: The Big Fire*, funded by NIH and available at the National Child Traumatic Stress Network.[101]

The mega Flatirons Community Church[102] headquartered in nearby Lafayette partnered with teachers and educators in the K-12 schools in the Louisville, Superior, and Lafayette area to help meet the needs of anyone who lost their home by providing gift cards to local stores and restaurants. They hosted events for these educators to care for, equip, and encourage them through these times, as teachers were often the first line of relief for students. Flatirons also worked with Avista Adventist Hospital to help care for their staff. They collaborated with other churches to create a streamlined approach for caring for the community with minimal overlap. An internal gift card drive at their five campuses raised $120,000, which was 100 percent donated to people affected by the fires and local relief agencies. Most importantly, Flatirons focused on caring for the emotional and spiritual needs of those affected in the community by sharing the love of Jesus.

The group A Precious Child supplied clothing for adults and children. The Jewish Family Service partnered with JEWISHcolorado Fire Relief Fund to provide direct financial assistance to anyone in need. They also provided free replacement Judaica, such as Ketubah, Mezuzah, and Shabbat candles. Sacred Heart of Mary Parish, just northwest of the devastation on S. Boulder Road and the original evacuation center, collected toys, clothing, food, and donations. Even though its property was singed, Boulder Valley Christian Church allowed many volunteers to stay in the church while they worked with Samaritan's Purse. They also served numerous meals to volunteers.

---

[101] This book can also be found at https://www.nctsn.org/resources/trinka-and-sam-big-fire

[102] Based on a June 22, 2022, email from Micah DeYoung, Social Media and PR Specialist, Flatirons Community Church.

One of the most unique offerings was provided by the members of Calvary Bible Church.[103] Founded in 1889, the church operates campuses in Boulder, Erie, and Thornton. An Evangelical Free Church, the Boulder campus first started Kingdom Assignments in 2003. During that first session, over four hundred Calvary members provided ninety minutes of service over ninety days to the community and donated over $100,000 to civic needs. In 2004, the Kingdom Assignment found seven hundred church volunteers refurbishing three Boulder schools. In 2005, three other churches pitched in, and one thousand four hundred volunteers refurbished five schools. By 2009, forty-five churches and four thousand five hundred volunteers served at over one hundred thirty-five sites.

With the Marshall fire and the weakening of COVID, Calvary Bible Church revived its Kingdom Assignments. Though only a few church families were hurt by the fire, Calvary challenged its members to support their affected neighbors and offered up to $2,500 in direct compensation to help meet the immediate needs of any affected family that church members knew. Over one hundred Calvary attendees reached out and touched 153 families affected by the fire. The church, with the help of three other organizations, distributed over $211,000 in unsolicited cash through their members to these families. Members also pledged to stand by those affected and help them in any way needed. Recipients were surprised by the church's "no strings attached" generosity and used the funds for all kinds of needs—from replacement clothes and shoes to auto repairs. They also appreciated the friendship shown and outreach of the Gospel.

Church groups reached out to help those affected by the blaze, not because they were paid, but because it was the right thing to do. They shared out of love for their neighbors in God's name and not in hopes of getting any reward.

Moving out of their daughter's home, Larry and Mary Boven stayed at a hotel on the Diagonal Highway northeast of Boulder for a couple of nights in early January. Larry did his normal running on the nearby trails, but Mary had a hard time adjusting. Larry used the time to visit the Disaster Assistance Center (DAC) and began the tedious process of restoring all their lost personal papers. He also signed up for assistance and a government rebuilding loan. He really loved Louisville and knew that Mary will be happiest rebuilding, staying near their three children and all that she knew.

---

[103] Based in part on emails from Kristen Reiner, Director of Community Outreach, Calvary Bible Church.

He reached out to the United Methodist Church for help, and the Edgewater UMC off Fenton Street in Denver contacted him and said they could stay in their furnished parsonage until they found something else. Mary loved it. The congregation was great and treated her royally. They helped them get clothing and basic needs. They helped them with meals. There were restaurants and many people and places nearby to keep Mary occupied and not concerned about rebuilding. Not far from Sloan's Lake, Larry had plenty of places to run.

Meanwhile, Larry kept working on how to get back to Louisville. As he owned their home free and clear, he expected to rebuild on the same site. However, they were not as young as they used to be, and a ranch design with a walk-out basement would be better than their previous two-story house. He contacted the original builder, Sheffield Homes, and asked if they would be interested in helping them rebuild. Sheffield responded positively and provided him with various ranch plans that fit onto their existing lot. Of course, costs had gone up significantly since they first built, but Larry thought with their insurance money and a small government loan, they could make it work.

With the help of friends and the DAC, Larry finally found a condominium in northeast Louisville that fit Mary's conditions to live in while they rebuilt. Though not in walking distance of the rec center, it was still in Louisville, and Mary will be able to see all her friends and get back to some semblance of normalcy. They moved in on Valentine's Day.

Figure 71 The remains of the Boven home in Centennial Heights West subdivision looking north.

Larry attended all the meetings on the demolition and rebuilding process put on by FEMA, Boulder County, and Louisville. He thought it will take them forever to get anything done. He talked with neighbors, and they put him touch with a private contractor who was clearing lots much faster and cheaper than waiting on the County and FEMA, what with the legal challenges and the equity scheduling process. He just wanted to get his home rebuilt and move back in as quickly as possible. So in May, he signed up with a private demolition contractor to do the cleanup. He also reached a deal with Sheffield on a ranch plan with a three-car garage and a walkout basement. He designed it with all the features that he knew Mary will want and need with her condition. With a little bit of luck and if the government doesn't intervene, he expects to move back home before Christmas 2022.

Rebuilding and Rebirth

Figure 72 Lush green grass meets blackened trees on Marshall Mesa from Marshall Road at Cherryvale June 15, 2022.

According to Owensby (1972), tallgrass prairies are "fire derived and fire maintained." And that is very true of the open space grasslands to the west of Louisville and Superior. The fire stimulated new growth. By mid-June 2022, these grasslands were as green as springtime in Ireland, and signs of the fire could only be seen in the occasional burned fence post and blackened tree. The fire brought rich rebirth to the prairie long grass. Though many homes and buildings were destroyed, the prairie rebounded quickly.

With the dismissal of the last lawsuit, lot clearing also progressed rapidly. By mid-June, over 50 percent of the lots in the Centennial Subdivision in Louisville were cleared and ready to be sold or rebuilt. Large dump trucks packed the roads to and from the area hauling out the toxic debris. Where they went was a mystery, but they continued day in and day out. Cleared lots sat side by side with lots still full of ash and burned-out relics. Lots in Marshall and unincorporated Boulder County were also flat and empty.

By March 21, 2022, Louisville issued its "Recovery Plan for Marshall Fire" stating the city's plans for ensuring a fast and safe rebuilding of the damaged and destroyed buildings. It broke the process into five stages—Emergency Response, Critical Services Restored, Debris Removal, Rebuilding Homes and Public Spaces, and All Homes and Businesses Reoccupied and Reopened. The city committed to providing the staffing and resources necessary to its residents to rebuild and to publicly track its progress. Roles for each city department in the process were clearly stated so that residents knew who to contact when encountering an issue. Contact methods were included. Tracking was provided on a real-time website.[104]

Figure 73 Coal Creek Drive debris still present with construction on Barcus Lane in Superior, June 15, 2022.

Superior also provided online tracking of its recovery progress on an open website[105] available to anyone. By June 20, most of the northern half of the Sagamore development lots, as well as about half of the affected lots in Original Superior, were cleared. In all, 108 of the active parcels were cleared in a very short time.

Boulder County did modify its building permit process to streamline it for Marshall fire victims. Owners who rebuilt the same structure (i.e., original location and footprint, same floor area or smaller, same height or shorter) could apply for a building permit immediately, so long as they committed to rebuilding with additional wildfire resiliency measures. Owners who made changes to preexisting structure plans could proceed per streamlined procedures for modifications falling under certain parameters. Per the county statistics,[106] by June 20, 2022, twenty-five lots were cleared, and two building permits were issued of the 157 homes destroyed in unincorporated Boulder County. Special rebuilding coordinators were assigned to help each homeowner navigate the county rebuilding requirements. As many of the buildings burned were quite old, the cost of new requirements, like requiring internal sprinklers and ignition-resistant materials, may be a surprise to homeowners rebuilding.

---

[104] The Louisville rebuilding dashboard is at https://louisvillecogov.maps.arcgis.com/apps/dashboards/e3a547529d32498ca7fbd0d3fd236bd0.

[105] The Superior recovery dashboard is at https://www.arcgis.com/apps/dashboards/b4a7cbaeb4ef43ba9b1e9c3c0f0d8c94.

[106] See Marshall Fire Rebuilding Dashboard at https://www.bouldercounty.org/property-and-land/land-use/building/marshall-fire-rebuilding/.

Xcel Energy set up a special webpage[107] for customers affected by the Marshall fire to help them with utility information. They committed to stopping service for both gas and electric for all destroyed buildings as of December 31 and suspended reporting defaults for nonpayment short term to allow homeowners to work through the loss. Both Louisville and Superior did the same for water and sewer utilities. For all properties rebuilt, utilities will be treated the same as new builds, but without additional tap fees.

Boulder County commissioners issued a statement on January 12, 2022, stating, "This fire was able to intensify and spread because of conditions created by the climate crisis."[108] Based partly on this, the State of Colorado passed SB22-206, Disaster Preparedness and Recovery Resources Bill to provide "resources for disaster preparedness and recovery, and, in connection therewith, creating the disaster resilience rebuilding program, the sustainable rebuilding program, the office of climate preparedness, and making an appropriation." Governor Polis signed this bill into law on May 17, 2022. A month later, Boulder County announced that the bill's first offering was a grant program providing up to $10,000 to Marshall fire homeowners who rebuild using high-efficiency electric homes with heat pumps for space heating, electric stoves, and heat pump water heaters. A special program advisor was hired by EnergySmart to offer free consultations to these rebuilders to meet the grant requirements.

After the NCAR fire, the Boulder City Council[109] held a special working session to discuss "fire resilience" on April 26, 2022. Boulder owns the largest acreage burned and mans the Open Space and Mountain Parks department that manages them. During their meeting, they concluded that grazing and tree thinning are effective at reducing the size of wildfires. This is also demonstrated by the few wildfires and overall health of the national forests and grasslands in South Dakota that already follows these practices. Most of Boulder's forty-six thousand acres of managed open space, including Marshall Mesa, are grasslands. Cattle grazing is effective at reducing fuel like tall oat grass for a wildfire. However, it impacts one of the major reasons why the open space was acquired originally—to keep the tall prairie grass natural. How Boulder and their Open Space and Mountain Parks department will respond long term to the Marshall fire was not announced during the special session.

Only time will tell how long it will take for Louisville, Superior, and Marshall to fully rebuild the structures damaged and destroyed. A similar 2012 fire in Colorado Springs took seven years to finish restoring all the

---

107 See https://www.xcelenergy.com/staticfiles/xe-responsive/Outages/Boulder%20County%20Wildfire%20Resources%20for%20Xcel%20Energy%20Customers.pdf

108 The lack of prescribed burns was not mentioned as a contributing factor, but additional burns were scheduled by the county in 2022.

109 Based in part from https://boulderbeat.news/2022/04/30/wildfire-resilience/.

buildings.[110] Housing in Santa Rosa, California, is still being rebuilt after a fire in 2017. With supply chain issues, inflation, and a tight labor market exacerbated by COVID, delays are inevitable. Nearby Denver reports two-thousand-five-hundred-square-foot houses that in previous years took four to five months to build now take eight to ten months to complete. Pre-2020, lumber prices ran $350 per 1,000 feet of lumber. In 2021, that price jumped to nearly $1,500, adding $30,000–$40,000 in cost to rebuild such a home. And the federal government is raising interest rates to reduce inflation, which will also make it more expensive.

Figure 74 Cleared lots in Louisville Centennial Subdivision below Harper Lake looking south toward the police department in mid-June 2022.

[110] Based in part from "Pandemic Adds Time, Cost to Rebuild after Colo. Wildfire," Patty Nieberg and Linda Whitehurst, Associated Press, January 7, 2022.

Even with these impediments, there is no doubt that rebuilding will occur. Demand to live in Colorado, where the sun shines over three hundred days a year and the mountains loom in the background, is still great. The prairie has already recovered, and new residents will ensure that rebuilding continues until finished. As Paul Williamson discovers, even if you don't rebuild, someone else will buy your lot and do it for themselves.

Cause and Effects

According to a government website[111], the Marshall fire can be boiled down to statistics—6,084 acres burned, 2 fatalities, 1,084 homes destroyed, 149 homes damaged costing $513 million to restore, etc., . . . etc., . . .etc. But reality is much more personal—the loss of a home of thirty years, the death of a beloved pet, personal mementoes destroyed, fleeing from an inferno burning seconds behind with only the shirt on your back. The aftereffects from the fire will haunt many for years to come.

In Colorado, county sheriffs are responsible for coordinating firefighting efforts for any conflagration that crosses firefighting districts. The Marshall fire quickly met these criteria within the first two hours, making Boulder County Sheriff Joe Pelle responsible. As of October 1, 2022, no official cause has been announced by the sheriff for the Marshall fire. Of course, the press and social media have provided four major theories of what started Colorado's most destructive fire.

That December, the grasslands west of Superior and Louisville were primed to explode. Extra spring rain let them grow thick and tall while the long, rainless season following made them bone dry. No monsoonal rains occurred in the summer of 2021. Both the Town of Superior and Mountain View Fire Rescue told Boulder County to address the open space grassland conditions, but their requests went unanswered.

The first call to 911 at 11:09 a.m. talked of smoke near CO-93 and CO-170. MVFR Engine 2209 arrived on scene within minutes and found no fire but discovered a low-hanging utility line that they assumed was electrical. They headed south on CO-93 Foothills Highway and discovered a brush fire at 11:20 a.m. In the 100 mph westerly winds, that fire expanded rapidly. The second 911 call was received at 11:30 a.m. for a fire at Marshall Road and Cherryvale, within half a mile downwind northeast of the original call.

The first hypothesis for why the fire started is electrical. Initial reports from the OEM on December 30 indicate that both reported initial fire locations might have been caused by downed power lines. However,

[111] See https://mars.colorado.gov/MarshallFire

the low-hanging wires first identified by MVFR Engine 2209 turned out to be communications wiring and not electrical. Xcel Energy quickly reviewed its equipment and stated on December 31 that there were no *downed* power lines near where the fire started.

That does not mean that the fire was not started by electricity. On March 31, KUSA 9News[112] aired a report showing a phone video taken by Edward Harrell at 12:10 p.m. on December 30 of Xcel Energy power lines arcing over the intersection of CO-93 and CO-170. The video was impressive as the wires danced in the winds and flashed as they touched in a large cloud of smoke. A class action lawsuit, filed by two businesses, Eldorado Enterprises Inc. and Eldorado Liquor Inc. with two unnamed persons (a married couple, characterized as "terrorized and damaged" by the fire), claimed Xcel equipment "were a substantial factor in the cause, origin, and continuation" of the fire. The plaintiffs filed the lawsuit on behalf of Coloradans who experienced property damage or suffered financial loss due to the fire.

But by 12:10 p.m., the time of the Harrell video, the fire was already racing to the east from the initial fire discovered by Engine 2209 south of that location. These arcing wires could not have started the fire discovered by Engine 2209, though they may have begun a secondary blaze, or another set may have started the original blaze.

The second hypothesis discussed is that the fire was accidentally caused by humans. Immediately following the fire, numerous videos popped up on the internet showing the shed fire on the Twelve Tribes property. Boulder Open Space Ranger 5077 shot a video at 11:19 a.m. of smoke rising that, from her angle, appeared to be coming from behind the Twelve Tribes property. Other videos near that time and later show the shed on fire. The Twelve Tribes are known to burn trash on their property, and firefighters visited the site previously in December for possible fire violations. The sheriff did obtain a search warrant for the property, took a few items for investigation, but later returned them all without issuing any arrest warrants.

The third theory is that the coal seam fires burning underground near Marshall flared up and started the inferno. Burning since 1869, these fires have simmered and smoldered until winds, or a blast of methane, reach their embers, causing them to explode in fury. They have caused several wildfires nearby in the past. The coal seam that was recently filled in with gravel and loose rock is near where Engine 2209 first discovered fire. Satellite images late on December 30 did show a hot spot still glowing near where the fire originated that

[112] The following is based in part on the 9News report of March 31, 2022, by Erin Powell and Marshall Zelinger. See https://www.9news.com/video/news/local/next/video-shows-unusual-activity-on-power-line-on-day-of-marshall-fire/73-bbc97b4e-0864-462a-a284-46f05c8f2a98

was not associated with any known buildings. It is very possible that the coal seam fires flared up due to the intense Chinook winds and started the inferno.

And the final theory is that the fire was set on purpose for some reason. The human-caused Oak fire in Jefferson County started near a popular trailhead two days prior on December 27, 2021. It burned 152 acres and caused numerous evacuations. Similarly, the NCAR fire began on March 26, 2022, near another popular trail, and produced many evacuations in Boulder. It was contained within three days at 190 acres burned. Both of these human-caused fires originated near popular hiking trails, just as the Marshall fire initial location was near the Marshall Valley and Coal Seam trailheads. Maybe someone with a fetish for flames started the Marshall fire or all three.

Images after the fire of its perimeter from the air clearly showed three prominent "U-shaped" or "V-shaped" patterns along its western edge. These were confirmed later by satellite images. These shapes are associated with fire spreading from a starting point in high winds. Analysts said that fire usually doesn't form different perimeter contours like that against the predominantly westerly winds. 9News[113] went so far as to quote wildfire investigator and consultant Brenda Rice that these "V-patterns" indicate that there were three ignition points. Maybe all three of the first hypothesis are true—the fire started in multiple locations by multiple causes and then combined due to the intensity of the winds. But air pictures do not take into consideration the ground contours and wind currents. Only ground analysis can determine the effect of these. 9News made no mention of the second 911 call of the fire at Cherryvale and Marshall. Most assume it is caused by flying embers carried by the high winds. Again, Xcel found no sign of a problem with their wiring at that locale either.

The "ignition area" is defined by the *Guide to Wildland Fire Origin and Cause Determination* (2016) as "the smallest location which a fire investigator can define . . . in which a heat source and fuel interacted with each other and a fire began." According to this field guide, locating this point and collecting evidence from it is the fire investigator's chief objective. This term has evolved from the earlier concept of "point of origin" because often in wildfire investigation, the start of the fire cannot be isolated to a single point. However, analyzing the relations between individual fire pattern indicators will reveal the overall fire pattern. Burn patterns on grass and trees tell the story of wind and fire. They demonstrate the fire's progression. Three main elements influence fire's development—weather, topography, and fuels. In the Marshall fire's case, fire investigators concentrate

[113] Based from https://www.9news.com/article/news/local/wildfire/marshall-fire/marshall-fire-may-have-multiple-causes/73-5d0fece4-516f-4a11-b3f5-bae9900e65ee

on the high wind speeds, dry grasses, and hilly terrain to determine the fire's spread. These investigators will search for fire pattern indicator vectors of head, flank, and heel, to determine how the fire spread.

According to the guide, once a fire has reached a certain size, it can create its own wind due to indraft airflow. In the case of the Marshall fire, the high-speed Chinooks pushed the fire at incredible speeds. However, later in the day and during the evening, the winds subsided, and back-burning against the wind was possible, depending upon terrain and available fuels. Thus, timing comes into play in explaining when the "V-patterns" occurred, which cannot be determined from pictures taken from the air.

Topography consists of slope, aspect, and terrain. In the Marshall area where the fire started, there are numerous small hills, irrigation ditches, and looming Marshall Mesa. The fire spread following the wind using these to its advantage. As Dr. Janice Coen from NCAR noted, the fire tended to follow the ditches and lowest areas as it burned eastward.

The third element is fuel. Near Marshall, it was mostly overgrown grasslands and ditches that were tinder-dry from the lack of rain late in the year. The fire exploded among these enough to create a firewall that consumed everything in its path. Trees and shrubs were also consumed, but these were a minimum in the early stages of the fire. Wooden houses didn't stand a chance to the high winds and intense flames.

The investigation into the start of the fire continued as of the end of September 2022. As the wind did shift and the heat from the flames can cause vortices and burn back, these three "U-patterns" may eventually be explained. It should also be remembered that the FBI was called out to investigate the start of the fire, and that may be delaying the release of the final report. Until the final report comes out, only hypotheses exist to describe how the Marshall fire began.

That doesn't mean that the Sheriff's Department hasn't continued other work on the Marshall fire. The fifty-four-page "Marshall Fire Operational After-Action Report" (AAR)[114] for the performance of the various government departments and agencies involved is complete. The intent of the AAR is to provide a concise review of the actions that occurred during the fire and analyze them and record what went well and what can be improved. As such, there is bound to be interagency posturing to ensure the best picture is presented

[114] See https://assets.bouldercounty.org/wp-content/uploads/2022/06/marshall-fire-after-action-report.pdf

to the public. Presented to Superior and Louisville elected officials before being signed, the press provided its take on the initial report on June 21, 2022.[115]

Though produced by the Sheriff's Department, the report includes sections written by different agencies directly involved with the fire. Besides the Sheriff's Department, Louisville Fire and Police include perspectives on their performance during the fire, as does the Rocky Mountain Type 1 Incident Management Team. The Boulder EOC also has a section commenting on their duties and improvement plan. Glaringly missing are any comments from Mountain View Fire and Rescue (MVFR), the fire department who first responded.

Among the key AAR findings are problems with public evacuation notifications, including gaps with cellphone alerts, and the lack of the use of the emergency sirens. Also noted are miscommunications between various first responders due to radio frequency issues, lack of personal protective equipment, no defined strategy for the large number of vehicles evacuating, and no plan to provide food and water to the first responders on-site for such long periods. Though warned in the 2010 wildfire protection plans, a colossal lesson learned is fires are not limited to the Colorado mountain forests, but also can quickly burn the plain's grasslands anytime of the year. The Boulder OEM quickly adopted FEMA's Wireless Emergency Alerts in early 2022 to notify cell phones in an emergency as a response to the problem with evacuation alerts.

The report also comments on the fire exploding quickly when it reached Superior, forcing firefighters to shift priorities from fighting the fire to evacuating homeowners. As radio frequencies were not shared, communications between firefighters and police lagged during those critical minutes performing the initial evacuations. Though miraculously 37,500 homeowners evacuated safely within four hours, traffic backed up in places for forty-five minutes. The lack of mental health support for first responders is also mentioned.

The AAR includes a section commenting on the unmaintained open space. Grasses that grew significantly with the spring rains were tinder-dry and unmanaged by Boulder County and the City of Boulder open spaces. Irrigation ditches suffered overgrowth as well. Superior Town Trustee Neal Shaw said that Superior notified Boulder County of the problem, but the county did nothing. Said Shaw, "We're now even talking about organizing a community mowing event to get the grass cut."

---

[115] Based partly on the *Denver Gazette* news article "Learning from Fire Mistakes," June 21, 2022, by Carol McKinley. The AAR is posted at https://assets.bouldercounty.org/wp-content/uploads/2022/06/marshall-fire-after-action-report.pdf. The author did review a preliminary AAR copy prior to its press debut.

Successes are also included in the AAR. When the need was identified, evacuation notices were issued promptly. Police and fire door-to-door notices cleared out neighborhoods with only two deaths and few injuries. Avista Adventist Hospital and many long-term care facilities like Balfour evacuated successfully. Roadblocks, once established, controlled traffic, and kept people out of the burn zones. Firefighters protected more structures than they lost, even with the loss of water pressure. Said Mike Chard, Boulder County Director of Emergency Services, "It's not 100%, but this report identifies where we have gaps and weaknesses. It's an attempt to bring everyone together."

The Boulder County OEM also updated the "2022–2027 Boulder Hazard Mitigation Plan," with a draft released May 17, 2022.[116] It states, "Within Colorado, Boulder County has the highest number of residential structures within 500m of public wildland and ranks tenth overall in the west in terms of existing wildfire risk[117]." As such, Boulder County rates wildfires as a "high" hazard significance with widespread potential impact. Separate annexes review specific hazards and risks for Louisville and Superior and other areas in the county. The study states Louisville has 1,095 structures within the wildland-urban interface fire risk area, of which 978 are at moderate to high risk. Both Louisville and Superior decided to participate in the hazard plan update. Louisville also hired its own company to review and comment on the wildfire hazards for the city. It adopted temporary twice-yearly mowing of its open space as a stopgap measure.

Louisville Police and Fire also developed an evacuation plan for any future event based on "polygons."[118] Regions within the city are predesignated by streets and addresses so that each polygon can be evacuated separately or several at a time. Tied into the county's new Wireless Emergency Alerts that broadcast messages to all cell phones in an area, the city feels that any future evacuations can be handled faster and safer. Additional personal protection equipment, including masks, will also be made available to all Louisville first responders.

[116] See https://assets.boulderoem.com/wp-content/uploads/2020/12/hazard-mitigation-plan.pdf

[117] 2022–2027 Boulder Hazard Mitigation Plan, pp. 4–87.

[118] Based on teleconference with Louisville Fire Chief John Wilson, June 30, 2022.

Conclusion and Final Thoughts

There is no doubt that the Marshall fire changed Boulder County. Its effects devastated those whose homes and businesses were damaged and destroyed. And yet miraculously, even among all the despair and destruction, only two human lives were lost. Thirty-seven thousand five hundred homeowners fled successfully, some in forty-five-minute traffic jams, without being overtaken by flames and smoke. Businesses and enterprises emptied into the smoke and chaos, and only eight people reported injuries during the fire. Health care and long-term care facilities evacuated without incident, some driving in a convoy to escape the flames. Firefighters battled the inferno with dropping water pressures, saving more buildings than they lost. Surely, even during this most egregious incident, there were many events that can only be described as miracles and acts of God.

The Boulder County Sheriff's Department recognized a few of the early heroes of the fire on June 27, 2022[119] during an evening awards ceremony. Sheryl Buchman, a Superior resident, woke a neighbor sleeping after a night shift, and both fled as the flames attacked their homes. Chris and Debbie Clyncke treated responding deputies to hot meals in their commercial kitchen during the fire. Bernadette and Joe Pflug, owners of the Black Paw, bathed and decontaminated first responders' dogs. These are a few of the individuals feted by the Sheriff's Department that evening. Volunteer organizations honored include the Southern Baptist Disaster Relief, Samaritan's Purse, and Search and Rescue Dogs of Colorado. Said Boulder County Sheriff Joe Pelle, "We honored the individual employees, agencies, partners, and community members who went to great lengths to save lives, both human and animal, save property where possible, and to begin the process of healing and recovery."

Bringing everyone together is the theme of the logo, "One Community—Together We Will Recover & Rebuild," as posted throughout the burn areas. It is the common commitment that Louisville, Superior, and

---

[119] Based in part on "Marshall Fire Heroes: Superior Woman Who Woke Neighbor, Residents Who Cooked Hot Meals for Deputies" by Carol McKinley, June 28, 2022, *Denver Gazette*.

Boulder County governments make to their residents. There is no doubt that the three communities of Marshall, Superior, and Louisville will rebuild. Within a few years, it will be impossible to tell where the fire occurred.

Figure 75 Marshall fire One Community signs are posted throughout Louisville.

But the communities will have changed. Though houses may be constructed on the same lots and as close together as before the fire, they will be built to new, safer standards, be more energy efficient, and be constructed better for the environment. Communities will change as many longtime residents chose not to rebuild and sell off, moving to another locale—some because of the memories of the fire and others due to the cost of rebuilding. But soon, folks like the Bovens will again be sitting on their porches, discussing the weather with their neighbors, and admiring the Colorado mountain views. Memories of the miracles that happened during the fire will fade away, and the Marshall fire will become just another part of history . .

About the Author

A native of Ohio, Tom Gormley graduated Ohio State University with a degree in Engineering and Colorado State University with a Master's in Business. With over forty years business experience in high tech industries, Tom is now writing. An avid history buff, his first book, "A Korean War Odyssey", tells of locating his wife's uncle, long lost during the Korean War. His second, "INFERNO!", is the story of the Colorado Marshall fire and the many miracles that surround it. Tom and his wife live in the Colorado countryside near the fire. They love to travel in their motorhome with their companion Havanese, Koko.

Appendix A—Partial List of the Marshall Fire Miracles

1. The Marshall fire burned over 6,000 acres and consumed more than 1,000 structures in four hours, forcing the evacuation of 37,500 residents, plus employees and workers, and yet only two people were killed and eight reported injured.
2. The large evacuation occurred smoothly over few roads with no "road rage" incidents and no evacuating vehicles overcome by the fire.
3. Even though city warning sirens did not sound, and most residents did not receive the reverse 911 evacuation notices, all evacuated safely and timely.
4. The fire occurred during a time when schools were out and most families were together, making evacuations simpler.
5. The Chinook winds that initially fueled the fire lessened and even reversed as the evening progressed, saving many buildings.
6. Snow moved in the following afternoon, further containing a fire that could have burned for days.
7. Bill and Karen Lerch missed the beginnings and the middle of the fire by minutes.
8. The smoke cleared at McCaslin and Main in Superior, allowing evacuees to quickly leave the conflagration even as the fire ravaged Original Superior and the Sagamore subdivision.
9. The quick thinking of Costco associate Bob Guerreri saved a 9,000-gallon gasoline delivery truck from exploding.
10. Other Costco associates quickly and safely evacuated the store and shut down its air system.
11. The many patrons and employees from the Superior shopping center evacuated safely even as nearby homes and businesses burned in the high winds.
12. Costco was miraculously reopened eight days after the fire.

13. Though firefighters responded to calls of flames four times at the facility, the Home Depot was undamaged and reopened the following day for business.
14. Many relatives like the Boven's daughter Anna returned to the burning areas to help with the evacuation and made it in and out safely through the flames.
15. The wind blew from the south-southeast around Avista Adventist Hospital, protecting it from the fierce flames and allowing it to be evacuated safely and remain relatively undamaged.
16. Avista Adventist Hospital reopened within nineteen days after the fire.
17. With Avista and Good Samaritan not taking new patients during the fire, other nearby hospitals feared they would be overwhelmed by injuries and limited activities in anticipation of fire victims, but only eight injuries were recorded.
18. An Adams County state trooper steadied Willie the Horse for four hours with the fire burning fiercely all around, and both survived unscathed.
19. Balfour Senior Living identified two facilities to receive both its ambulatory and skilled nursing residents and evacuated them safely with few issues.
20. Balfour returned all residents home safely and received truckloads of water to see them through the Louisville "boil water" advisory.
21. Though over sixty cases of COVID occurred at Balfour after the evacuation, none were life threatening to its elderly inhabitants.
22. The leftover truckloads of water at Balfour were needed at another Balfour facility once the Louisville "boil water" advisory was lifted.
23. Flatirons Health and Rehab successfully evacuated its convalescence patients via a convoy of vehicles provided by nearby health facilities through the fire.
24. Eighteen nursing homes, hospitals, and medical facilities safely evacuated during the crisis with no loss of life or injury
25. A brush truck and a Type 1 fire truck successfully saved sixty-one townhomes amid the conflagration. Typically, over twenty trucks would be required to fight such fires.
26. Division Tango saved 322 structures from the fire under the worst of conditions with few resources and unreliable fire hydrants.
27. The fire jumped six-lane US-36 at least three times but was stopped solidly by smaller S. Boulder Road.
28. When the water hydrants dried up, a water tender arrived just in time for the firefighters near Harper Lake.
29. The 4:30 p.m. minor train derailment did not require diverting fire resources for long.

30. No schools or churches were destroyed by the fire, and all their damage was superficial.
31. With fire hydrants drying up, Louisville water employees kept pumps operational, created a way to bypass safeguards, and diverted untreated water into the system.
32. Water employees safely drove a large explosive propane tank through the inferno to start generators at the south plant in the middle of the fire and kept water flowing.
33. Afterward, fire-caused emissions in Louisville and Superior were no worse than normal daytime air pollution.
34. The snow arrived the next day, keeping the wildfire in the grasslands contained and diluting ash and burn toxins, minimizing remediation needs.
35. Of the 37,500 residents evacuated, fewer than two hundred stayed at shelters. Shelters could have been overwhelmed.
36. All the evacuees found long-term housing rapidly, often in miraculous and in unexplained ways.
37. The capricious nature of the fire left some buildings standing unharmed and leveling others seemingly randomly.
38. Many farm animals and pets miraculously survived.
39. The outpouring of support from around the world for the burn victims was overwhelming within the first forty-eight hours.
40. Many personal items recovered from the +2700°F fire that melted aluminum and glass and warped steel support beams should not have survived.

If you would like to discuss miracles that you see (or lack in your life), reach out to one of these churches for more information:

https://calvarybible.com/online/

https://www.flatironschurch.com

https://www.ascentcc.org

Appendix B—Statistics and Fire Responders

Incident Period:[120]
December 30, 2021, through January 7, 2022
Location: Boulder County, Colorado, including Marshall, Superior, and Louisville
Size of Fire: 6,080 acres
Fatalities/Injuries: 2 fatalities and 8 injuries
Home Damage: 1,084 destroyed, 149 damaged, $513,212,589
Commercial Damage: 7 destroyed, 30 damaged, $65,979,347

Marshall Fire Initial Response:[121]

Mountain View Fire Rescue: Engine 2209 & Brush 2232
Open Space Ranger 5077

Working Fire Response:

Allenspark: Engine 5202
Big Elk Meadows: Brush 4934
Boulder: Utility 2552, Engine 2501
Boulder Emergency Squad: Rescue 3121
Boulder Rural: Engine 2301, Brush 2331, Brush 2332, Medic 2321, Chief 2360, Utility 2353, Engine 2302
Boulder Mountain: Brush 4332, Engine 4301

[120] Reference https://mars.colorado.gov/MarshallFire
[121] Adapted from the list at https://5280fire.com/2021-incidents/marshall-fire/.

Coal Creek Canyon: Tender 7042, Brush 7031, Engine 7003
Four Mile: Engine 4603, Brush 4631
Hygiene Fire Protection District: Engine 2803, Brush 2832
Lafayette: Brush 2631, Command 2662, Battalion 2660, Truck 2619, Brush 2632, Engine 2601, Engine 2602, Medic 2622
Longmont: Brush 2131, Brush 2133, Command 2167, Engine 2108
Louisville: Battalion 2760, Medic 2721, Medic 2722, Medic 2723, Training Engine 27, Training Medic 27, Engine 2702, Engine 2703, Brush 2732, Brush 2733, Tower 2718, Truck 2716, Chief 2761
Mountain View: Tower 2215, Truck 2216, Brush 2230, Brush 2234, Brush 2236, Brush 2238, Battalion 2260, Command 2262, Command 2266, Command 2269, Utility 2271, Rescue 2255, Medic 2225, Engine 2201, Engine 2203, Engine 2207, Tactical Tender 2242
Nederland: Rescue 5621
North Metro: Engine 66
Boulder County Fire Management:
West Metro: Wildland 1, Brush Engine 9, Medic 11
AMR Boulder: AMR 2

Departments / Agencies Assisting:

Adams County Fire Rescue, AirLife, Allenspark Fire Protection District, Ambulunz, AMR Boulder, AMR Pueblo, American Red Cross, Arapahoe County Sheriff's Office Wildland Fire Team, Arvada Fire Protection District, Aurora Fire Rescue, Banner Health Paramedics, Bennett-Watkins Fire Rescue, Berthoud Fire Protection District, Beulah Fire Protection District, Big Elk Meadows Fire Protection District, Black Forest Fire Protection District, Boulder County Fire Management, Boulder County Hazmat Authority, Boulder County Office of Emergency Management, Boulder County Parks & Open Space, Boulder County Sheriff, Boulder Emergency Squad, Boulder Fire-Rescue Department, Boulder Mountain Fire Protection District, Boulder Open Space & Mountain Parks, Boulder Police Department, Boulder Rural Fire Rescue, Brighton Fire Rescue District, Broomfield Police Department, Brush Volunteer Fire Department, Buckley Fire & Emergency Services, Bureau of Alcohol, Tobacco, Firearms, and Explosives (ATF), Byers Fire Protection District, Castle Rock Fire & Rescue, Centennial Valley Volunteer FD (WY), Central City Fire Department, Children's Hospital Colorado, Cimarron Hills Fire Department, Coal Creek Fire Protection District,

Colorado Bureau of Investigation, Colorado Division of Fire Prevention and Control, Colorado Department of Transportation-CDOT, Colorado National Guard, Colorado Springs Fire Department, Colorado State Patrol, Cortez Fire Protection District, Crook Fire Protection District, Denver Fire Department, Denver Paramedics, Durango Fire Protection District, East Orchard Mesa Fire District, Eaton Fire Protection District, Elk Creek Fire Protection District, Erie Police Department, Estes Valley Fire Protection District, Evans Fire Protection District, Evergreen Fire Protection District, Fairmount Fire Protection District, Falck Rocky Mountain, Federal Bureau of Investigation, Federal Heights Fire Department, Flight for Life, Florissant Fire Protection District, Foothills Fire Protection District, Fort Carson Fire Department, Fort Lewis Mesa Fire Protection District, Fort Lupton Fire Protection District, Fort Morgan Volunteer Fire Department, Four Mile Fire Protection District, Frederick-Firestone Fire Protection District, Front Range Fire Rescue, Galeton Fire Protection District, Genesee Fire Protection District, Gilpin Ambulance Authority, Glen Haven Area Volunteer Fire Department, Gold Hill Fire Protection District, Golden Fire Department, Greeley Fire Department, Highland Rescue Team Ambulance District, Hudson Fire Protection District, Hygiene Fire Protection District, iCare Ambulance, Indian Hills Fire Protection District, Inter-Canyon Fire Protection District, Jamestown Volunteer Fire Department, Jefferson County Fire Management, Jefferson County Sheriff, Lafayette Fire Department, Lafayette Police Department, Laramie County Fire Authority (WY), Larkspur Fire Protection District, Lefthand Fire Protection District, UCHealth LifeLine, Longmont Emergency Unit, Longmont Fire Department, Longmont Police Department, Louisville Fire Protection District, Louisville Police Department, Loveland Fire Rescue Authority, Lyons Fire Protection District, Manitou Springs Volunteer Fire Department, Manitou Springs Fire Department, Med Evac, Mesa County Sheriff Wildland Fire Team, Morgan County Ambulance Service, Mountain View Fire Rescue, Nederland Fire Protection District, New Raymer–Stoneham Fire Protection District, Northglenn Ambulance, North Fork Fire Protection District, North Metro Fire Rescue District, Oak Creek Fire Protection District, Pinewood Springs Fire Protection District, Platte Canyon Fire Protection District, Platte Valley Fire Protection District, Poudre Fire Authority, Pueblo Fire Department, Pueblo Rural Fire Protection District, Pueblo West Fire Department, Sable Altura Fire Rescue, Security Fire Department, South Adams County Fire Department, South Metro Fire Rescue, Stadium Medical, Stone Mountain Fire Protection, Strasburg Fire Protection District, Sugar Loaf Fire Protection District, Sunshine Fire Protection District, Team Rubicon, Thornton Fire Department, Timberline Fire Protection District, Upper Pine River Fire Protection District, United States Fish & Wildlife Law Enforcement, Vail Fire & Emergency Services, West Douglas County Fire Protection District, West Metro Fire Rescue, Westminster Fire Department, Westminster Police Department, Windsor-Severance Fire Rescue, Xcel Energy, Yoder Fire Department, many other agencies including law enforcement who responded to this disaster

Partial Bibliography

5280 Fire. (2022). *Marshall Fire*. Retrieved from 5280 Fire: https://5280fire.com/2021-incidents/marshall-fire/

A Superior Transformation. (2019, 07 01). Retrieved from Downtown Superior: https://downtownsuperior.com/a-superior-transformation/

Adams County Fire Rescue Podcast. (2022, 01 21). A first hand look back at the Marshall Fire-ACFR Firefighters tell their story. Colorado.

Amabile, Judy; Fenberg, Stephen (2022, 05 17). *Disaster Preparedness And Recovery Resources*. Retrieved from Colorado General Assembly: https://leg.colorado.gov/bills/sb22-206

Anchor Point. (2010). *Wildland-Urban Interface Community Wildfire Protection Plan*. Boulder, CO: Rocky Mountain Fire.

Automated Weather Logging. (n.d.). *PWS Weather Station*. Retrieved from PWS Weather: https://www.pwsweather.com

Avista Hospital. (2022, 01). *Fire viewed from Avista Adventist Hospital roof.* Retrieved from Vimeo: https://vimeo.com/661507003?embedded=true&source=vimeo_logo&owner=105818696

Barkley, Scott (2022, 01 03). *Colorado Baptists respond to wind-driven fire destruction*. Retrieved from Baptist Press: https://www.baptistpress.com/resource-library/news/colorado-baptists-respond-to-wind-driven-fire-destruction/

Boulder County. (2010). *Boulder County Community Wildfire Protection Plan*. Boulder, CO: Boulder County Government.

Boulder County. (2022). *Information on Boulder County's Emergency Notification System*. Retrieved from Boulder County : https://assets.bouldercounty.org/wp-content/uploads/2022/01/marshall-fire-emergency-notification-system.pdf

Boulder County. (2022). *Marshall Fire Rebuilding and Repairs in Unincorporated Boulder County*. Retrieved from Boulder County Org: https://www.bouldercounty.org/property-and-land/land-use/building/marshall-fire-rebuilding/

Boulder County. (2022). *Marshall Fire: Air Quality*. Retrieved from Boulder County.org: https://www.bouldercounty.org/disasters/wildfires/marshallfireaq/

Boulder County. (2022, 06 17). *New $10,000 incentive for Marshall Fire rebuilds*. Retrieved from Boulder County Org: https://www.bouldercounty.org/news/new-10000-incentive-for-marshall-fire-rebuilds/

Boulder County Commissioners. (2022, 01 12). *Boulder County Commissioners to the Boulder County Community and President Biden: This is a climate emergency*. Retrieved from Boulder County Org: https://www.bouldercounty.org/news/boulder-county-commissioners-to-the-boulder-county-community-and-president-biden-this-is-a-climate-emergency/

Boulder County Dispatch. (2021, 12 30). *Boulder County Sheriff and Fire Feed Archives*. Retrieved from Broadcastify: https://m.broadcastify.com/archives/feed/591

Boulder County Sheriff. (2022, 06 28). *Community members and valued partner organizations recognized*. Retrieved from Boulder Sheriff: http://http://www.bouldersheriff.org

Boulder County Sheriff Office. (2021, 12 30). Marshall Fire Videos. Colorado.

Boulder County Sheriff's Department. (2022, 06). *Marshall Fire Operational After-Action Report (AAR)*. Retrieved from Boulder County Org: https://assets.bouldercounty.org/wp-content/uploads/2022/06/marshall-fire-after-action-report.pdf

Boulder Daily Camera. (1895, 07 22). Will Protect Their Homes. *Boulder Daily Camera*.

Boulder OEM. (2022, 05 17). *2022 – 2027 BOULDER HAZARD MITIGATION PLAN*. Retrieved from Assets Boulder OEM: https://assets.boulderoem.com/wp-content/uploads/2020/12/hazard-mitigation-plan.pdf

Boulder Office of Emergency Management. (n.d.). *Boulder Office of Emergency Management*. Retrieved from Boulder Office of Emergency Management: https://www.boulderoem.com

Buffo, Ron (2014). Fear Rules Cities and Fight is On at Louisville Mines. *The Louisville Historian, Winter 2014*.

Castle, Shay (2022, 04 29). *As Boulder County burns, a new focus on fire resilience*. Retrieved from Boulder beat: https://boulderbeat.news/2022/04/30/wildfire-resilience/

Chief Niwot and the Curse of Boulder Valley. (n.d.). Retrieved from About Boulder: https://aboutboulder.com/blog/chief-niwot-and-the-curse-of-boulder-valley/

CIRES Communications. (2022, 01 13). *CSL and CIRES scientists investigate lingering air quality effects of the Marshall Fire.* Retrieved from Chemical Sciences Laboratory NOAA: https://csl.noaa.gov/news/2022/340_0113.html

City of Louisville. (2022). *CIty of Louisville Rebuilding Dashboard.* Retrieved from Louisville CO Government: https://louisvillecogov.maps.arcgis.com/apps/dashboards/e3a547529d32498ca7fbd0d3fd236bd0

CIty of Louisville. (2022, 03 21). *Recovery Plan for Marshall Fire.* Retrieved from Louisville Co Government: https://www.louisvilleco.gov/home/showpublisheddocument/34565/637844998923630000

Coen, Janice (2022). *Coupled Weather - Wildland Fire Modeling Case Studies - 2021 Marshall Fire.* Retrieved from NCAR: https://www2.mmm.ucar.edu/people/coen/files/newpage_m.html

Colorado Gives. (2022). *Boulder County Wildfire Fund.* Retrieved from Colorado Gives: https://www.coloradogives.org/bouldercountywildfirefund?step=step1

Colorado State University Extension. (2021, 12 31). *After the Disaster Guidebook - Boulder County.* Retrieved from CSU Extension: https://extension.colostate.edu/wp-content/uploads/2022/01/Boulder-County-After-the-Disaster-Guidebook-CSU-Extension-V3.pdf

Community Foundation Boulder County. (2022). *Boulder County Wildfire Fund.* Retrieved from Community Foundation Boulder County: https://www.commfound.org/wildfirefund

Conarroe, Carolyn (2001). *Coal Mining in Colorado's Northern Field.* Louisville, CO: Conarroe Publishing.

Division of Homeland Security & Emergency Management. (2022). *DR4634 Marshall Fire and Straight Line Winds.* Retrieved from Colorado.gov: https://mars.colorado.gov/MarshallFire

Dorsey, Larry (2009). *Ku Klux Klan: The Invisible Empire in Boulder County, Superior Historian, Summer 2009.* Retrieved from Superior Colorado Government: https://www.superiorcolorado.gov/home/showpublisheddocument/10569/636476249141770000

Dyni, Anne (2005, 12 27). *History of Irrigation in the Boulder Valley.* Retrieved from Boulder Area Sustainability Information Network: https://bcn.boulder.co.us/basin/history/irrigation.html

Eberhart, Perry (2018, 04 25). *The 1927 Columbine Mine Massacre: Trouble in Serene (reprint from Denver Posse of Westerners brand book, Vol. 29, 1973).* Retrieved from Lafayette History: http://www.lafayettehistory.com/the-1927-columbine-mine-massacre-trouble-in-serene/

Everbridge. (2022). *Emergency Alert System Information*. Retrieved from Everbridge: https://member.everbridge.net/453003085612231/login

Fraser, Clayton B. (1997). *Railroads in Colorado 1858 - 1948.* Loveland, CO: Fraserdesigns.

Galatowitsch, Susan; Baker, William (1985). *The Boulder Tall Grass Prairies.* Boulder, CO: Boulder County Nature Association.

Harrell, Edward (2021, 12 30). Phone Video of Marshall Fire and Xcel Power Line Arcing. https://www.youtube.com/watch?v=flWwWn6Lb84

Ippen, Chandra M. G. (2017). *Trinka and Sam: The Big Fire.* Retrieved from The National Child Traumatic Stress Network: https://www.nctsn.org/resources/trinka-and-sam-big-fire

Johnson & Ward. (1863). *Johnson's New Illustrated Family Atlas.* 113 Fulton St., New York: Johnson & Ward.

Linquist, J. Peter (2010). *The Louisville Historian, Issue 88, Fall 2010.* Retrieved from Louisville Colorado City Government: https://www.louisvilleco.gov/home/showpublisheddocument/1106/637122786507900000

Louisville City Council. (2022, 06 07). *APPROVAL OF RESOLUTION NO. 26, SERIES 2022 – A RESOLUTION APPROVING AND ADOPTING THE 2022-2027 BOULDER COUNTY, COLORADO MULTI-HAZARD MITIGATION PLAN.* Retrieved from Louisville Library: https://www.louisville-library.org/home/showpublisheddocument/35208

Louisville City Government. (2022, 01 01). *Fire Update: January 1, 2022.* Retrieved from Louisville Co City Government: https://www.louisvilleco.gov/Home/Components/News/News/5530/17?arch=1&npage=2

Louisville City Water & Operations Staff. (2022, 02 02). *The Heroic Story of the City's Water and Operations Staff.* Retrieved from Louisville Colorado Government: https://www.louisvilleco.gov/Home/Components/News/News/5679/17

Louisville Fire Protection District. (2022). *History.* Retrieved from Louisville Fire Protection District: https://www.louisvillefire.com/about/history/

Louisville Hisotrical Society et al. (2021). *Louisville Timeline.* Retrieved from Arcgis: https://experience.arcgis.com/experience/5afda61b96ed4793b49c3f55bc24e846/

Marshall Fire Survivors Network. (2022). Retrieved from Marshall Together: https://marshalltogether.com

McKinley, Carol (2022, 06 21). Learning from Fire Mistakes - Marshall blaze report outlines how agencies can better respond. *The Denver Gazette*, pp. 01, 08.

Michels, Ashley (2022, 5 11). *Local News: Boulder County grants first permit to rebuild after Marshall Fire.* Retrieved from KDVR : https://kdvr.com/news/local/boulder-grants-first-permits-to-rebuild-marshall-fire/

National Center for Atmosphic Research. (n.d.). *Who We Are - A Center of Excellence.* Retrieved from NCAR: https://ncar.ucar.edu/who-we-are

National Environmental Satellite Data and Information Service. (2022, 1 5). *Seen from Space: The Colorado Marshall Fire FacebookTwitterLinkedInRedditShare* . Retrieved from NOAA.Gov: https://www.nesdis.noaa.gov/news/seen-space-the-colorado-marshall-fire

National Weather Service. (2022). *High Winds and Marshall Fire on December 30th, 2021.* Retrieved from National Weather Service: https://www.weather.gov/bou/HighWinds12_30_2021

National Wildfire Coordinating Group. (2016, January). *Guide to Wildland Fire Origin and Cause Determination.* Retrieved from NWCG Government: https://www.nwcg.gov/sites/default/files/publications/pms412.pdf

Owensby, Clenton (1972). Burning True Prairie. *Third Midwest Prairie Conference Proceedings.* Manhattan, KS: Department of Agronomy, Kansas State University .

Powell, Erin; Zelinger, Marshall (2022, 03 31). *Xcel named in class action lawsuit alleging sparks from power line caused Marshall Fire.* Retrieved from 9news.com: https://www.9news.com/article/news/local/wildfire/marshall-fire/marshall-fire-class-action-lawsuit-xcel/73-e4ddd480-b2ee-41e6-9dce-a1dff3f25641

Rebuilding Better. (2022). *Rebuilding Better.* Retrieved from Rebuilding Better: https://rebuildingbetter.org

Roberts, Stephen B. (2007). *Coal in the Front Range Urban Corridor.* Reston, VA: U.S. Geological Survey.

Sampson, Joanna (2008). *Walking Through History on Marshall Mesa.* Boulder, Colorado: City of Boulder Open Space and Mountain Parks.

Shinn, Mary; Wyloge, Evan; Earls, Stephanie (2022, 02 20). *Dangerous legacy: Tens of thousands of Coloradans live near one of the state's many underground coal-mine fires.* Retrieved from The Denver Gazette: https://denvergazette.com/news/local/dangerous-legacy-tens-of-thousands-of-coloradans-live-near-one-of-the-state-s-many/article_e534bc8c-476f-5bb5-be96-61e25ba55b3a.html

Sister Carmen. (2022). *Marshall Fire Relief.* Retrieved from Sister Carmen: https://sistercarmen.org/marshall-fire-relief/

Superior Historical Commission. (2004). *"Shootout at the Superior Depot," Superior Historian Fall 2004.* Retrieved from Superior Colorado Government: https://www.superiorcolorado.gov/home/showpublisheddocument/82/635548425414100000

Superior Rising. (2022). *About Us.* Retrieved from Superior Rising: https://www.superiorrising.org/about/

Town of Superior. (2022). *Superior Recovers.* Retrieved from Superior Colorado Government: https://www.arcgis.com/apps/dashboards/b4a7cbaeb4ef43ba9b1e9c3c0f0d8c94

U.S. Department of Homeland Security. (2022, 05 31). *Wildfires.* Retrieved from Ready: https://www.ready.gov/wildfires

Vaughan, Kevin (2022, 01 27). *Wildfire expert: Marshall Fire may have started in multiple places as a result of multiple ignition points.* Retrieved from 9News: https://www.9news.com/article/news/local/wildfire/marshall-fire/marshall-fire-may-have-multiple-causes/73-5d0fece4-516f-4a11-b3f5-bae9900e65ee

West Metro Fire Rescue. (2022, 1 20). *West Metro Fire Rescue: On the Front Line- The Marshall Fire.* Retrieved from You Tube: https://www.youtube.com/watch?v=cVXMch9X2D8

Whitehurst, Lindsay; Niebrg, Patty (2022). Pandemic Adds Time, Cost to Rebuild after Colo. Wildfire. *Associated Press.*

Xcel Energy. (2022). *Boulder County Wildfire Resources for Xcel Energy Customers.* Retrieved from Xcel Energy: https://www.xcelenergy.com/staticfiles/xe-responsive/Outages/Boulder%20County%20Wildfire%20Resources%20for%20Xcel%20Energy%20Customers.pdf

Index

A

AAR (After-Action Report") 197-9, 212
aboutboulder.com 19, 213
access code 140
accident 101, 112-13, 141
    multicar 140-1
    two-car 106, 138
Acme 11-12
Acme Place 12
Adams County 89, 91, 101
Adams County Station 89-90
After-Action Report" *see* AAR
agencies 115, 163, 165, 197, 200, 210, 215
Aikens 19-20
air 9, 104-6, 123, 133, 135, 155, 161, 175, 196-7
Air Quality Index (AQI) 136
Airbnb 59, 140, 157, 175, 179
    original 178
alarm 86, 93, 95, 99, 107, 116, 140
    intrusion 118, 122
ambulances 38, 77-8, 86, 124, 146
American Medical Response (AMR) 46, 209
AMR (American Medical Response) 46, 209
AMR Boulder 209
Andrea 22
announcement 44, 52, 72, 88, 179-80
apartment 69, 123, 126, 142, 146
Appia 15, 17, 66, 72, 76, 81, 84, 86, 91, 93, 95, 97, 100-1, 107, 112
application 11, 32, 96
Applied Technology Council (ATC) 161
AQI (Air Quality Index) 136
Arapaho 19-20
Arapahoe 108, 117, 120, 141
Arapahoe Circle and Willow Place in Louisville 158
Arapahoe Circle in Louisville 100
areas evacuating 68
Arkansas Rivers 1
Arvada 51, 63, 86, 122
Arvada Truck 98-9
ash 42-3, 52, 81, 83, 89, 91, 101, 105-6, 135, 157-8, 161, 168, 172, 183-5, 189
assets.bouldercounty.org 34, 68, 172, 197-8, 211-12
assets.boulderoem.com 199, 212
assistance 40, 88, 138, 153, 159, 179-80, 185-6
ATC (Applied Technology Council) 161
avalanches 69, 71
Avista 41, 77-8, 86, 117-18
Avista Adventist Hospital 41, 76-7, 163, 185, 199, 206, 211
Avista Hospital in Louisville 79, 139

B

backyard 57-8, 138, 141, 177
Balfour 69-71, 76, 84, 87-8, 121, 125, 155, 199, 206
Balfour's buildings 70-1
bankruptcy 110-11
Baseline north of Louisville 76
Battalion 209
batteries 28
bcn.boulder.co.us 61, 213
Becki Siemers 70, 76, 87, 122, 155
beds 23, 41, 58, 71, 100, 106, 121
Bender 89-91
Bender, Katie 89-90
bids 171
bill 28, 35, 77, 191, 205, 211
blacksmiths 4, 6
blanket 177
blaze 8, 65, 99, 114, 145, 147, 149, 152, 186
blocked Marshall Road 35
blocks xii, 17, 26, 49, 72, 74, 80, 86, 93, 96, 100, 104-5, 116-17, 130, 143
blocks west 42, 118
bloodhound 176-8
blowing xii, 72, 104-5
bluestem grasses 24-5
board 73, 84, 86, 96, 106, 122, 147
Boarding homes 4
bond 15
booklet 153
Boulder 2-3, 5-7, 9-10, 13, 15-16, 24-5, 29, 31-2, 34-5, 41, 43-7, 115, 131-2, 191, 211-15
  north of 20, 32, 133
Boulder All-Hazard Incident Management Team 32, 45
Boulder and Weld Counties 33, 110
Boulder campus 153, 186
Boulder Canyon 19, 107, 111
Boulder City Council 191
Boulder Colorado 10
Boulder Colorado Banner xv
Boulder County 9-11, 15-16, 26-7, 34, 46-7, 67-8, 114-15, 152-3, 162-3, 169-71, 173-4, 179-81, 190-1, 198-9, 211-15
Boulder County evacuation centers 115
Boulder County Fairgrounds 80-1, 83, 94, 117
Boulder County Fire 32, 47
Boulder County Fire Management 209
Boulder County Marshall 87
Boulder County OEM 153, 199
Boulder County OEM and Xcel Energy 128
Boulder County Org 212
Boulder County O˚ce of Emergency Management 38, 209
Boulder County Sheri xii, 26, 32, 40, 44, 46, 194, 200, 209, 212
Boulder County Sheriff and Fire Feed Archives 212
Boulder County Sheriff's Office xii
Boulder County Type 163
Boulder County Wildfire Fund 213
Boulder County Wildfire Resources for Xcel Energy Customers 216
Boulder Creek 19-20
Boulder Daily Camera xv, 12, 212
Boulder Emergency Squad 46, 208-9
Boulder Engine 81
Boulder EOC 80, 163, 198
Boulder Fire Department 46, 95
Boulder Hazard Mitigation Plan 199, 212
Boulder IMT 45
Boulder IMT Type 80, 91
Boulder OEM 46, 68, 99, 147, 149, 151, 156, 163, 198, 212
Boulder O˚ce of Emergency Management 44-5, 87, 212
Boulder Police Department 46, 209
Boulder Road 10, 13, 38, 41, 67, 72, 81, 84, 86-7, 93, 99, 106-7, 112, 130-1, 184-5
Boulder Road east of town 76
Boulder Road in Lafayette 76, 116, 122
Boulder Road in Louisville 106, 112, 117
Boulder Rural 80, 208
Boulder Rural Engine 117

Boulder Sheri 76, 92, 212
Boulder SWAT 94
Boulder Tall Grass Prairies 214
Boulder Tallgrass Prairies 24
Boulder Type 40
Boulder Valley 19, 183, 213
Boulder Valley Christian Church 112, 185
Boulder-Weld coal˛eld 23
boulderbeat.news 191, 212
Boven, Larry 17, 72
Boven residence in Louisville 17
Bovens 72-3, 122, 164, 201, 206
boxes, moving 176
boys 19, 58
Brave Louisville xi
brie˛ng 114-15, 147
broadcast 32, 35, 47, 67-8, 71, 94-5, 104, 112
Broom˛eld 51, 77, 86, 90, 104, 106, 116
Brush 32, 37-8, 40, 208-9
    tasked Boulder Rural 66
    toned Boulder Mountain 112
brush truck 35, 38, 76, 89-91, 96, 99, 206
Buckthorn Way in Louisville 105
building Louisville farther 12
buildings xi, 18, 25, 37, 52, 91, 95, 121-2, 139-40, 148-9, 155-7, 161, 174, 181, 189-90
burn xii, 7, 27, 35, 37, 65-6, 75, 81, 83, 91, 99, 107, 124, 135, 197-8
burn area 37, 104, 129, 136, 138, 150-1, 156, 161, 163, 174, 200
burn zone 129, 134-5, 147, 150, 152, 163, 184, 199
burning 8-9, 25, 28, 37, 40, 55, 59, 66, 72, 74, 78, 80, 91, 134-5, 143-4
burning buildings 74, 91
burning homes 73, 123, 144
    started xii
buses 70-1, 87, 107, 122
businesses 3, 29, 66, 114, 118, 129, 156, 170, 172, 179-80, 195, 200, 203, 205-6

C

CAD (computer-aided dispatch) 47
callers 47, 51, 147
Calvary Bible Church 186
campuses 185-6
Canary Lane 105-6, 117, 126, 144, 146
canyon 3, 111
Capt 20, 98
cards 161
care facilities, long-term 199-200
caring 153, 185
Carnegie Library for Local History 4-5, 7, 13-14, 21, 23, 29, 31, 109, 111
carts 52, 54, 94
casualties 13, 114
cat 68
CAWFE (Coupled Atmosphere-Wildland Fire-Environment) 133
CC (Colorado Central) 109-10
cell phones 44, 67-8, 198-9
cement board 43, 167
Centaur Circle, block of 118
Centennial Heights 106
Centennial Heights West 154
Centennial Parkway in Louisville 86, 116
Centennial Subdivision in Louisville 189
Centennial Valley of Louisville 17
Century Drive in Louisville northwest of Lowes 84
Century Drive Louisville 81
Ceres lawsuit 173-4
checkout conveyors 52-3
Cherryvale 34, 37-8, 40, 44, 48, 92, 189, 194, 196
Cherryvale Command 40, 48
Cherrywood 70-1, 86, 88
Cherrywood Lane 76, 98-9
Cherrywood Village 69
Cheyenne 19-20, 110
Chief Niwot 19-20, 213

Chief Willson 96
 contacted Louisville Fire 129
children 10, 13, 20, 69, 71, 95, 182, 185-6
Chinook winds xii, xv, 85, 153, 205
 high velocity ix
 high-velocity xv
 intense 196
Chinooks xvi, 9, 104-5
churches 4, 181, 185-6, 207
CIRES (Cooperative Institute for Research in the Environmental Sciences) 132, 135
CIRES Communications https 135
citizens 12, 29, 119
city xi, 14-16, 25-6, 30, 46, 66-8, 80-1, 87, 110, 129, 156, 158, 168-9, 173-4, 199
City of Boulder 6, 9, 32, 35, 43, 46, 198, 215
City of Boulder and Boulder County 45
City of Boulder Police and Fire Communications 47
City of Boulder voting 13
City of Louisville 94, 213
CIty of Louisville 213
CIty of Louisville Rebuilding Dashboard 213
city o˚cials 96, 160, 162, 165
cleanup 135, 168-9, 171, 173-4, 188
cleanup contract 171
Cleared lots in Louisville Centennial Subdivision 192
closures, soft 160, 165
cloth grocery bags 58-9
clothes 59, 73, 88, 175
Club 69-71
Club Circle in Louisville 85, 104
CO 115, 211, 213-14
CO-93 xv, 28, 32, 35-7, 39-40, 43-4, 66, 77, 105, 117, 194-5
CO-170 28, 32, 35-8, 40, 43, 52, 194-5
CO-170 Marshall Road xv, 28
coal 3-6, 8-10, 12, 15, 20, 22-3, 29, 94, 108, 215
 million tons of 20, 23
 ton of 6, 9
 tons of 11-12
coal beds 9, 24
Coal Creek 19, 24, 57, 74, 80, 133
Coal Creek Circle 99
Coal Creek Ranch 57, 75, 78-9, 99, 144, 175
Coal Creek Ranch development in Louisville 107
coal lands 3, 6
coal mines 5-6, 15, 29
coal mining 4-6, 23-4
Coal Mining in Colorado 12, 213
coal seam 3, 6-9, 11, 20, 137, 195-6
Code x, 26, 33, 48, 60, 82, 84, 98, 125, 127, 131, 137, 139, 142, 156-7
coen 133, 135, 213
Coen, Janice 133-5, 197
Col 20
collection point 30
Coloradans 195, 215
Colorado xi-xii, 1-2, 10-11, 18-19, 24-5, 30, 43-4, 60-2, 68-70, 108-11, 133, 175, 178, 193-4, 211-15
 eastern 20
 railroads in 108, 214
 state organization 179
Colorado Central *see* CC
Colorado City 108
 usurped 108
Colorado coal 7
Colorado history ix, xv, 25
Colorado Marshall 203
Colorado mountains 108-9, 201
Colorado National Guard 94, 162, 210
Colorado Springs 111, 180, 191
Colorado State Patrol 47, 210
Colorado state politics, dominated 25
Colorado State University 203
Colorado State University Extension 153, 213
Colorado Territory 2-3, 20, 108-9
Colorado's Northern Field 12, 213
Columbine 14, 213

command 37, 40, 45, 51, 66, 72, 80, 90, 92-3, 99, 101, 106, 149, 209
Command, Marshall xiii, 37-8, 40-1, 65, 73-4, 76, 80, 84, 86, 91-3, 100, 106, 116, 122-4, 137-8
Commander Wilber 32, 80, 91, 147, 149, 152, 165
committee 171
communities xi, 6, 16, 34, 43-4, 69, 96, 102, 135, 157, 179, 185-6, 200-1, 213
Community Ditch 61, 112, 116, 118
Community Foundation 179
Community Foundation Boulder County 179, 213
Community Park 76, 99, 116, 123
Community Wild˛re Protection Plan 34
companies 6, 10, 15, 28-30, 149, 156, 171, 199
  ditch 61
  electric 28
  local distribution 30-1
completion 40, 110, 173
complexity 162-3
computer ix, 42, 58-9, 73, 159
  personal 69
computer-aided dispatch (CAD) 47
connected Marshall 5
construction 77, 110, 135, 181, 190
contacts 38, 51, 66-8, 72, 74, 86, 124, 138, 161, 178, 190
contract 30, 111, 171, 173
contractors 18, 30, 169, 172-3
con˙agration xi, 126, 144, 153, 194, 205-6
Cooperative Institute for Research in the Environmental Sciences (CIRES) 132, 135
coordinates xii-xiii, 45-6, 171
Copper Lane 100, 142
Costco xii, 40, 50-2, 55, 66, 77, 104, 127, 205
Costco gas station 40, 52, 55, 65
Costco shopping xiii, 51, 66, 134
costs 68, 94, 115, 169, 173, 181, 187, 190, 192, 201, 216
cottages 13
country 29-30, 83, 110
county 9, 16, 34, 44, 111, 138, 162, 165, 168-9, 171, 173-4, 181, 188, 191, 198-9
County Dispatch 26, 37, 63, 66, 71-2, 74-6, 80-1, 85-6, 92-4, 99-100, 106-7, 116-18, 122, 124-6, 138-43
County Dispatch and Police Dispatch 126, 144
County of Boulder Colorado 10
Coupled Atmosphere-Wildland Fire-Environment (CAWFE) 133
court 171, 173-4
Courtesy 4-5, 7, 11, 13-14, 19, 21, 23, 26, 29, 31, 51, 54, 64-5, 90, 95
Courtesy of Boulder Co 87
Courtesy of Boulder County 62
Courtesy of Boulder OEM 164
Courtesy of NOAA NWS-Boulder 39, 85
Courtesy of Xcel Energy and Boulder OEM 166
COVID 107, 153, 155, 163, 186, 192
COVID-19 16
CR-170 Marshall Road 66
Cramer 53, 55
Cramer, Joe 52-4
creek 20, 24, 60, 111, 133
crews xi, 8, 55, 66, 80, 89, 94, 96, 114, 156, 172
cubic feet 9
Culebra Creek 60

D

DAC (Disaster Assistance Center) 153, 159, 178, 183, 186-7
dad 175-6
debris 102, 157-8, 168-9, 172-4, 184
debris removal 173-4, 180, 189
Demand Integrity in Government Spending (DIGS) 171, 173
demolition 169, 174, 188
Denver 3, 5, 15, 18, 29, 42, 91, 95, 108-10, 121, 136, 182, 187
Denver & Boulder Valley Railroad 110
Denver-Boulder Turnpike 41, 152
Denver Paci˛c *see* DP

department xii, 6, 33-5, 40, 47, 73, 122, 197-8, 200, 209, 212
Department Operations Center (DOC) 45
deploy 40, 66, 94, 132, 162-3
deputies xii-xiii, 42, 65-6, 147, 200
deputies evacuating houses 32
Deputy 37, 74-6, 80, 112
desert glass 178
destroyed buildings 96, 129, 149, 189, 191
devastation 91, 149-50, 153-4, 164, 167, 185
DIGS (Demand Integrity in Government Spending) 171, 173
Dillon 99-100, 105, 117-19, 147
directed Edward 100, 106, 124
Disaster Assistance Center *see* DAC
disaster preparedness 191, 211
disasters 44-6, 67, 69, 95, 153, 161, 210, 212
dispose 168-9
dispute, domestic 106
distance 13, 61, 67, 110, 187
disturbance, domestic 118
ditches 10, 34, 60-2, 133, 197
diversions 62
Division Tango 96, 98-9, 112, 206
di˚culty breathing 86, 117, 124, 126
DOC (Department Operations Center) 45
dogs 51-2, 73, 200
donations 83, 157, 179, 185
  physical 157, 179
Donner 89, 91
down Marshall Mesa 144
downtown 12, 95
Downtown Louisville 95, 141
DP (Denver Paci¸c) 109-10
drainages 133
DRC 171-4
dug 60
dumpsters 158, 168
  large 168

E

Earth 132
east 11, 14, 20, 25, 35, 37-8, 40, 51-2, 57, 66, 71-2, 98-9, 104-5, 109, 118
east Boulder 108
east Louisville 69, 124
eastern Colorado plains 105
ective 89, 91, 96, 99, 135, 145, 173, 191
ects 35, 73, 135, 152, 161, 194, 196, 200
Edgewater UMC 182, 187
educators 185
Edward 86, 93, 100, 105-7, 112, 116-19, 122-6, 214
Eighty-eighth Street 41, 139-40
Eighty-eighth Street in Louisville 118
elderly persons 81, 123-4
Eldorado Springs 33-5, 144
Eldorado Springs-Marshall Fire Protection District 34
electricity 28, 30, 74, 78, 128, 147, 156, 158, 160, 163, 195
Element Hotel 72, 74-6, 90, 92, 114, 138, 149, 156
embers 35, 74, 85, 91, 112, 125, 133, 195-6
EMD (Emergency Medical Dispatch) 47
emergency 31, 42, 44, 67, 69-71, 94-5, 108, 115, 198
  medical 96
Emergency Medical Dispatch (EMD) 47
Emergency Operations Center *see* EOC
emergency room (ER) 77
Emergency Support Functions (ESFs) 45
Emerson 53, 55, 118
Emerson, George 52-3
employees ix, 33, 41, 52-3, 55, 71, 77, 88, 132, 149, 153, 165, 200, 205
Engine 32, 35, 37, 101, 107, 112, 138, 195, 208-9
engines 35, 73, 91, 101-2, 145
EOC (Emergency Operations Center) 44-5, 94
equipment 32, 34, 40, 88-9, 92, 108, 121-2, 129, 151, 181, 195
ER (emergency room) 77
Erie 3, 9, 15, 18, 24, 28, 33, 106, 108, 110, 120, 186

ESFs (Emergency Support Functions) 45
evacuate 38, 42, 49, 52-3, 58-9, 68, 70, 72-7, 80-1, 86-8, 99, 107, 115-18, 124-6, 130
evacuating residents 71, 119
evacuation centers 157, 179
evacuation order 38, 72, 74, 86-8
evacuation tra˚c 75, 77, 128
evacuations 38, 53-4, 66-9, 71-3, 78, 80-1, 93, 107, 116-18, 124, 137-8, 155, 196, 199, 205-6
evacuees 67, 69, 76, 100, 122, 139, 142-3, 151, 207
  blind 143
evening 22, 28, 43, 58, 73, 115, 118, 138, 145, 147, 197, 200, 205
Everbridge 214
ex-wife 58
exchange, telephone 95
expeditions 1
exploding Marshall 51
eye protection 184

F

facilities 25, 47, 70-1, 73-4, 77, 88, 107, 118, 121-2, 147, 155, 206
factors 133, 135, 172, 191, 195
families xi, 6, 49, 58, 96, 112, 153, 158, 178, 182, 186, 205
family photograph 49, 51
farm animals 82-3, 207
farmers 10, 60, 62, 82
fatalities 115, 194, 208
faults 3
Federal Emergency Management Agency *see* FEMA
Federal troops camping in Louisville 14
feeling ill 58
fees 169, 181
FEMA (Federal Emergency Management Agency) 68, 71, 115, 159, 161, 168, 188
FEMA Administrator Deanne Criswell 161, 164
FEMA-funded cleanup 173
female 118, 124
few miles northwest 108
Fire, Marshall iv, 98, 114, 174, 189, 211-16
Fire-ACFR, Marshall 211
Fire Dispatch 76, 84, 86, 93, 99-100, 105-8, 112, 116-17, 119, 123-4, 126, 137-8, 140, 143, 145
Fire Management Assistance Grant (FMAG) 115
Fire˛ghters xii, 44, 65, 147, 153, 160-2, 199-200, 211
Flagsta 25, 33-4
FlatIron Crossing Mall xiii, 40-2, 45, 51, 66, 74, 80, 82, 89, 91-2, 94, 98, 101, 116
Flatirons 107, 185
Flatirons Health and Rehab 107, 206
FMAG (Fire Management Assistance Grant) 115
food 18, 59, 117, 157-60, 162, 177-9, 182, 185, 198
Foothills Highway xv, 66, 100, 112, 117
Foothills Highway east to Louisville 74
foundation 45, 157, 172, 178, 180, 184
Francisco 129
frantic radio calls xii
Frasier Meadows 88, 121
Frasier Meadows in Boulder 88, 155
Frederick 3, 15, 28
freight 110
friend 3, 58, 68
front 42, 51, 55, 59, 66, 93, 95, 176
fuels 135, 196-7
function 45-6

G

Galina 68
game camera 177-8
garage 59, 100
garden 35, 121-2, 168
gas 9, 30-2, 78, 160, 191
gas meter 32
gas station 42, 52, 138, 182
gates 61

Gazette, Denver 8, 83, 200, 215
generators 129, 143
Getty Images ii
goats 51-2, 83
GoFundMe page 168-9, 178
Gold City 108-10
Gold Lexus 124-5
gold seekers 19
Golden 5, 10, 28, 77, 108, 110
Golden Town 10
Good Sam 77-8, 83, 117
Goodhue and Marshallville ditches north of US-36 93
Gorham 5-6
government 9, 11, 179, 188, 211
    federal 68-9, 169-70, 192
government agencies 181
governor 5-6, 14, 25
Governor Polis 115, 161, 191
grab 69
grading 10, 109, 111
Grand Junction 70-1
Granddaughter Layla Cornell 51
Grant Avenue in Louisville 143-4
grasses xii, xvi, 24, 26, 35, 42, 58, 62, 66, 71-2, 81, 93-4, 100, 116, 198
grasslands xv-xvi, 24-5, 76-7, 189, 191, 207
grasslands west 34, 194
group 41, 43-5, 109, 181, 185
guards iii, 13, 15, 99
Guerreri, Bob 52, 55, 205
guide 196-7
gusts 9, 35, 104, 115, 133
gym 58

H

Hake 20-2
hard closures 158-9, 165
Harper Lake 15, 73, 86, 92-3, 100, 102, 122, 126-7, 192, 206
Harper Lake in Louisville 101, 118, 124
Harper Lake Louisville 86
Healthy Forest Restoration Act (HFRA) 34
heart 92
heat 8, 65, 74, 78, 155, 159, 172, 197
heaters 157
Hecla 12-14, 69, 76, 117
helmets 35
help evacuate 100, 106, 112, 116, 118, 146
help evacuating 119, 142
hematite 3-4
HFRA (Healthy Forest Restoration Act) 34
high-performance homes, constructing 181
high winds knocking 67
Highway 11, 101, 124, 152
hill 17, 41, 57, 80, 197
Hillside Lane 17, 72-3
history x-xi, 3, 7, 61, 201, 213-15
hit-and-run 125-6
Home Depot 66, 118, 122, 206
Home Depot in Louisville 66, 72, 118-19, 134, 138
homeowners 68, 93, 152-3, 172-3, 181, 184-5, 191, 198
homes 10-12, 16-17, 35, 42-3, 63, 65-6, 72-4, 77-8, 85-6, 93, 106, 122-4, 147-50, 152-3, 187-90
    arrived 42
    car-garage 17
    cheap 21
    comfortable 181
    cottage 69
    damaged 16
    daughter's 168, 186
    destroyed 129
    dream 18
    electric 191
    family 83
    few 6
    headed 121
    heat 15

manufactured 180
member's 155
nearby 51, 135, 167, 205
new 16
nursing 107, 206
resilient 181
return 152
surviving 135
transfer 155
two-story 11
Homes and Businesses Reoccupied 189
homes blazing 117
homespun clothing 43
Horse Evacuation Boulder Fort Collins Fire 82
horses 3, 51-2, 60, 81, 83, 94, 110, 206
hoses 35, 63, 73, 81, 91, 94, 99, 184
hospital 41, 77-8, 85, 107, 117, 206
hot spots 89, 134, 150, 152, 157, 162, 195
hotel 74, 76, 154, 186
house xv, 18, 21, 30, 35, 51, 58-9, 73, 101-2, 117, 121-3, 150, 154, 158, 174-5
house-to-house ordering evacuations 105
houses burning 63, 73
Housing and Urban Development (HUD) 170
https iii, 19-20, 43-4, 67-9, 78, 104-5, 132-3, 158-9, 161-2, 171-2, 179-81, 190-1, 194-9, 207-8, 211-16
HUD (Housing and Urban Development) 170
human services 159, 161
hurricanes 69, 105
Hwy 133
hydrants 63, 99, 101, 128-9, 143, 206
hydro-mulching 171

I

ICP (Incident Command Post) 40, 45
ill 58
images ii, 133-5, 196
satellite 195-6
impacted-by-marshall-¿re 153
IMT *see* Incident Management Team
IMT1 163
Incident Command Post (ICP) 40, 45
Incident Management Team (IMT) 40, 45, 162, 198
Incident Team 162
incidents 45, 121, 163, 200
including Marshall 208
including Marshall Mesa 191
inferno x, 35, 43, 92, 99, 167, 176, 195-6, 200, 207
information ii, 32, 43-4, 47, 58, 69, 78, 81, 94, 115, 128, 161, 171, 177-81, 207
Information on Boulder County 211
informed Marshall Command 92, 107, 117, 130, 138, 141
injuries 14, 81, 107, 114-15, 121-2, 138, 206, 208
instruments 135
International Workers of the World (IWW) 14
internet ii, 58-9, 104, 152, 195
intersection 11, 37, 44, 105, 160, 195
interviews ix, 17-18, 26, 28, 32, 52, 68, 96, 171
investigation 150, 152, 157, 195, 197, 210
investigators 196-7
in'ation 192
iron 10
iron ore 3-4
irrigation ditches 20, 60, 197-8
IWW (International Workers of the World) 14

J

Jase 57-9, 153, 175-8, 182
Jase's folks 59
Jase's parents 175
Jean 58-9, 175, 177-8, 182
Johnson 2-3, 214
Julesberg 10, 109
jump 66, 104

K

Kansas City 109-10
Kansas Paci¸c (KP) 109-10
Kestrel Lane 146
kids 57-9, 168, 175, 178
Kingdom Assignments 186
Klan 25
Kowar 128-9
KP (Kansas Paci¸c) 109-10

L

La Niña 136
Lab for Atmospheric and Space Physics (LASP) 132
Lafayette 14-15, 29, 68, 82-3, 99, 104, 117-18, 161, 181, 209
Lafayette Battalion 37-8, 40
Lafayette Engine 106, 112, 117, 141
  toned 100, 118, 139-40
Lafayette Medic 139-40, 143
Lafayette northwest of downtown Louisville 123
Lafayette YMCA 94, 115-16, 151, 157
Lake, Marshall 24, 92, 127, 138
land xvi, 6, 10, 15-16, 19, 61, 82, 162, 181
Langford 4-5
Larry 17, 73, 154, 182, 186-8, 213
LASP (Lab for Atmospheric and Space Physics) 132
law enforcement ix, 35, 67, 91-2, 149
law enforcement o˚cers ix
law enforcement units 143
lawsuit 13, 171, 173, 189, 195
ld-marshall-¸re 215
Lincoln 99-100, 105, 108, 112-13, 117-19, 122-4, 138, 141, 147, 168
line winds, straight 115
list 69, 84, 87, 94, 157, 160-1, 208
living residents 76, 88, 121, 155
  independent 125
locations 8, 12, 37, 40, 43, 67, 69, 76, 80, 88, 106, 140, 152, 184, 194-5
Longmont 29, 47, 66, 73, 76, 88, 106, 115, 118, 143, 145, 147, 154, 209
Longmont Emergency Unit 46, 210
Longmont law enforcement units Paul 131
Longmont Unit 117, 143
Longmont United 78, 107
Longmont units Paul 126
Longs Peak 112
Longs Peak Drive in Louisville nonemergency 145
looming Marshall Mesa 197
lots 12, 174, 189, 201
Louisville 10-17, 24-6, 28-30, 39-41, 65-72, 92-6, 98-101, 104-7, 116-19, 126-9, 142-7, 156-9, 174-5, 187-9, 198-201
  attacked 50
  attacking 105
  east side of 69-70
  eastern 70, 76, 94, 100
  loved 186
  reached 15
  south 80
  southeast 41
  southern xv, 67
  started listing 16
  study states 199
  subdivision of 57, 106
  west 69
  western 71, 99, 128
Louisville and Superior Cleanup 167
Louisville area 104, 126
Louisville Battalion 37, 40, 80
Louisville Brush 71
Louisville Bus 93-4, 106, 143
Louisville Cemetery 126, 130
Louisville Chief Water Plant Operator Greg Venette 128
Louisville City Water & Operations Sta 214
Louisville Co City Government 214
Louisville Co Government 213
Louisville Coal Creek Golf 123

Louisville Coal Creek Ranch 80, 176
Louisville Colorado City Government 214
Louisville Colorado Government 214
Louisville crew 95
Louisville deploys 96
Louisville Engine 38
Louisville evacuation orders 152
Louisville Fire xi, 46, 80, 96
Louisville Fire and Police 198
Louisville Fire Chief John Wilson 199
Louisville Fire chief Willson 73
Louisville Fire Department iii, 72
Louisville Fire Protection District xi, 95, 210, 214
Louisville Fire Station 72, 91, 97-8, 101-2
Louisville Firehouse 81
Louisville handling north of US-36 and MVFR 80
Louisville Harper Lake area 74, 103, 116
Louisville Historian 10, 13, 94, 212, 214
Louisville Historical Museum 11, 14
Louisville Historical Society 26, 95
Louisville home 12, 135
Louisville hydrant pressure 138
Louisville law o˚cer 140
Louisville Library 214
Louisville Manorwood 121
Louisville Manorwood Lane 149
Louisville mayor Ashley Stolzmann 152
Louisville McCaslin Boulevard east 72
Louisville Medic 106, 119, 126, 140, 143-4
    now-free 118
    toned 106, 117, 119, 124, 143
Louisville Middle School 95, 141
Louisville miners 13
Louisville Mines 13, 212
Louisville North 10, 128
Louisville north of US-36 72, 92
Louisville Open Space 34
Louisville Police and Fire 199
Louisville Police Department 46, 76, 210
Louisville Police Department building 76
Louisville Police Station 72, 84, 98
Louisville Police Unit 83-4
Louisville Public Works 138
Louisville Rebuilding Dashboard 190
Louisville Rec Center 72
Louisville Recreation and Senior Center 17
Louisville Recreation Center 66, 76, 91, 96, 101, 164
Louisville Reservoir 127
Louisville residents 158
Louisville Size of Fire 208
Louisville south 76, 87, 128
Louisville South Howard Berry 128
Louisville south of South Boulder Road 75
Louisville Tactical 84
Louisville team 94
Louisville Timeline 214
Louisville Trucks 72, 99
Louisville Unit 76, 145
Louisville wastewater treatment plant 11
Louisville Water 96
Louisville Water and Operations staff 130
Louisville Water Department 138
Louisville water employees 207
Louisville Water Treatment Plant 104
louisvillecogov.maps.arcgis.com 190, 213
Louisville's Centennial 156
Louisville's community hospital 41
Louisville's El Dorado Lane 124
Louisville's equipment 72
Louisville's population 13
Louisville's South 128
Louisville's water supply 138
Luckily 42, 69, 74, 93, 101, 125, 141, 152, 163
Ludlow 13-14

M

MAC (Multi-Agency Coordination) 45
MAC group 45
machine guns 6, 13, 15
Macy 74, 80, 89, 94, 98, 100-1, 106, 149
Main Street 15-16, 95
mall 40, 90-1
map iv, 34, 96, 131, 136, 150-1, 157, 159
mars.colorado.gov 194, 208, 213
Marshal 22, 80
Marshal Angelo D 22
Marshal Fire 81
Marshall xi-xiii, xv, 3-9, 24-5, 27-8, 33-40, 44-7, 49, 66-8, 132-6, 161-5, 179-82, 189-91, 194-7, 200-1
Marshall, Joseph 3
Marshall area 161, 197
Marshall blaze report 215
Marshall circa 5
Marshall coal 7
Marshall Consolidated Coal Mining Company 11
Marshall Drive 44, 86
Marshall Fire FacebookTwitterLinkedInRedditShare 215
Marshall Fire Heroes 200
Marshall Fire Initial Response 208
Marshall Fire Miracles 205
Marshall Fire Operational After-Action Report 197, 212
Marshall Fire Rebuilding 212
Marshall Fire Rebuilding Dashboard 190
Marshall Fire Relief 215
Marshall Fire Survivors Network 214
Marshall Fire Videos 212
Marshall northeast 23
Marshall Open Space areas 35
Marshall rate 9
Marshall Road CO-170 51
Marshall Road intersection 32
marshall-꜀re 196, 208, 211, 215-16
marshall-꜀re-relief 215
MarshallFire 194, 208, 213
Marshall's smelter 3
marshalltogether.com 180, 214
Marshallville Ditch 61
marshall꜀reaq 212
Mary 17, 72-3, 154, 186-8, 215
masks 16, 53, 161, 167, 184
Maxar Open Data Program 64-5
McCaslin 17, 20, 41-3, 51, 55, 65-6, 72-5, 80, 84, 86, 90-1, 99, 107, 119, 122
  east of 89, 149
  west of 18, 104, 106
McCaslin Boulevard 15-16, 67, 69, 74, 98, 128, 152
McCaslin Boulevard in Louisville 137
McCaslin Command 72, 76, 83-4, 86, 93
Meadow Court 124
meals 13, 116, 121, 159, 183, 185, 187
Medic 208-9
medivac team 108
Melzer 101-2
members 41, 43-4, 52, 91, 121, 147, 155, 162, 185-6
memories 73, 201
mergers 28, 34
Meridian Lane 117, 126
Mesa, Marshall 3, 6-7, 189, 215
metal, twisted 149, 156-7
methane gas 9, 30
MHz 47
Middle Fork 27, 32-3, 37-8, 40-1, 44-5, 114, 133, 161, 163
miles xiii, 9, 23, 26, 28-30, 35, 37-8, 41-2, 49, 51, 71, 77, 105, 107-8, 147
miles northeast 120
million 9, 109, 171, 173-4, 180, 194
miners 4, 6, 12-13, 15, 21-2
mines 6, 10, 12-15, 23, 29, 108
mining 3, 6, 8, 10
minutes xii, 26, 28, 37-8, 40, 52, 59, 66, 69, 71, 77, 112, 134, 138, 186
miracles ix, xvi, 43, 55, 67, 78, 88, 156, 200-1, 203, 207

mitigation 46
model ii, 133
moisture 24, 135-6
monsoons 136
Mont Alto Park 111
Montoya, James 52
Mountain Parks 191, 215
Mountain View 34-5, 99, 209
Mountain View Fire Rescue *see* MVFR
mountain wave 85, 104-5
mountains 1-3, 9, 16-17, 25, 33, 47, 104, 118, 169
mph 1, 9-10, 18, 28, 42, 57, 77, 80-1, 85, 89, 101, 104-5, 114, 121, 132
mph winds 65
Mulberry Street 98-9, 106
Mulberry Street in Louisville south 80
Multi-Agency Coordination (MAC) 45
Museum of Boulder Collection 4, 13-14, 21, 23, 29, 31, 109, 111
mush 184
MVFR (Mountain View Fire Rescue) 32-4, 80, 194, 198, 208, 210
MVFR Command 37, 40, 116
MVFR Engine 35, 37, 76, 106, 194-5
MVFR south of US-36 and Louisville north 92
MVFR Truck, toned 107-8

N

nap 58-9
National Center for Atmospheric Research *see* NCAR
National Institute of Standards and Technology (NIST) 132
National Oceanic and Atmospheric Administration *see* NOAA
National Renewable Energy Laboratory (NREL) 132
National Science Foundation (NSF) 132, 135
National Weather Service 9, 68, 104, 215
native languages 19
natives 1, 19-20
natural gas 15, 30-1, 147, 152, 155-6, 158
natural gas leak 100
Nawatny 10-11
NCAR (National Center for Atmospheric Research) 25, 132-3, 191, 196-7, 213, 215
ne-on-day-of-marshall-¸re 195
neighborhoods 57, 63, 72, 93, 115, 124, 149-50, 154, 171, 199
  burned-out 158, 175, 177
neighboring xi, 25
neighboring homes 172
  attacking 58
neighbors iii, xv, 17, 49, 58, 67, 72-3, 118, 180, 186, 188, 200-1
New Illustrated Family Atlas 2-3, 214
New Year's Eve 10, 59, 141, 150-1, 153
news 44, 58, 135, 153, 195-6, 212-13, 215-16
next-door Louisville South Howard Berry water treatment plant 49
Nighthawk Circle 93
Ninety-sixth 117, 119, 145, 147
Ninety-sixth Street in Louisville 124
NIST (National Institute of Standards and Technology) 132
Niwot 19-20, 33, 115-16, 147, 151
NOAA (National Oceanic and Atmospheric Administration) ix, 39, 85, 132, 135
NOAA noon surface winds 39
noaa.gov 215
non-evacuated city residents 152
nonpro¸ts 171, 179-81
noon xii, 39-41, 44, 49, 51, 58, 105, 128, 151, 160-1, 165
Nordstrom 45, 91-2, 147, 149, 152, 156, 165
north 2, 11-12, 24-5, 40, 51, 57, 66, 69, 72-4, 81, 85-6, 91, 93, 99-100, 104-6
  houses 80, 104
north Boulder 25
North Boulder Recreation Center 100, 115-16, 151
North Broadway xii, 26
north plant 127-8
northeast 37, 48, 102

northeast Louisville 187
Northern Coal¸eld 3, 110
Northern Colorado 29
Northern Colorado Conservation District 127
Northern Colorado Power Company 29
Northern Water 127-8
northwest 66, 139, 185
Northwest Parkway 72, 95
NREL (National Renewable Energy Laboratory) 132
NSF (National Science Foundation) 132, 135
nursing residents 125, 155
    skilled 88, 121, 206

O

occasions, special 28
OEM (O˚ce of Emergency Management) 27, 38, 40, 44-5, 51, 63, 66-7, 72, 87, 100, 116, 150-2, 156-7, 159, 161
Oklahoma 19-20
Old Colorado City 17
Old Louisville Inn on Front Street 95
Old Marshall Road 35, 37
Old Marshall Road north 28
Old Santa Fe Restaurant in Louisville 89
Old Town Louisville 11
on-site 29, 32, 71, 100, 112, 141, 146, 161-2
Open Homes Program 157, 179
open space 8, 15, 24, 26, 34, 91, 135, 191, 198-9
Open Space and Mountain Parks 191, 215
ord.com ii
organizations 25, 181, 186
Original Marshall 94
Original Superior xiii, 18, 74, 81, 134, 138, 169, 190
orts xii-xiii, 73, 82, 111, 129, 149-50, 152, 155, 157, 162, 165, 179-82, 194
Overland Route 108-9
overnight bags 88, 121, 155
Owens 128-9
Owl Drive 112
owners 3, 20, 44, 68, 141, 169, 172, 190, 200
o˚ce, post 4, 11-12, 26
O˚ce of Emergency Management *see* OEM
Oxford Road 118-19

P

Paci¸c, Denver 109-10
page ii, 34, 49, 138
park 26, 73, 99
parking 51-2, 55, 71, 77-8, 91, 124, 178
particulates 136
party 1-2, 13, 112, 119, 124, 138, 141, 145, 147
passenger 35, 110
patients 47, 70, 77-8, 88, 106-7, 118
    critical 77, 117
Paul 18, 126, 131, 143-7, 168-9
pdf 191, 213, 215-16
peak Louisville gust 105
Pelle 35, 115, 150, 156-7
People's Ditch 60
perimeter 135, 162, 196
Perrella Garage 95
personnel 34, 162
Peterson 129
pets 69, 207
Photo 33, 38, 48, 60, 82, 84, 98, 125, 127, 131, 137, 139, 142, 144, 156-7
Photo courtesy of Louisville Public Works and Utilities 130
Photography x, 26, 33, 48, 60, 82, 84, 98, 125, 127, 131, 137, 139, 142, 156-7
pictures x, 19, 21, 26, 30, 53, 69, 80, 102, 105, 144, 177-8, 197
Pikes Peak 1, 108
Pinyon Way in Louisville south 112
pipes 31, 128, 153, 156, 158, 165
plans 46, 71, 152, 158, 160, 165, 172-3, 198
    ranch 187-8
plant 29, 128-9

plastic 69
plat 11
plows 60
podcast 89
police ix, 46, 59, 91, 126, 152, 164, 198-9
Police Dispatch 93-4, 99-100, 105-8, 116-19, 122, 124-6, 130-1, 137-8, 140-3, 145-7
police unit 94, 99, 107, 131, 138, 140-1, 147
Polk Avenue and Owl Drive in Louisville 117
pollutants 135
polygons 199
population 6, 10, 16, 21, 26
power 29-30, 74, 100, 105, 143, 149-50, 152, 161
power lines 30, 128, 152, 215
    downed 26, 28, 114, 149, 151, 157, 194-5
power outages 41, 150, 153
prairie 189, 193
pre-evacuation xii, 25, 66, 68, 86, 99
preparedness 46
present-day Denver 1-2, 19
President Biden 115, 212
press brie‹ng 114
pressure 30-1, 35, 128-9, 138
process 45, 59, 129, 156, 169, 171, 173-4, 178, 189-90, 200
property iii, 6, 11-12, 44, 49, 51, 66, 132, 140, 153, 158-9, 168-9, 171-2, 184-5, 195
property owners 171, 173
Ps 69
PSAPs (Public Safety Answering Points) 47
Public Safety Answering Points (PSAPs) 47
Public Service Company 29-30
publisher ii
pumps 128-9, 207

Q

Quail 121-2
Quality Inn in Louisville east 66

R

radio 32, 92, 100, 117-18, 163
railroads 5, 10-11, 108, 110-11, 214
rails 109-10
railways 110
ranger 37, 145
RASEI (Renewable and Sustainable Energy Institute) 132
rebirth 189
rebuild ix, xi, 154, 168, 173-4, 180, 187, 190-3, 201, 215-16
rebuilding 174, 181, 187, 189-90, 193, 201
Rebuilding Better 215
Rebuilding Homes and Public Spaces 189
rebuildingbetter.org 181, 215
rebuilt 95, 174, 187, 189-90, 192
recovery 46, 162, 191, 200
reference https 208
refrigerators 150, 158, 160
Regal Square evacuation request to Louisville Police 93
region xv, 1, 9, 23-4, 34, 68, 94, 104, 108, 116, 199
relatives 11, 28, 88, 119, 122, 206
relief 115, 143, 153, 182, 185
relights 156, 165
Renewable and Sustainable Energy Institute (RASEI) 132
request 51, 57, 71, 74, 81, 106, 115, 123, 145
requested Marshall Command 49
rescue 47, 63, 71, 81, 83, 89, 112, 198, 208-9
Reservoir, Marshall 129
residences 12, 49, 69, 174
residents ix, xv, 33-4, 67-8, 87-8, 118-19, 121-2, 146-8, 150-3, 155-6, 158-61, 164-5, 190, 200-1, 205
    ected 161, 180
    longtime 49, 201
    new 28, 193
    returning 152, 155
residents east 117
resource mobilization 44-5
resources 32, 37, 40, 43, 45, 47, 51, 63, 66, 68, 72, 152-3, 162-3, 180-1, 190-1

responders 84, 96, 117, 163, 183, 198-200
restaurants 15-16, 89, 95, 185, 187
Retrieved 211-16
reverse 63, 72, 75-6, 87, 205
Richmond Homes 26
ride 55, 88, 142
Ridgeview Drive 147
Ridgeview Drive in Louisville 145
risk ix, 30, 34, 65, 95, 107, 110, 149, 168, 199
    moderate 34
rivers 1, 3, 60, 108
RMFD (Rocky Mountain Fire District) 33-4
Road, Dillon 16, 57-8, 75, 80, 85-6, 89, 99, 112, 119, 122, 126, 144, 149, 175
Road, Marshall 8, 32, 35, 37-8, 42, 49, 52, 55, 65, 67, 104, 114, 127, 129, 138
roadblocks 35, 90, 92, 118, 122, 142-3, 149, 152, 154, 162, 199
roads 14-15, 28, 43, 66, 71, 99, 101, 109-10, 126, 141, 153, 163, 189
Roberts 51, 215
rock 6, 12-13, 15, 24, 195
Rock Creek 19, 34, 91, 116, 124, 147, 173
Rock Creek Parkway 118, 123-4, 152, 160
Rocky Mountain Fire District *see* RMFD
Rocky Mountain Type 162-3, 198
Roger 184
rooms 57, 71, 78, 88, 122, 155
Roosevelt 130-1
roo¿ng 168
route 108-9, 111
ruins 168, 176, 178
runways 171-2

S

safety 8, 70, 82, 88, 96, 153, 162
Safeway 116
Sagamore neighborhood 63, 65, 114
Sagamore subdivision xii-xiii, xv, 50-1, 55, 60, 73, 205
saloons 4, 12-13, 21
Samaritan's Purse 178, 183-5, 200
Sans Souci Community 100
school buses 117-18
schools 4, 10, 12, 112, 175, 185-6, 205, 207
scientists 132-3, 135
seam 3, 8, 23-4
Searcy 22
SEEC (Sustainability, Energy, and Environment Complex) 132
Serene 3, 14-15, 213
Sergeant 49, 51, 53
sergeants xiii, 92
service xi-xii, 34, 67, 90, 119, 122, 143, 149, 157, 165, 179, 186, 191
service line 31
Servpro 78
set 1, 15, 76, 91-2, 98, 118, 153, 168, 184, 195-6
Seventy-¿fth 141
shaft 10, 12, 20
Sharpe, Robert 49
shelters 116, 207
sheri xiii, 37, 42, 47, 65, 147, 194-5
Sheri 27, 32, 35, 40, 47, 49, 51, 53, 66, 75-6, 80, 149-50, 156-7, 164-5, 197-8
sheri, quoted Boulder 34
She°eld 187-8
She°eld Homes 187
shift 143, 183-4, 197, 200
Siemers 71, 88, 155-6
sirens 58, 67, 72
Sister Carmen 157, 179, 182, 215
situational awareness 44-5
skilled nursing 69-71, 76, 122
skilled nursing residents home 155
smoke xii-xiii, 7-9, 32, 35, 37, 40-3, 51-2, 54-5, 58, 66-7, 71-2, 77-8, 91, 101, 194-5
    intense 41, 52

smoke alarm 33, 100, 112, 116
smoke blowing east 105
smoke damage 122, 158
smoke plume 37, 49, 56, 105-6, 132
smoke smell 55, 155
snow 24, 71, 134-6, 152-3, 156-7, 160, 163, 168, 184, 205, 207
solar panels 18
son, elder 58, 175, 178
south Boulder 25, 38-9, 67, 81, 100, 105, 132, 143
South Boulder Creek 61, 127
South Boulder Recreation Center 67, 94, 100
South Boulder Road in Louisville 142
South Foothills 32
South Foothills Command 35, 37
South Howard Berry 127-8
South plant 128-9, 207
southbound 65-6
Southern Arapaho 19
southwest 51, 55, 73, 76, 78, 139
space 105, 121, 215
Spanish Hills 10, 75-6, 92, 94, 104, 133, 141, 174
 west of 93, 112, 116-17, 184
speculators 10
spring 20, 24, 61, 94, 109, 198
sta 41, 45-6, 71, 78, 87-8, 96, 107, 121-2, 155, 185
state xiii, 7-8, 21, 25, 28, 37, 44, 46-7, 68, 94, 96, 110-11, 149, 162-4, 170
state militia 6, 13-15
State of Colorado 191
stations xi-xii, 26, 34-5, 66, 72, 81, 95, 99, 101, 103-4
 gate 31
statistics 174, 194
stock imagery ii
stories ix-x, xvi, 83, 153, 196, 203, 211, 214
street 57, 59, 72, 83, 98-9, 101, 122, 140, 149, 199
Street, Cherry 69, 72, 80, 92, 99, 107, 147, 149
strike 3, 6, 13-15, 22
strikers 6, 13-15, 22
 hundred 15
structures ix, xi-xiii, xv, 34, 72-3, 80, 85-6, 98-9, 101, 126, 157, 160-1, 190-1, 199, 205-6
 residential 199
sturdy rock homes 4
subsidiary 110-11
Summit View Drive in Louisville 125
Sunset 111
Superior Colorado Government 213, 216
Superior east of McCaslin 105, 118
Superior residents 26, 181, 200
Superior Rising 180-1, 216
Superior Sagamore 64-5
Superior train depot 22-3
Superior's water plant 74, 128
support 44-5, 132, 153, 178, 185-6
support Marshall Command 92
surface 3, 8, 24, 104, 133
surface temperatures 8
survey 9, 135
Sustainability, Energy, and Environment Complex (SEEC) 132
Sycamore Court in Louisville 74
system 30, 47, 67-8, 207
 transmission 30

T

tactical channels 37, 92, 100, 126, 138
tallgrass prairies 24, 189
tanks 128-9
 storage 128-9
taxes 6, 181
teachers 185
teams 3, 45, 60, 80, 91-2, 129, 135, 156, 162-3, 165, 184
temperatures 8, 105, 150, 152-3, 168
Terminal reservoir 128
terrain 197
territorial capital 10, 108-9

territory 1, 109
Texas 15, 30, 59, 153, 171, 175, 178, 182
thickness 24
thrift 181-2
Together, Marshall 180-1, 214
Tom 203
tones 32, 67, 92, 106, 126
tons 3-4, 8, 174
topographic features 133
topography 196-7
tornado 67
tower 13, 209
town xv, 5, 10-12, 15, 21-2, 24, 26, 33, 41, 66, 76, 94-5, 109, 168-9, 180-1
town of Louisville 12
townhomes 91
townhomes amid 206
townsfolk 14
toys 37, 175, 177, 182
Tra ii
track 30, 92, 108-9, 111, 190
    miles of 108-9, 111
Trail Ridge and Washington in Louisville 143
trails 8, 26, 126, 150, 176
train xi, 13-14, 108, 110-11
training sessions 183-4
transit 76, 112, 146-7
transition, started Louisville's 15
transmission lines 29-30
transport 77-8, 83, 108, 121, 125, 184
transporting 5, 122, 124-5
tra˚c 32, 40-2, 55, 59, 63, 65-6, 73, 76-7, 81, 86, 90, 105, 108, 112, 116
tra˚c control xiii, 37, 40, 81, 84, 92
tra˚c lights 55, 63, 66
tra˚c management 129
trees 30, 57, 75, 80, 149, 154, 173, 196-7
    blackened 189
Tribes 43-4, 195
Tribes property 8, 37, 44, 195
trooper 81
troops 14, 20
trucks xii, 35, 37, 42-4, 51, 65-6, 90-1, 94, 96, 99, 101-2, 122, 175, 206, 209
Turnberry Circle in Coal Creek Ranch Louisville 86
Turnbull 51-2
Turnbull residence 66, 83
twelvetribes.org 43
Tyler 100
Type 45, 89, 91, 101, 162-3, 206
Tyvek 184-5

U

UMCOR (United Methodist Committee on Relief) 182
unincorporated Boulder County 6, 145, 157-8, 172, 174, 189-90, 212
Union Paci˛c 10-11, 108-11
Unit 35, 40, 76, 83, 93, 99-100, 105-6, 112, 116, 118-19, 122-4, 126, 130-1, 137-43, 145-7
Unit Edward 81, 84
United Methodist Committee on Relief (UMCOR) 182
United States 1, 16, 30, 43, 104, 110, 162
units 27, 32, 35, 37-8, 40, 48-9, 51, 66, 72-3, 76, 86, 93-4, 105-6, 112, 143
University of Colorado 132, 135, 153
University of Colorado campus in Boulder 47
Uni˛ed Command 94, 124
Unluckily 49, 69, 72, 74, 76, 86, 93, 109, 121, 178
untreated water 127, 129, 138
updates 55, 68, 92, 156-7, 162-3
uploads 34, 68, 172, 197-9, 211-13
US-36 15, 20, 40-1, 49, 51, 66, 72, 75, 80, 90-1, 93, 101, 116, 134, 149-50
US-36 Boulder-Denver Turnpike, large xv
US-36 north of Boulder 27
Ute 19
utilities 78, 128, 130, 163, 173, 191, 208-9
utility line 35, 37

V

V-patterns 196-7
vacant 69, 71, 106, 175
Valley, Marshall 196
vegetation xii, 8, 24, 66, 116
vehicles 80, 107, 112-13, 121, 138, 155, 172-3, 206
Venette 129
vents 8
vicinity 3, 5, 8
victims 117-18, 157, 179-81, 190, 206
videos 40, 44, 195
Vigil, Misty 52
VIIRS (Visible Infrared Imaging Radiometer Suite) 133
Villa 70
Violet 57, 59, 175-8
Visible Infrared Imaging Radiometer Suite (VIIRS) 133
Vista Lane 106
volunteers xi, 43, 55, 95-6, 157, 179, 183-5
    hundred 186

W

walls 6, 72-4, 95, 133, 163
Walnut Street in Louisville 124
Washington 105, 112, 122, 143, 145
Washington Lode 3
water 6, 8, 10, 24, 29-30, 35, 60-2, 89, 91, 102, 110, 127-30, 155-7, 160, 206-7
    boil 138, 206
    bottled 155, 159
    buckets of 78, 107
    diverts 60, 127
    potable 155-6, 158
water levels 128-9
Water Plant Operator 128
water pressure 80, 128-9, 138, 145, 199-200
water rights 60, 62
water supplies 12, 96
water tanks 6, 74
water treatment plant 128, 138
water truck 172
WEA 68
website 67, 69, 157, 181
website https 43
Welch 11
wellhead 30
west xv, 1, 9, 11-12, 20, 24, 39, 42, 51, 57, 72-3, 101, 104-5, 107-10, 116-18
West Metro 98-9, 101, 209
West Metro Brush Trucks 98
West Metro Fire Rescue 98, 210, 216
west side 63, 65, 72, 81, 91-2, 99
Western United States ix, xv
wife ix, 11, 17, 20, 22, 51, 62, 72, 89, 106, 164, 203
wildland xii-xiii, 33-5, 89, 91, 209
wild¸res ix, xii, 9, 30, 32, 34, 40, 43, 67-9, 71, 112, 132, 191-2, 195-6, 215-16
Williamson, Paul 18, 42, 69, 149, 167, 170, 173, 193
Willie 81
Wilt, Roger 184-5
winds xii, xv, 27-8, 34-5, 39, 42-3, 51-2, 58-9, 66, 77-8, 91-2, 101-2, 104-5, 135-6, 194-7
    60-mile-per-hour 74
    blinding 42
    high xii-xiii, xvi, 9, 28, 35, 38, 44, 48, 85, 94, 100, 115, 122, 196-7, 205
    high-speed 105
    horri¸c 68
    intense 42
    strong xv, 63, 104, 153
    surface 85
    swirling 112
winds abating 145
winds light 25
winds subsiding 147
windshield 55
Windsor-Severance Fire Rescue 210
windstorms 9

windstorms fanning xv
windswept 77
winter 6, 20, 24, 212
Wisconsin 20, 22, 30, 149
woman 74, 100, 106, 117-18, 122
women 13, 15, 20
workers 111, 173, 205
    utility 149, 152, 165
wp-content 34, 68, 172, 197-9, 211-13
www 195-6, 207, 211-13, 215-16
www.bouldercounty.org 136, 171, 190, 212
www.boulderoem.com 44, 67, 100, 114, 150, 158, 162, 212
www.bouldersheri 212
www.commfound.org 179, 213
www.louisville-library.org 214
www.louisvilleco.gov 128, 159, 213-14
www.louisville˛re.com iii, 96, 214
www.superiorcolorado.gov 25, 213, 216
www.tra ii
www.youtube.com 44, 53, 93, 214, 216
WY 209-10

X

Xcel 30-1, 74, 128, 152, 156, 158, 165, 196, 215
Xcel Energy 9, 30, 128, 149-51, 156, 160, 162, 195, 210, 216

Y

yards 80
YMCA 106, 119, 143, 146, 152, 157
YMCA of Northern Colorado in Lafayette 80

Z

Zelinger, Marshall 195
zone 61, 104, 128, 140, 150, 165

Printed in the United States
by Baker & Taylor Publisher Services